BRITISH INDUSTRY
An Economic
Introduction

BRITISH INDUSTRY

An Economic Introduction

PETER JOHNSON

Basil Blackwell

First published 1985

Basil Blackwell Ltd
108 Cowley Road, Oxford OX4 1JF, UK

Basil Blackwell Inc.
432 Park Avenue South, Suite 1505,
New York, NY 10016, USA

British Library Cataloguing in Publication Data

Johnson, P. S.
    British industry : an economic introduction.
    1. Great Britain—Industries
    I. Title
    338,0941   HC256.6

    ISBN 0–631–14205–3
    ISBN 0–631–14206–1 Pbk

Library of Congress Cataloging in Publication Data

Johnson, Peter, 1908–
    British industry.

    Includes index.
    1. Industrial organization—Great Britain.
2. Competition—Great Britain. 3. Industry and state—Great Britain. I. Title.
HD70.G7J64 1985   338.0941   84-28263
ISBN 0–631–14205–3
ISBN 0–631–14206–1 (pbk.)

Typeset in Great Britain by Photo·Graphics, Honiton, Devon, England.

Printed in Great Britain by Page Bros (Norwich) Ltd

To Malcolm

Contents

Preface

This book arose out of a conviction that students taking introductory courses in economics could usefully benefit from a rather more detailed treatment of industrial organization and activity than can be given in a basic 'principles' text.

In planning and writing a book of this kind it is important to have at least some feel for the kind of coverage provided in an introductory economics course. In this respect I have derived considerable benefit from two sources. The first is my experience as one of the lecturers on the first year elements of economics course at Durham University. The second is my involvement in the writing of Part V: The Structure of Industry in *Economics: An Integrated Approach*, published by Prentice Hall in 1984. This text, which is based on the first year course at Durham, was written by John Creedy, who took overall responsibility for the book, Lynne Evans, Barry Thomas, Rodney Wilson and myself. I am most grateful to my colleagues for the insights that this collaborative venture provided. My thanks are also due to Adrian Darnell and Norman Gemmell who helped to clarify my thinking on a number of issues.

I owe a substantial debt to Julie Bushby and Kathryn Cowton who typed successive drafts of the book with unbelievable patience and great competence. I am also grateful to my family, and especially to my wife, who showed considerable forbearance while this book was being written.

I am indebted to the Controller of Her Majesty's Stationery Office for permission to reproduce Crown copyright material. My thanks are also due to a number of publishers and authors who have allowed me to use extracts from works in which they have the copyright. Full acknowledgement is given in the text.

Peter Johnson,
Durham

Introduction

THE PURPOSE OF THE BOOK

This book provides an economic introduction to the organization and operation of British industry. It will enable the reader to stand back a little from the everyday contact that he already has with firms and industries and to gain a broader and more knowledgeable perspective on them. Introductory courses in economics and related disciplines are usually unable, because of time constraints, to examine firms and industries in any depth. A good deal of abstraction is therefore involved. Such abstraction often serves as a source of frustration and disappointment to those students who expect their subject, even at an elementary level, to be obviously related to 'the real world' in which they live. This book, which focuses on the realities of industrial organization and activity, should provide some reassurance for these students.

THE USE OF ECONOMIC AND STATISTICAL CONCEPTS

The book uses a number of important economic and statistical concepts. The degree of prior knowledge that is assumed in the treatment of these concepts does, however, vary. For example, while the nature of production is discussed in some depth in chapter 1 because it is central to the rest of the book, the notion of a demand curve is assumed to be already familiar to the reader (to construct such a curve from first principles would require a substantial digression). It should be clear from the text itself how much prior knowledge is taken for granted.

The level of mathematics used in the book is very elementary. Calculus is used only very briefly in the appendix to chapter 8. This appendix may be ignored by the uninitiated.

THE PLAN OF THE BOOK

The book divides into three parts. Part I examines various aspects of industrial organization with particular reference to the UK. Chapter 1 is concerned with the meaning of 'production' and particular emphasis is placed on the wide ranging and complex nature of the productive process. The chapter also considers the measurement and valuation of inputs and output, and the relationship *between* inputs and output ('efficiency'). It is hoped that this chapter will encourage the reader to think of production in a much broader sense than is usually the case, and to be a little more aware of the very extensive co-ordination process that lies behind the production of even relatively insignificant items. In chapter 2, alternative ways of *organizing* production are considered. Key features of centrally planned and market systems are outlined. The particular way in which production is organized in the UK is then examined. Special attention is paid here to the role of the state.

Chapter 3 focuses on UK industry. After considering the method of industrial classification used in official statistics, it uses these statistics to examine changes in various aspects of the structure of industry over the past two decades. It also looks at the mechanisms by which industrial change comes about. Chapters 4 and 5 are devoted to specific aspects of UK industry which have attracted widespread interest in recent years. Chapter 4 examines market concentration and its relationship with efficiency and profitability. In chapter 5 attention is focused on the largest firms and on the implications for market power which arise when firms operate in several markets. This chapter also considers the effects of multinational operations and the activities (and control) of the nationalized industries. Chapter 6 concludes part I by comparing UK industrial performance with that in some other industrialized countries. It also looks at the notion of deindustrialization in the UK context.

Part II is devoted to the analysis of competition between firms. Chapter 6 provides an overview of the competitive process under conditions of uncertainty. Interdependence between firms, and potential entry are seen as key elements in this process.

The next four chapters examine particular aspects of competition. Chapter 8 looks briefly at pricing. After examining what 'price' means, it describes the procedure of average cost pricing under different assumptions about firm objectives. It also looks at why firms sometimes discriminate in price between different consumers. Advertising is the subject of chapter 9. Data on advertising in industry are first considered. Attention is then concentrated on the firm's advertising decision, and the relationship between advertising and market structure, prices and profitability. The chapter concludes with a brief review of the welfare effects of advertising. In chapter 10 competition in innovation is explored. Data on industrial research and development (R & D) are presented and the relationship between such activity and market structure is examined. A discussion of the diffusion of innovation concludes the chapter.

Chapter 11, the final chapter in part II, looks at investment, an activity which has an important part to play in a firm's competitive strategy. After examining various investment concepts and the extent of investment in the UK, it considers different methods of investment appraisal. Sources of investment finance are then briefly explored. The possibility of merger or take-over as an alternative to new investment, and investment in human capital are dealt with in the last two sections of this chapter.

Part III of the book considers some issues of industrial policy. Chapter 12 is concerned with competition policy. It sets out the theoretical case for a competition policy, and looks at the various options that policy makers may adopt. The operation of competition policy in the UK is then briefly surveyed. The appendix to this chapter gives some extracts from the relevant statutes. Attention in chapter 13 concentrates primarily on selective policies designed to raise international competitiveness. The chapter reviews the development of such policies since 1974, and examines some of the 'market failure' arguments that might be used to support government intervention. It also examines a number of ways in which governments may 'fail' in policy implementation. The chapter concludes with a brief discussion of policy evaluation.

PART I
Industrial Organization

1

The Nature of Production

1.1 INTRODUCTION

When the customer drives his new car out of the showroom, his action represents the culmination of a process of co-ordination which stretches over a vast array of activities. The final assembly of a mass produced car involves not only the more obvious 'shop floor' activities, such as fitting and paint spraying, but also a wide range of other functions including purchasing, design, personnel, marketing and cleaning. Each item required in this assembly operation has itself to be made. Even the humblest items such as first aid plasters, radiator hoses and office pencils can boast of histories which often involve a long and complex chain of activities. This chain can ultimately be traced back to the exploitation and processing of raw materials somewhere in the world. When the car finally reaches the end of the assembly line, it has to be distributed to car dealers who in turn engage in selling and marketing activities. These distribution activities are themselves dependent on numerous other activities: for example the building of showrooms, the making and delivery of office supplies, and electricity generation.

Each separate activity may be viewed as having certain inputs – labour (often consisting of many different types of skill), machinery and equipment, premises and materials (in raw or processed form). These inputs are co-ordinated and transformed into output. It is the process by which inputs become output that is referred to as production. Cars are of course only one example of output. Hundreds of thousands of other types of output exist. Each involves the fairly precise co-ordination of a unique network of activities. These networks vary in their extensiveness and complexity. The next two sections provide a closer examination of inputs and output. The latter is taken first.

1.2 OUTPUT

'Final' and 'Intermediate' Output

Output may be of two basic types. Where it goes to the final consumer, it is labelled as *final*. Where it becomes the input for another productive activity it is referred to as *intermediate*. How much intermediate output is produced in an economy is of course crucially dependent on how 'activity' is defined in that economy. Such definitions are inevitably rather arbitrary. It is for example possible to define a country's car production as one vast activity stretching back to the sources of the raw materials (or to the dockside if imports are involved) and forward to the final transaction in the showroom. The only inputs then are labour, domestic raw materials, and any imports. Machinery and equipment, premises and supplies manufactured in the country are simply raw materials or imports which have been processed *within* the activity. There is thus no intermediate output. For most purposes it is unlikely that such a conglomerate activity would be a helpful basis for analysis. 'Car production' usually refers to a more narrowly defined activity – or *industry* – which has as its core the final assembly line. Definitional issues are further considered in chapter 3.

Many activities that contribute to car production (as usually defined) also provide inputs for other activities. For example, electricity generation provides power for a wide range of other uses. Indeed, less than 2 per cent of the sales of the UK electricity supply industry go to the production of motor vehicles and parts. Steel manufacturing similarly has many outlets apart from car production. The latter accounts for only about 10 per cent of total UK sales of steel. Feedback also exists. Glass making is required if windows and windscreens are to be available for assembly line operation, but cars are also required as an input for glass making (for transporting personnel on official business). In this context cars are intermediate output.

Goods and Services

Output may be divided into goods and services. The former, of which cars are an example, are tangible whereas the latter are intangible. Hairdressing, shipping, chiropody and banking are some examples of services. Like goods, services may be further classified as intermediate or final. The output from the office activities associated with the vehicle assembly line are intermediate. Government services such as law and order and defence are usually treated for national accounts purposes as final although some economists have argued that they are essentially intermediate in nature. The argument here is that without these services the rest of the economy would not be able to function. The same argument could however be applied to a whole range of outputs. The distinction between goods and services is sometimes used in the analysis of structural change in industry. In this book goods and services are often grouped together under the heading of 'output' or 'products'.

Production and Wants

The ultimate purpose of production is to satisfy wants. This function is performed primarily by final output although it may also be argued that intermediate output sometimes meets wants: for example, workers may gain some psychic satisfaction from the process of production itself and from seeing what is (to them) the 'end product', even though the latter may feed into other activities as an input. The satisfaction of wants as the goal of productive activity raises a number of fundamental economic questions. For example, given limited resources, only a proportion of wants can be satisfied. Which wants should be included in that proportion? The existence of the state also raises further issues. Does the state have wants that are independent of the individuals in the country concerned? Or is it simply acting on their behalf? There are probably no policies initiated by the UK government which have the unanimous approval of UK citizens. Thus for some individuals the state has wants which they themselves do not have. Again, some individual wants, for example national defence, may only be realizable if there is a 'collective' want. An extensive discussion of the role of the state cannot be provided here. However activities paid for by the state (for example tax collection, defence, policing, the Foreign Office) are treated as forms of production in this book. The part played by public authorities in production is examined further in chapters 2 and 3.

Public Goods and Services

Some goods and services display the characteristic of non-rivalness, that is, the consumption by one individual of a unit of the good or service does not stop another individual from consuming the *same* unit. This characteristic is absent in most products. If an individual consumes a tin of baked beans, no other individual can also consume that *same* tin of beans. However the 'consumption' of street lighting is not similarly restricted: many individuals can enjoy the *same* product. Theatre performances, defence, the beams from lighthouses are other examples of products which, to a greater or lesser degree, display the characteristic of non-rivalness. It should be noted however that it is not always totally the same product that is being consumed: a seat in the 'gods' is rather different from one in the stalls, even though it is the same stage performance that is watched. Furthermore, the nature of the product may change as the number of consumers involved changes. The last night of the Proms would be a very different product if attended by only a handful of people. A moment's reflection on these examples also suggests another limitation on the concept of non-rivalness: it only exists up to capacity limits. If the theatre has empty seats, non-rivalness is present; a full house, however, means that no one queueing outside can see the show unless someone else gives up his or her seat.

Non-rivalness may also be associated with non-excludability. The latter characteristic refers to the inability to exclude from consumption. While it is possible to do this with theatre performances – non-ticket holders are not admitted – it cannot usually be done with, say, defence or street lighting. It may not always be *impossible* – no doubt legislation could be drafted that excluded certain individuals from areas where street lighting existed – but it would doubtless be extremely complex. Where *both* non-rivalness and non-excludability are characteristics of output, pure public goods (and services) are said to exist. Pure private goods and services do not have either of these characteristics. A range of variations is of course possible between these two extremes.

Goods and services which, to a greater or lesser degree, are 'public' in character present special problems in relation to the identification of wants. For example, non-excludability may mean that consumers attempt to obtain 'a free ride', thereby enjoying the consumption while avoiding the costs involved. This in turn may have implications for the way in which the production of public goods and services is organized, financed and controlled (see for example p.156).

The Valuation of Output

The use of market prices

For many purposes it is desirable to know how much output has been produced in a country or in an area of a country over some time period. Such a calculation provides a guide to what has been obtained for the inputs that have been used up. The total amount of goods and services produced is one important indicator of a country's economic prosperity. (It does, however, have to be used very carefully and in conjunction with a range of other measures.) It is also sometimes necessary to know how much output has been produced over some time period in a particular industry or sector. To undertake such a task some means of adding together quite distinct forms of output is required. Even the output of a fairly narrowly defined industry is likely to be heterogeneous.

One fairly straightforward way of adding together heterogeneous output is to take the total value of that output based on market prices (i.e. what the output fetches or would fetch in the market). Of course such a procedure requires the assumption that these prices are an appropriate yardstick of value. This measure is referred to in UK industrial statistics as gross output. It includes not only the value of those goods and services that have actually been sold during the period – usually referred to as sales revenue (or just revenue) but also the value of work in progress and of output going for stock. It is sometimes desirable to adjust this figure to allow for the presence of subsidies and/or taxes; this complication is not however considered here.

Double counting

It was indicated earlier that output may be either final or intermediate. If the market value of *both* types of output is added together double counting would of course occur. The following example illustrates this point. It is assumed that a country has only two industries, *A* and *B*, and that there are no imports. Industry *A* produces its output from scratch and buys nothing from elsewhere. It sells its output to industry *B* for £100. Industry *B* then adapts it in some way and sells the output to final consumers for £300. This £300 *includes* the £100 purchase by industry *B*. Thus a total market value of output of £400 would be misleading. One way round this problem is to count only the value added: £100 in industry *A* (remember it buys in nothing) and £200 in industry *B* (£300 minus £100). The value added is equal to the value of the final output *less* the value of intermediate output bought in. (In an open economy, such intermediate output would include any imports.) In the UK the value added term most commonly used in official production statistics is gross value added at factor cost. This is defined as gross output less the cost of purchases of intermediate output bought in, rates, the cost of licensing motor vehicles and where applicable, duties.

Output with no market price

A market prices approach to the valuation of output faces is not especially helpful when output is not exchanged in a market. The output produced by a tax inspector or a policeman are obvious examples: there is no market in which these services are sold. In such cases the value of inputs, primarily the wage bill, may have to be used as the nearest approximation to a value of output measure. In the UK national accounts, there are a number of outputs which are valued in this way. Such an approach can lead to distortions. For example a bigger Civil Service wage bill will be represented as higher output from that Service. There may be other explanations for the increase in wages!

1.3 INPUTS

A Classification of Inputs

Inputs, or factors of production as they are often called, are basically everything that goes into the production process. They have been traditionally divided into three categories: labour, capital and land. 'Labour' is all human activity. 'Capital' includes all man-made inputs. Thus it embraces machinery and equipment, and premises as well as supplies of components and processed materials. 'Land' is usually taken to include all natural resources. In a closed economy taken as a whole, the only inputs are land and labour. Capital ultimately derives from these. But for any *particular* industry, the threefold classification is a useful starting point. Within each category there is of course substantial heterogeneity. 'Labour' for example embraces a very wide range of skills: the present classification of occupations used in the UK lists about 3,500 categories. 'Occupation' is not of course synonymous with 'skill' but it is near enough for present purposes. Similarly the machinery and equipment under the 'capital' heading may vary from the simple hand tool to the highly sophisticated electronic robot. Variations in the quality of 'land' are also easy to find.

Because of the general scarcity of inputs it is useful to know how much of these inputs are utilized in the production of different goods and services and indeed in production as a whole.

Stocks Flows

When the utilization of inputs in production is considered two concepts should be kept distinct: the stock of an input at some point in time and the flow of input services during some time period. It is the latter that measures the contribution of an input to production. If, for example, it is necessary to know how much labour contributed to chemicals production in 1982, it may not be very helpful to know that in June of that year 390,000 were employed in the industry, unless some idea of what that figure implies for the man hours or man years that were put in is also given. Only then would a flow measure be provided. Of course if all industries have roughly the same degree of stability in their labour force, and if employees all work similar hours during a week, the stock figures provide some information about the relative sizes of labour flows. Although these assumptions are not always wholly valid, such stock figures are often the only measure available. Most of the labour data used in this book are therefore of this kind. Even a man hours or man years measure may not reflect the heterogeneity in the labour force, in terms either of its skills, or of the *intensity* with which it is employed. Of course data on labour in individual industries may be disaggregated into various skill categories but such a procedure makes comparisons across industries difficult. One simple way of tackling the heterogeneity problem is to take the total wage and salary bill. Such a measure implies that the wage structure accurately reflects the differences in contribution made by the different types of labour.

Measuring the flow of input services is more complicated when it comes to capital, not only because of the heterogeneous nature of these inputs but also because they vary considerably in the length of their productive lives. Factory premises may last for 50 or a 100 years, whereas a body press may have a five year life. Some hand tools may last less than a year. The life of any particular item of capital depends in part on the intensity with which it is used as well as on technological progress. The latter may render a machine obsolete even though it may not be physically worn out. The measurement of the flow of capital services for any given period may therefore require some means of apportioning the total flow across time periods. Any apportionment procedure is bound to raise difficulties and in any case comparisons on a physical basis across different types of capital is not possible. Again, one widely used approach employs monetary values, and measures the depreciation of the item, i.e. the loss in value resulting from its use during the period.

Some natural resources ('land') are so plentiful that there is no point in measuring their contribution. Others however are scarce and it is important to measure their contribution to production. Many of the problems that arise here are similar to those relating to capital.

The Entrepreneur

The person or persons who undertake the crucial role of co-ordination and organization or 'management' have been included under the 'labour' heading. Such a role may however involve much more than simply routine co-ordination. Key decisions have to be made on the nature of output and technology. Such decisions may involve substantial risk. These risks may not be limited to those of a financial character only but may also be related to status, reputation and self-esteem. Some decision takers (for example in government) may face only the last two kinds of risk. If the wrong decisions are made, the consequences can be disastrous not only for the decision taker but also (perhaps more so) for others. For example when Laker Airways collapsed early in 1982 as a result (in part at least) of the collapse of sterling and the recession in the airline industry, the banks were owed £230m, 2,500 staff were made redundant and 6,000 passengers were stranded overseas.

Because of the distinctive nature of these decisions some economists have identified a fourth factor of production which they have labelled as 'entrepreneurship'. A number of views have been expressed on what constitutes the essential characteristics of such a factor. For example, Schumpeter equated it with innovative activity which he defined 'as any "doing things differently" in the realm of economic life' (1939, p. 84). Knight (1921) associated it primarily with risk bearing. Kirzner (1973) more recently has characterized it by 'alertness' to market opportunities (see pp. 107–8). All of these views have some additional insight to offer into business behaviour. Although in this book entrepreneurship is included under the labour heading the vital role of the functions mentioned is acknowledged. They are discussed later in chapter 7.

1.4 EFFICIENCY

It is sometimes useful to consider the relationship between inputs and outputs in a firm, industry or nation. This relationship measures the efficiency of production. This term is often used in different ways and it is important to be aware of the various concepts that are used. Three main types of efficiency are considered in this book.

Technical Efficiency

Production is technically efficient when it is impossible to reduce the amount of any one factor going into the production of a given output, while the amounts of all other factors are held constant (all factors and output being measured in physical terms). There may be several technically efficient ways of producing a given output. Consider for example the building of a brick wall. One method might use 40 man hours, the relevant hand tools (for example, trowels) and a hired cement mixing machine. Another might use 80 man hours, and only the relevant hand tools. (In this case the cement is mixed manually.) Both methods may satisfy the requirement for technical efficiency.

It is sometimes helpful to make comparisons – for example, over time or across countries or industries – of technical efficiency. The measures available to do this usually provide only a partial picture. One such measure which is widely used is labour productivity. This is defined as the ratio of output to labour input. Capital productivity measures are also possible but are rather more difficult to calculate. The partial nature of both measures is readily apparent. For example, rises in labour productivity may occur primarily because more machinery and equipment is employed in the productive process and may not result from increased effort by labour itself. Some investigators have therefore attempted to examine changes in total factor productivity. Such an indicator requires the indices of *both* labour and capital productivity to be spliced together. How this splicing is done is of course crucial. It is usually achieved by weighting the two indices by their share of the total factor incomes from the industry or industries under examination. (Thus if wages and salaries account for 0.7 of the latter, then the labour productivity index is given a weight of 0.7 in the construction of the total index). Fortunately the growth of labour productivity appears to be fairly closely related to the growth of total factor productivity, at least as far as UK manufacturing and retailing is concerned, (Wragg and Robertson, 1978, p. 42). Even if this were not the case, labour productivity measures would still provide a useful spur to further investigation: differences in the growth of labour productivity still have to be explained.

Cost Efficiency

A given output level is produced in a cost efficient way when it is impossible to reduce further the total expenditure on the factors used in its production. Production that is technically efficient is not necessarily cost efficient. For instance in the earlier example of the building of a brick wall, one of the methods used may be more expensive, i.e. less cost efficient, than the other. Cost efficiency necessarily implies technical efficiency.

In recent years, the concept of X inefficiency (first developed in Leibenstein (1966)) has received considerable attention. X inefficiency arises because of such factors as management's desire for a quiet life and its inability or unwillingness to motivate the work-force. As a result, organizational 'slack' develops. X inefficiency may be regarded as a form of cost inefficiency. It serves to highlight the important point that people may sometimes gain from cost inefficiency. For example managers may find the quiet life, which gives rise to higher costs, more congenial.

Allocative Efficiency

Allocative efficiency, as its name implies, is concerned with how resources are allocated among possible uses. Allocative efficiency is achieved when it is impossible to change the allocation in such a way as to make one person better off without making someone else worse off. Particular attention is paid to this type of efficiency when price and output distortions under monopoly are considered (pp. 188–90). Allocative efficiency is usually considered in the context of a given distribution of income.

1.5 UNRECORDED PRODUCTION

Non-Marketed Activities

'Production' as defined in the first section of this chapter can be interpreted very widely and can be extended to cover a wide range of activities. For example, domestic tasks undertaken by a household – washing up, bed making, weeding – may all be regarded as forms of production. Do-it-yourself activities may be similarly labelled. These activities are all undertaken without payment. Many are of significant proportions: for example over a third of all drivers now undertake their own car servicing. Some of the outputs from these activities, or something like them, may also be bought and sold in the market place. For example many DIY activities have marketed equivalents available. There may therefore be information on market prices which may be used to value some of this output. However there is a problem here: if domestically produced output *were* to be sold on the market, market prices themselves might well be affected, especially if the amount of output involved were substantial. Thus current prices might be a poor guide to true market values. Furthermore, even if this problem were ignored, existing prices would only be of use in valuing output if data were available on the quantities of each service produced. Such data would be extremely difficult to collect and it is hardly surprising that official statistics do not usually record these types of production. For this reason they are ignored in this book. However it is important to be aware of the existence of unrecorded production, at least of the more obvious kind, in order correctly to interpret the statistics that *are* collected. For example, an increase in a country's recorded output may occur as a result of people who formerly performed domestic services at home going out to work. Yet the very act of doing so inevitably reduces unrecorded output produced at home. Thus the gain in recorded output overestimates the real increase.

The Black Economy

The output discussed above is not traded, and therefore does not have a market price attached to it (even though it may be possible to establish the market prices of similar output that is traded). There is however another category of output which *is* traded but which nevertheless might not be recorded in certain official statistics. For example some traders may attempt to avoid or reduce their liability to income tax by not declaring their earnings (or by declaring only *some* of them) to the tax authorities. Traders who are registered as unemployed may be anxious to avoid the disqualification for unemployment or Social Security benefit that the disclosure of self-employment brings. Such traders usually prefer a cash transaction and the minimum of paperwork! (Cheques are an unattractive form of payment as they involve a recording operation at the bank which may then be utilized by the tax authorities.) Although there may be an underreporting of sales or income from production as a result, expenditure data, collected, for example, from surveys of consumers, may not be affected to the same extent, as consumers do not have the same incentive to underreport especially as they are not usually required to indicate the precise destination of their expenditure. The UK *Censuses* of *Production* and *Employment* data used in this book are obtained direct from businesses and are therefore subject to underreporting.

Another way in which tax liabilities may be avoided is through barter. An electrician may for example agree to undertake electrical repairs for a farmer who pays him with a meat carcase. Both may thereby share in the gains from tax avoidance. (The farmer may in real terms have to 'pay' less because the electrician has no liability to tax.) No recording of the transaction is necessary.

That part of a country's output that should be, but is not recorded by the tax authorities is said to be produced in the 'black economy' or the informal sector. Estimates of the size of the black economy in the UK vary considerably and range from 2.3 to 7.5 per cent of Gross Domestic Product (Dilnot and Morris, 1981).

1.6 SUMMARY

Production is a complex activity. Output from production may be final or intermediate, and may be in the form of goods or services. Its ultimate purpose is the satisfaction of wants. Some of this output may have a public good (or service) character; this creates special problems in relation to the identification of wants. One way of adding heterogeneous output together is through the use of market prices, although not all output has such a price attached to it. Factors of production are usually divided into labour, capital and land; however, some economists have added entrepreneurship as a fourth factor. Measurement of the flow of heterogeneous factor services usually require some monetary valuation.

Efficiency is concerned with the relationship between inputs and output. This relationship may be viewed in different ways, and it is important to distinguish between technical, cost and allocative efficiency. Some types of production are not recorded in official statistics either because they are not marketed or because they are in the black economy.

This chapter has looked in some detail at the nature of productive activity, at the output that flows from it, and at the inputs that go into it. No attempt has been made to look at the ways in which such activity might be organized in an economy. This is the subject of the next chapter.

2

The Organization of Production

2.1 INTRODUCTION

The previous chapter highlighted the complexity of production in a modern economy. Some idea of this complexity may be obtained from the number of components going into the production of different types of output. For example, Unipart, the BL parts subsidiary, lists 5,200 replacement items for the Metro range of cars. In a large computer there are more than a hundred thousand different components, and in the Apollo rocket system, ten *million* (Freeman 1982, p. 91)! Clearly many thousands of activities contribute in one way or another to the production of output. Final output is itself made up of large numbers of different items. For example, a large UK department store, a channel through which only a proportion of goods and services are sold, may carry 250,000 different lines. Co-ordination of activities – and of the inputs within each activity – is therefore an immense but vital task. Small errors in this co-ordination process can make it impossible to produce the intended good or service.

Many important questions arise in relation to the co-ordination process. Three are of particular interest here. First, what kinds of output, and how much of each kind, should be produced? The possible configurations of final goods and services that an economy could produce, given time for adjustment, are infinite. Secondly, who should receive this output? Finally, how is the output to be produced, i.e. what technology should be employed? The answer to this last question determines what kinds of inputs are employed and how they are combined. Again the possibilities are endless: for example car production could be undertaken in ways quite different from those currently utilized by Ford or BL. It is even conceivable that one man working by himself and starting from scratch could produce – but probably only after an extensive period – a car bearing at least some resemblance to one produced on an assembly line. The three questions posed above are of course interrelated.

The ways in which these questions are answered vary from one economy to another. Each economy is probably unique in the particular combination of decision-making mechanisms that it adopts. Nevertheless it is possible to make certain basic distinctions between different types of economic system and this is attempted in the next two sections.

2.2 THE CENTRALLY PLANNED ECONOMY

Co-ordination through Central Planning

In this economy – perhaps best typified by the Soviet Union – most of the key decisions on production are taken by the state and its agencies. State planners set the output targets and attempt to co-ordinate production in such a way as to ensure consistency between outputs and input demands. The fact that an economy is *centrally* planned does not necessarily imply that *all* production decisions are taken at the centre; much decision making may be devolved to subordinate agencies. However these agencies are ultimately responsible to the former.

The co-ordination required in a modern economy is a massive task. In the Soviet Union, the central planning and supply organizations co-ordinate the production of 20,000 key commodities (Buck, 1982, p. 67). Their subordinate agencies are responsible for even greater numbers.

At the factory level, these plans are translated into targets against which performance is measured. Managers and workers may be offered various incentives (for example, bonus payments) to fulfil plans. The setting of targets is a difficult task. Those who have to meet such targets are likely to play some part in their initial determination; this provides scope for distortions to creep in. For example managers may press for targets that can be easily achieved. Furthermore, distortions in the output mix may occur if too much emphasis is placed on a single target. For example targets set in volume terms may lead, at the factory level, to an emphasis – not intended by the planners – on bulky items.

Markets and Prices

Many final goods and services even in a centrally planned economy are sold in markets. Central planning does not usually extend to telling consumers what they shall buy in the shops although it will certainly influence the extent of the choice that they have. It is therefore necessary for the planning agencies to set prices. If shortages or unsold stocks are to be avoided these prices have to be set to 'clear the market'.

This is not always achieved (nor sought) in the Soviet Union (Nove, 1977, p. 187). Intermediate goods and services also have prices, but these prices are primarily for purposes of accounting and of evaluating managerial performance. The setting of prices is a mammoth task in itself: one estimate suggests that Soviet planners have to fix over ten million prices (quoted in Buck, 1982, p. 66). Factories which make losses do not have to close down, as additional funds can be made available by the state to cover any difference between sales revenue and costs.

The execution of plans is of course facilitated if inputs are owned by the state. (Private ownership of inputs is compatible with central planning, provided the authorities have extensive powers to control their usage; however, where such powers exist, private ownership does not mean very much anyway.) Most machinery and equipment, premises and natural resources are publicly owned in the Soviet Union. Except in an economy where slavery is the norm, however, labour still remains the property of the individual. The state may engage in the detailed direction of labour to different uses but such controls are difficult to enforce, and it is hardly surprising that there is relatively little direction of labour in the Soviet Union. There are some restrictions on the movement of labour – for example, from rural areas to towns – but the restrictions do not amount to administrative allocation. This means that the pattern of wages must be set in such a way as to attract the required amount of labour to the different purposes set out in the production plans.

To describe an economy as 'centrally planned' does not necessarily imply that *every* production activity is controlled by the state. In the Soviet Union, for example, about a quarter of agricultural output is produced from private plots. Although the workers concerned do not own these plots, they work for themselves and do own any livestock that uses them. They also own the produce. (Nove, 1977, p. 122). A number of private service activities, for example shoe repairing, also exist. However such activities are heavily taxed.

2.3 THE MARKET ECONOMY

The Co-ordinating Role of the Market

The 'invisible hand'

In the market economy, the process of co-ordination is primarily achieved through the 'invisible hand' of the market. Ultimately, only those goods and services whose production costs customers are willing to cover are produced. Prices are free to adjust. In markets in which the quantity demanded exceeds the quantity supplied prices tend to rise. Where the reverse is true, prices tend to fall. As prices change so consumers and producers adjust the quantities demanded and supplied respectively. A market system is usually (although it need not necessarily be) associated with the private ownership of inputs. Decision taking is in the hands of private individuals and organizations who do not engage in the conscious co-ordination of production and consumption decisions. It is the market that is seen as providing this function. Because there is no central body which has overall control of the economy, decision making is often said to be decentralized. (However, it should be noted that in the very large business organizations which sometimes exist in a market economy, ultimate control lies with a central management, which clearly wields substantial power as far as the organization of production is concerned.)

It is sometimes argued that the market system works only very imperfectly as a co-ordinating mechanism because firms do not adjust very rapidly to market signals. Thus shortages and unwanted stocks appear. Various obstacles may stop new supplies coming on to the market. Furthermore in some circumstances firms may seek to restrict output below and raise prices above the level that would occur if market forces were allowed to operate freely. Such firms may also be able to manipulate consumers – for example through advertising – to demand what they want to produce. Thus consumer demand ceases to be an independent force in the market place. Some further difficulties which may arise from the operation of the market are considered on pp. 215–17.

The key role of transactions

The market system revolves round the transaction through which output is transferred from the seller to the buyer in exchange for some kind of payment. For a transaction to occur a seller and a buyer must first search for, and find each other. They then have to negotiate and agree the terms on which the exchange is to take place. For example the seller may agree to give certain guarantees on the quality of the product, while the buyer may promise to provide payment in a particular way. Sometimes one of the parties may have to take steps to enforce the terms of the agreement. Transactions therefore give rise to costs. These transactions costs are likely to be particularly heavy where there is no well developed market for the output in question and where there is a high degree of uncertainty in relation to the performance characteristics of that output. Anticipated transaction costs may sometimes be so heavy that a potential buyer or seller may decide not to proceed with a transaction. Transactions costs are considered more fully later in this section.

The State in a Market Economy

Even the strongest supporters of the market system would acknowledge (even if they did not accept the argument that such a system does not do the job of co-ordination particularly well) that there are some areas in which the market would fail to provide the optimal amount of goods and services. Sources of market failure are more fully considered in chapter 13 in the context of industrial policy. However, two particularly important ones are worth noting here. First, externalities may be present. These arise when the costs incurred by, and the benefits accruing to, the private decision taker in the market system do not fully reflect all the social costs and benefits. In these cases private decisions may not be optimal from society's viewpoint. Secondly, some output may have a 'public good' character and underprovision may therefore result (see pp. 5–6). Defence and law and order are two forms of output where such underprovision is likely.

To undertake even these basic tasks and to obtain the finance for them from tax payers requires labour and other inputs. It should be noted, however, that the state may perform these functions in a variety of ways. There is no reason in principle why, for example, some of the policing function should not be provided by private organizations which offer their services in the market place to the state rather than by employees of the state. More attention is paid to the issue of 'privatization' in chapter 5.

Most proponents of a free market system would also accept that society as a whole has some basic responsibility to assist the less fortunate, such as the mentally handicapped, the ill and the elderly.

The Nature of the Firm

In most economies where the market plays an important part in the co-ordination process, the majority of individuals do not work for themselves but are employed by a firm or a business. The firm is a device for bringing together in one or a number of locations a range of different inputs. It may produce final or intermediate output. Each employee agrees to work at a location and at a wage agreed with the firm. The firm owns or rents machinery and equipment. By co-ordinating these inputs, the firm produces output which it then sells, either to final consumers or to other firms.

Firms and Transaction Costs

It might of course be possible for the final consumer to co-ordinate the production of a particular good or service himself. To do this he would have to contact each individual input owner. However, even for relatively simple products, this would be a mammoth task. In many cases it would require a substantial knowledge of technology to know what inputs are required in the first place. The customer would have to enter into a large number of contracts, each of which would have to be separately negotiated. These contracts would have to be specific and detailed. Part of the contract would involve an agreement on price. Such an agreement would in turn, require the customer to be well informed on prices in general (so that he could avoid being over-charged). Once the contract was negotiated, he would have to monitor its execution and enforce its terms. Some input owners might be reluctant to sign a contract with one customer without at the same time signing contracts with other customers and indeed with other input holders. For example, a designer may be unwilling to design a car (or part of it) unless he knows that many other customers will also purchase his services (no one customer would be able to cover all the designer's costs). Contracts between input owners and customers may be dependent on contracts *between* input owners. One input owner may be reluctant to supply his services unless he also knows that other input owners with whom he has to work closely are also willing to supply. Thus without a firm, a web of multilateral contracts might be necessary. It is quite likely that many, perhaps most, modern goods and services would not be produced at all.

How does this complex picture alter when a firm is introduced? First, the consumer contracts *only* with the firm. He no longer needs to negotiate with *each* input owner; in consequence it is not necessary for him to acquire extensive information on technology and input prices. Secondly, monitoring and enforcement functions are left to the firm. Thirdly, each input owner need contract only with the firm. Such bilateral contracting means that a contract between any one input and the firm can be renegotiated without changing any other contract. (In multilateral contracting, the whole package would have to be renegotiated.) Fourthly, the firm's contracts with labour may not be very detailed. In return for an agreed wage or salary, the workers agree, within limits, to accept the direction of the firm's management.

Some of the gains that may be obtained from the existence of firms have been outlined. These gains are usually described in terms of savings in transactions costs, i.e. the costs of negotiating in the market place. If these gains exist, why is the whole of a market economy not organized in one giant firm? One answer is that the costs of organization *within a firm* may eventually outstrip savings in transactions costs.

Incomes Received through the Firm

The income of inputs is received from the firm. The owners of a firm also have an entitlement to income. This latter income arises from the difference between what the firm receives from customers (sales revenue) and what it pays out for inputs (costs). There is an important distinction between the income received by an input and that received by an owner. The former is contractual in nature. It has to be paid, whatever the firm receives in the market (provided it does not become insolvent). The income that owners receive, however, cannot be guaranteed in this way. No firm in a world of uncertainty can be sure of what the final outcome of all its transactions may be. This income may therefore be described as residual. It is of course the profits of the business.

2.4 THE UK ECONOMY

The Importance of the Private Sector

Most productive activity in the UK is undertaken by privately owned firms. These businesses operate within a legal framework which gives them certain rights and obligations. Provided they conform to legal requirements they are left largely free of state involvement in the running of their activities. They can start up, expand, contract or go into liquidation without reference to any kind of central planning agency. Similarly they can reduce or increase their product range or introduce new technology and new methods of working as they wish. There is no administrative body which tells them what inputs they should buy. The only requirement for the continued existence of a business is that it is profitable: unprofitable businesses eventually cease operations (unless rescued by the state).

Types of firm in the UK

In the UK a firm may take one of three basic legal forms.
(1) *Sole proprietorships*. The sole proprietorship is a single owner firm. This is the most common – and simplest – form of business. Any individual can set himself up in this way, so long as he does not infringe planning and other general legal requirements. He is obliged to show his accounts only to the tax authorities. He can finance the initial stages of the business either from his own resources or by borrowing (for example, from friends or his bank). A sole proprietorship may or may not have employees.

The owner receives any profits the business makes. However, he is personally liable for all its debts. Thus, if the firm is unable to meet all its commitments, the owner can be forced to sell his personal assets (including, for example, his car, house, or boat) to pay the debts. If the assets are insufficient then the owner can be made bankrupt.

The sole proprietor is likely to have difficulty in borrowing substantial sums from banks and other financial institutions. These institutions know that if the business fails, the amount that they can recover will be limited to the value of the assets of the business and of its owner. The latter often does not have extensive personal wealth.

(2) *Partnerships*. One way in which access to funds can be improved is through the formation of a partnership in which several individuals (usually no more than 20) share the profits and are jointly and severally responsible for any debts of the business. Partnerships may also enable diverse skills to be brought together in one business. The sole proprietorship and partnership are particularly suited to activities which have relatively low capital requirements and which are not particularly risky. The production of many services lends itself to these particular forms. For example, estate agents require only a small capital outlay to set up. Office premises and equipment, together with finance for working capital, are all that is required. Both premises and equipment may be rented or bought. The risks are quite low. Doctors, dentists and lawyers are in a similar financial position. They face the additional risk (unknown to estate agents) of lawsuits relating to professional negligence. But insurance against this risk can be obtained.

(3) *Limited liability companies*. A limited liability company is an organization with a legal identity which is distinct from that of its owners. For example, such a company can sue and be sued and can enter into contracts. The owners of a limited liability company are those individuals and institutions which hold its shares. A share is a document which indicates that the holder participates in the ownership of the company and is entitled to a share of the profits. Some of the shareholders may of course be the company's employees, but the latter are not required to be shareholders. When a company is formed it issues shares, the sale of which provides a source of finance for the company. A company may also issue new shares after formation in order to raise additional finance. Shares may be transferred between people.

There are two main kinds of share. The preference share gives the holder priority over other shareholders in the distribution of the company's profits. The entitlement of the preference shareholder is usually fixed in relation to the (nominal) value of the shares that he owns. Sometimes a company may make insufficient profits to pay in full the preference shareholder's entitlement; at other times it may make more than enough to meet his claims. In the latter case however he still only receives his fixed entitlement (unless he owns participating preference shares, in which case he may receive a further share in the rest of the profits). Where preference shares are cumulative, any short-fall in payment in one year is carried forward to subsequent years. The preference shareholder also has priority over other shareholders, as far as the repayment of his capital is concerned, if the company fails.

The ordinary share confers no priority of payment on the holder. The amount of the company's profits he receives varies from year to year, and depends on the total profits made by the company, and on the company's distribution policy. In good years, the ordinary shareholder does well; in bad years he suffers. However, he usually has more say – through his voting rights at company meetings – in the operation of the company than the preference shareholder. Ordinary shares are sometimes called equities.

In the post-war period the financial institutions have become steadily more important as shareholders. For example in the UK, such institutions increased their shareholdings from 29.0 per cent of the total in 1963 to 47.7 per cent in 1975. The main casualty of this trend was the individual shareholder whose share fell, over the same period, from 57.5 per cent to 40.2 per cent (*Economic Progress Report,* July 1979). It is likely that the relative importance of financial institutions has continued to grow since 1975.

The process by which a company is set up is known as incorporation. Before this can take place, a number of documents have to be filed with the Registrar of Companies, who is a government official. The two most important documents required are the *Memorandum of Association* and the *Articles of Association.* The former sets out, among other things, the objectives of the company to which its management must adhere and the latter gives details of the relationship between the shareholders and the company. Every company must have a board of directors (which may be very small). The role of a director is to manage the company. However, not all managers are directors.

If a limited liability company is forced to close because it is unable to pay its debts, the shareholder's personal assets cannot be used to meet creditors' claims. Such limited liability facilitates the raising of finance by reducing the risks attached to ownership participation. The shareholder may of course lose the value of his shares if the company is forced into liquidation. However, the shareholder may 'spread' risks by dividing his total shareholdings between several different types of company.

The vast majority of companies are not allowed by law to offer their shares to the general public. These are private limited liability companies. Even with this limitation, however, their ability to raise funds is likely to be greater than that of the sole proprietorship or partnership. The public limited liability company which must put the initials 'plc' after its name faces no such restriction. It is therefore able to draw on a potentially very large source of funds. In return, its activities have to face more public scrutiny and legal regulation. The shares of a public company may or may not be bought and sold on the London Stock

Exchange. A private or public company may of course raise capital without issuing shares. For example, a company may borrow from a bank. Sometimes directors have to provide personal guarantees for borrowings. Such guarantees are, however, of a specified value, whereas the sole proprietor's liability is not limited in this way.

Numbers of firms in the UK

In 1982 there were 2.2 million people self-employed in the UK. This represents a rise of over 10 per cent on the 1972 figure. Sole proprietors and partners are usually self-employed; and the majority of them are in non-manufacturing. For example over 50 per cent of self-employment tax assessments in 1979 were in building, distribution and professional services. The number of companies (public and private) in existence has risen steadily in the post-war period. At the end of 1983 there were 855,710 companies registered in Great Britain. This figure, which also includes a small proportion of companies not covered by the classification given earlier, is nearly 64 per cent higher than that for 1970. Both the number of births and deaths has risen steadily over the period, with the former outstripping the latter. Less than 1 per cent of companies in 1982 were public companies. Many companies are not actively trading.

A business may go through more than one legal form during its life. For example, many new businesses start off life as sole proprietorships and only become incorporated after they have grown to a reasonable size. Some private companies eventually convert to public status often to improve their access to finance. (There were 184 such conversions in Great Britain in 1983.)

The Activities of Government

Although privately owned businesses play a central role in UK production, the government at both central and local levels is also heavily involved. Even UK governments which have identified themselves with *laissez-faire*, the doctrine of 'free' markets, have not restricted themselves to providing the basic functions of law and order and defence.

The nature and extent of government involvement in production (in its widest sense) in the post-war period has varied considerably. However, the ways in which successive governments have concerned themselves with the production of goods and services may be classified into four main categories: the public sector, shareholdings in companies, economic policies and indicative planning. Each category is briefly considered below.

The public sector

Central and local government departments, the public corporations and the armed forces are usually referred to as the public sector.

(1) *Government departments.* The state may own productive capacity. A department run by central or local government is the most direct form of such ownership. In the UK at the present time, government departments are responsible for a wide range of activities, including not only the basic functions of defence and law and order referred to earlier, but also education, health care and construction. Central administrative services are required to collect revenue and to conduct foreign policy. By the very nature of these activities, the government is directly involved in organizing production. Most of the goods and services government officials produce are not sold in the market place; nor do government departments go into liquidation if they are not profitable.

(2) *Public corporations.* These corporations are public trading bodies set up by Act of Parliament. They are intended to operate at arm's length from the government departments ultimately responsible for them. However, the government appoints, directly or indirectly, the whole or a majority of the corporations' boards of management. Furthermore in practice governments have exercised considerable influence over the corporations' activities (see pp. 79–80 for some of the ways in which this influence has been felt).

In April 1982, there were 49 public corporations in existence varying from the Royal Mint, the body responsible for producing notes and coins, to the Covent Garden Market Authority. Of these public corporations 17 were nationalized industries. These included the National Coal Board, the British Railways Board and the British Steel Corporation. The nationalised industries are examined more closely in chapter 5. It may be noted here, however, that they may continue to exist despite heavy losses. They are able to do this – unlike private businesses – by virtue of their access to public funds. In 1981/82, the operating loss for the British Railways Board was over £1,000m. Substantial operating losses were also incurred by the National Coal Board (£248m) and the British Steel Corporation (£343m). Any interpretation of these losses must, however, bear in mind that the nationalized industries are subject to responsibilities and constraints that are not imposed on private enterprises.

Table 2.1 gives an indication of the size of the public sector in employment terms in 1983. In total, it accounted for nearly 30 per cent of the total labour force. In employment terms, the biggest individual parts of the public sector are the nationalized industries and the education and health sectors.(Trends in the public sector are considered in chapter 3.)

The public sector does of course have enormous influence on the rest of the economy through its purchases of goods and services. For example, central and local government's total consumption of final output was 26 per cent of all domestic consumption of such output in

Table 2.1   Employment in the UK public sector, 1983*

Function	Numbers (000s)	% of total UK employed labour force†
Central government	2,353	9.9
H.M. Forces and women's services	322	1.4
National Health Service	1,246	5.3
Other central governments	785	3.3
Local authorities	2,879	12.1
Education	1,434	6.0
Health and social services	360	1.5
Construction	130	0.5
Police	187	0.8
Other local authorities	768	3.2
Public corporations	1,663	7.0
Nationalized industries	1,465	6.2
Other public corporations	198	0.8
Total UK public sector	6,895	29.1
Total UK private sector	16,825	70.9
Total UK employed labour force	23,720	100.0

*Preliminary estimates only.
†Figures subject to rounding errors.
Source: *Economic Trends*, March 1984.

1982 (purchases by public corporations are of course intermediate output). In the same year the public sector accounted for 12 per cent of all capital expenditure.

Government shareholdings in limited liability companies

The government also owns shares in companies. For example it has 48.4 per cent of the shares of British Aerospace and nearly 100 per cent of BL's shares. This mode of ownership places a considerable distance between such companies and the relevant government departments. Nevertheless it is inevitable that such an ownership stake, especially where coupled with extensive government financial assistance should bring some element of accountability. For example although it is the government's declared aim that BL should to all intents and purposes act as an independent company, some of that company's decisions are bound to be subject to close public scrutiny. The sale of its agricultural tractor business at Bathgate was one instance where such scrutiny was applied. This particular decision was investigated by the Public Accounts Committee of the House of Commons. Even where the government holds a minority shareholding, it normally has power to appoint directors.

Government economic policies

(1) *Types of policy.* The third way in which UK governments have involved themselves with production is through their economic policies. These policies have ranged from those related to the management of aggregates such as total demand or the money supply to those concerned with more specific objectives. In the post-war period, the latter type of policies have embraced a wide variety of measures, including wages and price controls, selective and non-selective grants and loans to industry, the regulation of monopolies, and restrictive practices and measures to improve the quality of the labour force and industrial efficiency.

(2) *Small firms policies: an illustration.* The diverse nature of government policies in respect of industry may be illustrated by its present involvement in the small firms area. On the financial side, it has introduced a number of measures. The Loan Guarantee Scheme, under which the government guarantees 70 per cent of the loans of commercial banks to small firms which would not otherwise get financial backing was launched in 1981. Other recent financial initiatives include the Business Expansion Scheme, which provides tax relief for investors who put money into small businesses; the Venture Capital Scheme, which permits losses on the disposal of shares owned by individuals in small companies to be set against income rather than capital gains; and the Small Engineering Firms Investment Scheme, which is designed to help small firms invest in advanced capital equipment. The government also provides training for would-be entrepreneurs through the Manpower Services Commission's sponsorship of courses. Trainees on these courses are paid a training allowance. Information services are provided through the Department of Industry's Small Firms Centres. No charge is levied on enquirers. Many local authorities also run information bureaux. Advisory and counselling services are offered through a variety of channels. Small businesses can utilize the counselling services of the Small Firms Centres: no charge is made for the first (exploratory) session; thereafter a modest fee is imposed. They may also use the services of the Management Extension programme which involves the

secondment to them of redundant executives who can provide management advice. Technical advice may be obtained under the Small Firms
Technical Enquiry Service.

In order to increase mobility of unemployed people into business, the
government has introduced the Enterprise Allowance Scheme which
provides a weekly payment (for a period of a year) to unemployed
people wishing to set up in business. Many other measures designed to
reduce the burden of taxation, company, employment and planning
legislation have been introduced.

The true cost of all these measures is not known and would be difficult
to estimate although a recent estimate suggests that the cost to the
Exchequer is around £500m (see *British Business*, 6 May 1983, p. 199).
The question of whether these policies are worthwhile in a cost benefit
sense cannot be examined here. However, they were all designed to
influence, in one way or another, the productive activities of a particular
part of the private sector.

Indicative planning

Governments have sometimes involved themselves in production
through attempts to co-ordinate private plans and decisions. Perhaps
the boldest experiment in this area in the post-war period was the
publication in 1965 by the (then) Labour government of a *National Plan*
(HMSO, 1965). The plan accepted that most production would continue
to be governed by market forces but argued that 'the assembly of the
forecasts and plans of private industry is a great help in planning the
public sector. Similarly, industrialists should benefit, both from the
collection of the plans of other industries which are their customers and
from a knowledge of the intentions of government – by far the largest
buyer in the country' (*ibid*, p. 3). However, the *Plan* never spelt out
precisely what those benefits were. For various reasons the targets set by
the *Plan* did not materialize and the *Plan* – and indeed the principles
behind it – quickly faded into obscurity. Such a detailed exercise (in
what has come to be known as indicative planning) has not been tried
since. There have, however, been lesser attempts by government to
achieve greater co-ordination of decision making in the economy (see
pp. 210–12).

One mechanism for co-ordination that has managed to survive
successive changes in government is the National Economic Development Council (NEDC) which was set up in 1962. Its membership
consists of government ministers, trade union officials and management.
(In 1984, however, the trade unions temporarily withdrew from NEDC
following the government's decision to ban union membership at its
communications headquarters at Cheltenham.)

A number of NEDC committees have been set up for particular industries (see p. 211). These bodies are able to discuss a wide range of issues in relation to the encouragement of competitiveness and obstacles to growth. They do not, however, have any formal powers.

2.5 SUMMARY

The co-ordination of production in an economy may be achieved in a variety of ways. Central planning is one option. Another possibility is the 'invisible hand' of the market, where the key element is the transaction. State involvement in production may still be justified in such a system by reference to market failure. The firm, which in the UK may take one of three basic forms, provides a means of reducing transactions costs in the market place.

The UK economy is a mixed economy in the sense that it involves a combination of private and public sector activities. The public sector now accounts for about 30 per cent of the total UK employed labour force. Governments have also involved themselves in production through shareholdings in companies, through a variety of economic policies and through attempts to co-ordinate private plans and decisions.

In the next chapter attention is focused on what has been happening to UK industry in the post-war period.

3

The Structure of Industry in the UK

3.1 INDUSTRIAL CLASSIFICATION

The Basis for Classification

In chapter 1 it was pointed out that an industry may be defined in various ways. It may therefore be helpful to have a standard set of definitions which can be utilized across a wide range of studies. Such a classification system may also be a useful means of grouping together firms with similar interests.

The interests of firms may be linked in a variety of ways. They may sell products which are close substitutes for each other, i.e. they may operate in the same output market. They may buy in the same input market. They may employ similar production techniques. The grouping together of firms with common interests may be valuable for at least two reasons. First, such firms are likely to be affected by the same kind of influences. For example, all firms selling drugs have to conform to the same legal regulations on clinical trials and on advertising. They may all be affected by a general change in attitudes towards the use of drugs. Firms which employ deep sea divers, i.e. who operate in the same input market, are all covered by the same safety regulations, and by the availability of trained manpower. Firms using the same techniques of production are all likely to be affected by the same changes in technology. Secondly, firms with similar interests may be interdependent. Each firm's decisions may influence, and be influenced by those of other firms. It is often useful therefore to study the behaviour of interdependent firms as a group. However, there is no guarantee that firms which have similar interests in *one* aspect of business operations will also have them in another aspect. For example, manufacturers of suits compete in the same output market yet one firm may use natural fibres and another synthetic materials, i.e. they buy in different input markets. Again similar techniques of production may be used by the producer of warships and the merchant shipbuilder, but they sell in very different output markets. Thus different criteria may produce different groupings of firms.

Once a criterion for grouping firms with similar interests has been established, it is then necessary to specify the level of aggregation at which the industry is to be defined. Even if it is agreed (for example) that output markets are to be the basis for classification, different *degrees* of substitutability of products remain. The market for suits again provides a useful example. Should the industry include only producers of suits selling in a particular price bracket, or should it cover producers of *all* kinds of suits? The industry definition could be further extended to include all types of outer garments or even all clothing. Indeed in the last resort all goods and services compete with each other for limited consumer purchasing power. (Some consumers may well find themselves choosing between a new suit and, say, a better holiday or a bicycle.) In the end, the line must be drawn rather arbitrarily.

The 1980 Standard Industrial Classification

In the UK, the Standard Industrial Classification (SIC), 1980, is the basis for industry definitions. A number of different factors are taken into account in arriving at these definitions. They include the nature of the process or of the work done, the principal raw material used, the type or intended use of goods produced or handled and the type of service rendered. Different factors predominate in different parts of the classification and it is sometimes the case that a broad grouping based on one common factor is subdivided by reference to another.

The classification is undertaken at four main levels of aggregation. The full range of activities is first divided into ten broad Divisions each denoted by a single digit from 0 to 9. Each Division is divided into Classes of which there are 60 in total. A Class is assigned a two digit number, the first digit being that of the Division in which it is found. Classes are subdivided into 222 Groups. Each Group is given a three digit classification (the first two numbers of which denote the Class). Finally the groups are subdivided into Activities of which there are 334. The four digits assigned to each Activity provide information on the Group, Class and Division in which it is found. For example, as table 3.1 shows, Activity 3523 (Caravans) is part of Group 352 (Motor vehicle bodies, trailers and caravans) which in turn is part of Class 35 (Manufacture of motor vehicles and parts thereof). Class 35 is in Division 3 (Metal goods, engineering and vehicle industries).

Table 3.1 Extract from Division 3 of the Standard Industrial Classification, 1980

Class	Group	Activity	
35			MANUFACTURE OF MOTOR VEHICLES AND PARTS THEREOF
	351	3510	MOTOR VEHICLES AND THEIR ENGINES
	352		MOTOR VEHICLE BODIES TRAILERS AND CARAVANS
		3521	Motor vehicle bodies
		3522	Trailers and semi-trailers
		3523	Caravans
	353	3530	MOTOR VEHICLE PARTS

Source: *Standard Industrial Classification, 1980*, HMSO, 1979.

It is conventional to group Divisions 2–4 (Extraction of minerals and ores other than fuels; manufacture of metals, mineral products and chemicals; Metal goods, engineering and vehicle industries; and Other manufacturing industries) under the general heading of Manufacturing. Not all the data presented in this book are based on the 1980 SIC. The precise SIC used is not, however, usually crucial to the interpretation of such data especially where very broad groupings such as 'Manufacturing' are used. Some data are available at regional and sub-regional levels. It is therefore often possible to talk of an 'industry' in different geographical contexts.

The above classification is applied to the statistical unit, i.e. the unit for which the relevant statistics are available. The definition of this unit may vary with the type of data being collected. For example, the unit used for employment data usually consists of the address at which there are employees whereas in retail distribution the unit is frequently that used for the collection of value added tax. For most of the present book the unit may be equated with the 'establishment' or 'plant', often equivalent to a single factory or office.

A firm may have several statistical units. For example, it may run several separate establishments each of which keeps its own statistical records. Each may produce different types of output. A unit is classified to an industry on the basis of its biggest single activity. It is possible, therefore, to have units belonging to the same firm allocated to different industries. It is also possible for a unit to be classified to an industry on the basis of a *minority* activity.

Much of the analysis in this book is devoted to the behaviour and performance of firms in output markets. In empirical work on such markets, however, it is often necessary to rely on data collected for SIC 'industries'. The differences between these two concepts should be borne in mind.

Since most of the references to market in the following chapters refer to output markets the word 'output' has been dropped. Input markets, however, will continue to be explicitly identified as such.

3.2 CHANGES IN UK INDUSTRIAL STRUCTURE

A variety of different yardsticks may be used to analyse changes in industrial structure over time. Employment, output and sales are among the more obvious possibilities. Which particular measures are chosen depends of course on the purpose of the exercise, and on data availability. In this chapter, attention is focused on output and employment data as these are probably the most informative summary measures.

Changes in the Pattern of Industry

Some data

In table 3.2 data on trends in the UK's industrial structure over the period 1961–83 are presented. Most of the data are given at Division level, although a further breakdown is possible for Division 9 (Other services). Data for the manufacturing sector as a whole are also given. Annual growth rates (on a compound basis) for output and employment are provided in columns 3 and 5 respectively. Output growth is measured in *real* terms in the sense that it is calculated after allowance has been made for any increase in the general level of prices. In column 4, each industry's share of total output in 1961 and 1983 is shown for comparative purposes. The same comparisons are made for employment in column 6. The output and employment measures are not calculated on a strictly comparable basis. For example the former includes the contribution made by the self-employed; such people are excluded from the latter. However, these discrepancies are not substantial.

Some important trends

The following features of the table are particularly worthy of note.

Table 3.2 Trends in the UK's industrial structure, 1961–83

1 Industry	2 Division number (1980 SIC)	3 Annual (real) growth rate of output 1961–83*† (%)	4 Share of output* (%)		5 Annual growth rate of employment‡ 1961–83 (%)	6 Share of employment (June)‡	
			(a) 1961	(b) 1983		(a) 1961	(b) 1983
Agriculture, forestry and fishing	0	2.5	2.0	2.3	−1.9	3.1	1.6
Energy and water supplies	1	4.4	6.4	11.0	−1.6	4.9	3.1
Manufacturing	2–4	1.0	30.7	25.2	−1.3	37.6	26.3
Extraction of minerals and ores other than fuels; manufacture of metals, mineral products and chemicals	2	0.8	6.1	4.8	−1.7	6.6	3.8
Metal goods, engineering and vehicles	3	0.7	14.0	11.0	−1.1	16.2	12.4

Other manufacturing	4	−1.3	10.7	9.4	−1.4	14.8	10.0
Construction	5	−0.1	9.0	6.1	−1.3	6.5	4.7
Distribution, hotels and catering repairs	6	1.3	15.2	12.7	0.5	16.8	19.6
Transport and communication	7	2.4	6.5	7.1	−0.8	7.4	6.2
Banking, finance, insurance, business services	8	4.3	7.9	13.4	3.7	3.7	8.6
Other services	9	1.9	22.2	22.3	1.6	19.9	29.8
Public administration and defence	9	0.7	8.7	6.7	na	na	10.2§
Education and health services		2.9	7.6	9.4	na	na	13.5
Other services		2.0	5.9	6.1	na	na	6.1
Total		1.9	100.0	100.0	0.2	100.0	100.0

na = not available

*Output in this table is broadly equivalent to gross value added at factor cost (see p. 7). Figures subject to rounding errors.

†Growth rates are based on the indices of output at constant factor cost published by the Central Statistical Office.

‡Employees in employment, Great Britain. Figures subject to rounding errors.

§Includes the armed forces.

Source: Derived from *National Income and Expenditure*, 1983; *Economic Trends*, October 1983; Department of Employment *Gazette*; Historical Supplement, No. 1, August 1983; Central Statistical Office.

First, only in three Divisions (Distribution, hotels and catering, repairs; Banking, finance, insurance, business services; and Other services) was employment growth positive. All other Divisions declined in employment terms. However, in all but two of the Divisions which experienced negative employment growth, output growth was positive. Secondly, in all Divisions, output growth exceeded employment growth. Thus all sectors experienced growth in labour productivity. In some Divisions, notably 0, 1 and 7, productivity growth was particularly rapid.

Thirdly, manufacturing declined considerably in relative importance over the period. By 1983 it accounted for only about a quarter of both total output and employment. Such a decline also occurred in many other advanced economies (Brown and Sheriff, 1979, p. 240), although the process seems to have gone further in the UK. The overall decline in manufacturing does, however, disguise substantial variations in growth records across individual industries in that sector. A few industries have experienced fairly rapid growth. For example, chemicals and man-made fibres (both part of Division 2) and electrical and instrument engineering (part of Division 3) have all had average annual output growth rates of 3 per cent per annum or above. At the other extreme, output of metals (part of Division 2), has experienced substantial decline – over 2.5 per cent per annum. The experience of some industries has of course varied over the period in a way which is not apparent from the growth figure for the period as a whole. For example, motor vehicle manufacturing (part of Division 3) experienced an almost consistent expansion of output up to 1973, but its decline since that year has almost exactly offset that expansion.

Fourthly, Banking, finance, insurance and business services, education and health, and Transport and communication experienced relatively rapid expansions in output. (However, employment declined in Transport and communication.)

Distribution – the major element in Division 6 – is of course closely tied in with the fortunes of manufacturing. This may be part of the explanation why this industry, unlike other service industries, has grown so slowly. Divisions 6–9 – the Divisions in which all the services (including public administration and defence) are found – accounted for nearly 56 per cent of total output in 1983 (and 64 per cent of 1983 employment).

Part of the growth in some services may be more apparent than real in that manufacturers may now be providing fewer services in-house, preferring rather to buy them in from outside. Such a trend would show up in the official statistics as an increase in the relative importance of services, even though no real increase in the service activities associated with manufacturing had occurred. However, it is unlikely that the shift away from in-house provision of services by manufacturers is the dominant factor behind the increasing importance of the service industries.

Finally, the most rapid growth of all has been in Energy and water supplies with the primary generator of growth being North Sea oil and gas. The latter's growth has been phenomenal: between 1961 and 1983 its output went up by well over 1,000 per cent. This expansion, which of course started from very small beginnings, is in marked contrast to the considerable decline in what was once a very large coal industry; coal output more than halved over the period. The output growth rate for Energy and water supplies overall reflects these conflicting trends. The production of North Sea oil and gas is substantially more capital intensive than coal mining. Even rapid expansion of the former has not been sufficient to offset the decline in employment in the latter. Thus for the Division as a whole, employment has declined.

The data in columns 4(b) and 6(b) taken together, imply substantial differences across industries in the output to labour ratio. These differences in part reflect differences in the capital intensity of production. Thus Energy and water supplies which is relatively capital intensive, has a share of total employment that is less than a third of its share of gross value added. Many services – for example, distribution, education and health – on the other hand are relatively labour intensive; hence their share of employment is higher than their share of output. This is not the case across all services: commercial services which rely extensively on computerized operations are an obvious exception.

Factors behind the changes

The reasons for these changes in UK industrial structure are complex. However, two fundamental factors may be identified. First there are changes in the pattern of demand. These may arise for a wide range of reasons: changes in tastes and fashion; changes in the structure of the population; and changes in incomes. The last mentioned factor may be especially important in explaining the shift towards services: many services have a relatively high income elasticity (defined as the proportionate change in quantity demanded divided by the proportionate change in income). As incomes increase with economic growth so it would be expected that such service activities, particularly those connected with tourism and leisure pursuits, would grow in relative importance.

The second factor is changes in conditions of supply. Technological change, expressed in new products and processes, may lead to the development of new industries, and to the decline of some existing industries. The expansion of chemicals and man-made fibres, electrical and instrument engineering owes much to this source. Technological advance may come more easily in some industries than in others (see p. 157). Productivity increases may also be relatively easier to achieve in some industries than in others.

Demand and supply factors may be closely interwoven. For example some innovations may be developed *in response to* pressures of demand. Others may emerge independently of such demands and *generate* new demands.

Changes in the UK industrial structure must be seen in the context of international trade. Any variations in the UK's relative competitiveness across industries would be expressed in changes in industrial structure. For example, Japanese competition in motor cars has had a major effect on the UK car industry.

The Public Sector

Figure 3.1 traces the development of the public sector and its major components in terms of their share of the total employed labour force for the period 1961–83. (The break in the series in 1966 is due to a slight change in the data base.) Overall the public sector has expanded its share (from 23.0 per cent in 1961 to 29.1 per cent in 1983). The main contributors to this expansion were central government and the local authorities.

The Size Distribution of Firms

One facet of industrial structure which has attracted a good deal of attention in the post-war period has been the size distribution of firms and establishments in the private sector. This attention has focused on three main considerations. The first concerns market concentration, the extent to which individual markets are dominated by a small group of firms. The second is the level of aggregate concentration, the extent to which the private sector as a whole, or a substantial segment of it, is dominated by a few firms. Market and aggregate concentration are considered in greater detail in chapters 4 and 5 respectively and are not therefore considered further here.

The third aspect of the size distribution which has attracted interest and which is considered in more detail here concerns the relative importance of firms and establishments of different sizes. The size of a firm may affect the cost efficiency with which it operates (see chapter 4) and its ability to invent and innovate (see chapter 10). There is still a good deal of debate over whether the UK has the 'best' mix of firm sizes. In this context it is interesting to note the very considerable change in policy emphasis that has occurred in the last 20 years in respect of firm size. In the mid-1960s, the emphasis in industrial policy

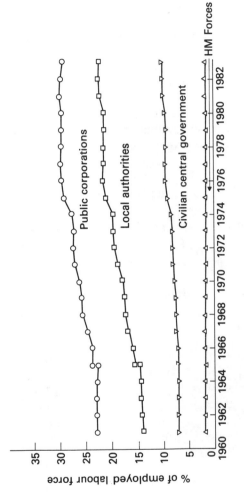

Figure 3.1 Employment in the public sector
Source: derived from *Economic Trends*, March, 1984.

was on restructuring to achieve greater firm size. Technological development in many industries was seen as depending on large firms. In
the 1970s, however, the emphasis shifted to stimulating the development of small firms. Such firms were seen as an important channel for
new competition and new products and processes.

Manufacturing

In table 3.3 data on trends in the relative shares of small and large firms
(or 'enterprises' as they are referred to in official statistics) and
establishments in manufacturing since 1958 are given. Overall there has
been no dramatic change in these shares, although there appears to have
been a tendency, particularly marked in the early 1980s, for small firms to
expand their share and for large firms to reduce theirs. This is a reversal
of the pattern in the inter-war and immediate post-war periods. Similar
trends are apparent among establishments. The data must, however, be
interpreted carefully. An expanding small firm sector does not neces-

Table 3.3   Size of enterprises and establishments in UK manufacturing

	Percentage of total employment in manufacturing			
	Enterprises		*Establishments*	
Year	*less than 200 employees*	*more than 10,000 employees*	*less than 200 employees*	*more than 1,000 employees*
1958	24		32	
1963	20		31	
1968	19		29	
1971	21.0	36.6	27.9	41.1
1972	21.5	35.0	27.4	42.1
1973	20.7	37.0	27.4	42.3
1975	21.5	36.4	28.9	41.8
1976	22.6	35.3	29.8	40.7
1977	22.5	34.8	29.5	41.0
1978	22.8	34.6	29.6	41.4
1979	23.1	34.9	29.8	40.9
1980	24.3	33.9	31.9	38.5
1981	25.9	31.3	33.9	36.8

Note: A line between years indicates a break in the series. Data for previous
      and subsequent years are not necessarily comparable.
Source: HMSO, 1971, chapter 5; *Censuses of Production*, various years.

sarily mean that more new firms are surviving or that existing small firms are growing relatively faster. The figures may reflect *declining* fortunes of larger firms. As they reduce in size, so they swell the share of the smaller size category. Unfortunately it is not possible, on the basis of existing data, to say why the shares have moved in the way they have.

Share of employment is only one measure of relative size. Other measures may yield different results. For example small and large enterprises (as defined in table 3.3) accounted (in 1981) for 97.2 and 0.1 per cent respectively of the total *numbers* of enterprises.

Non-Manufacturing

Manufacturing is of course only one industrial sector. However, many other industries have experienced a trend towards larger scale. In agriculture, the post-war period has seen a very clear shift towards larger holdings, partly as the result of the need to take full advantage of greater mechanization. (In 1982, over 37 per cent of holdings were over 40 hectares.) In retailing, the larger multiple stores have steadily grown in relative importance, at the expense of the independent shops. The percentage share of retail turnover of the former rose from 28.2 per cent in 1961 to 40.1 per cent in 1976; the latter's share fell between the same years from 53.9 per cent to 43.0 per cent. In 1980, retail businesses employing less than ten persons accounted for 90.2 per cent of the total number of businesses but only 24.6 per cent of total turnover, whereas businesses with a thousand employees or more had only 0.08 per cent of the total number of businesses, but accounted for 50.5 per cent of total sales.

The move towards larger scale in retailing has been due to many factors. These include greater mobility (through car ownership) of consumers which has in turn permitted the setting up of large stores which serve an extensive area and which are thereby able to take advantage of various economies of large scale production. Developments in technology, particularly the use of computers in stock control, have also favoured the larger units. The buying power of the large businesses does of course give them a price advantage. The small outlets have tried to counter this by setting up their own voluntary buying groups (Livesey, 1980).

In business and financial services, there has almost certainly been a considerable expansion in the share of the largest firms in many areas of activity in the post-war period. In commercial banking, there were 11 London clearing banks in 1958, but a series of mergers in the 1960s reduced it to five. In 1978, these banks were responsible for 56 per cent of all sterling advances by UK banks. The number of Building Societies has also fallen: from 755 in 1957 to 316 in 1978 (HMSO, 1980a, p. 436). The five societies with assets over £2,000m in 1978, controlled over 54

per cent of total assets. In insurance credit and finance there has also
been substantial growth in the share of the largest companies. At the
end of 1978, ten insurance companies (19 per cent of the total number)
each with assets of over £1,000m controlled over 50 per cent of the total
assets held by insurance companies. Sixteen finance houses (32 per cent)
controlled 66 per cent of the total assets in their sector.

The construction industry is a little unusual in that there has been
relatively little change in the size distribution. Small firms have continued to play a substantial role throughout the post-war period.
Fleming (1980) points out that although the size of the very largest firms
has tended to increase, the mean size of firms in terms of operatives
employed was very much the same at the end of the 1970s (at nine) as it
was in 1948. The reasons behind the continued persistence of the small
firm in construction are not difficult to find. Demand is geographically
dispersed and the product is non-transportable. Both these factors tend
to lead to a wide geographical dispersion of independent firms. Furthermore, the work itself is very diverse, and encourages the growth of
specialist firms.

3.3 THE MECHANICS OF CHANGE IN THE PRIVATE SECTOR

In the previous section, recent trends in industrial structure were briefly
considered. As far as the private sector is concerned these trends are the
net result of changes taking place at the level of the individual firm. This
section examines the mechanisms through which such changes came
about. Consideration is restricted to factors which influence the size of
an industry measured, say, by gross value added or employment.
However, much of the discussion below is relevant for explaining
changes in other features of industrial structure such as the size
distribution of firms.

Ownership Changes

It is important to realize at the outset that changes in the pattern of
ownership in an industry may not necessarily affect the size of that
industry. For example an entirely new firm may come in and take over
existing capacity. As a result, the firm from whom the capacity is bought
may be reduced in size or may even go into liquidation. Another
possibility is for existing firms in the industry to buy and sell capacity
among themselves. In both these examples of a switch in ownership, a
change in the total size of an industry is not a *necessary* consequence.
However, it is sometimes the case that ownership changes *do* have

implications for an industry's size. Productive capacity may be taken over by new entrants or by other firms already in the industry precisely because they believe that they can expand output by increasing cost efficiency through (for example) the replacement of inferior management. Some of the effects of merger activity on efficiency, and the relative merits of internal expansion and 'external' growth through merger are examined in chapter 11.

A firm run by an ageing owner may well be revived (and its output consequently increased) if taken over by a young dynamic entrepreneur. Management 'buy outs' – in which managers buy part or the whole of a company in which they are employed and run it for themselves – are another means by which an ownership change may affect the scale of operations. Many such buy outs lead to the preservation of capacity that would otherwise close down. For example when Rank decided to close down its precision industries division in Leeds in 1979, a number of managers in the division used their redundancy money to buy out part of the company's operations. In 1983 six of the companies formed as a result were still in operation.

The effect of ownership changes on output may not, however, always be positive: a firm may buy up capacity in order to close it down and thereby protect its own position.

Provided these possible relationships between ownership and output changes are borne in mind, a useful distinction between two basic types of mechanism through which changes in industrial structure come about may be made. These are examined below.

Two Mechanisms for Change

Births and Deaths

Changes in industrial structure may occur as the result of differences across industries in the rate at which new firms are born and existing firms die. Expanding industries may experience a relatively high birth rate and a relatively low death rate; the reverse may be the case in declining industries. Births and deaths may not of course be unrelated: sometimes the former may *cause* the latter.

Some idea of the birth and death rates in the UK economy as a whole may be obtained from Value Added Tax (VAT) registration data. (Every business with sales of £18,000 or over must register.) These data have a number of pitfalls. For example, some new businesses do not have to register because they do not reach the minimum turnover required. Conversely, some removals from the register may not reflect the demise of a business but rather a fall in turnover below the threshold. Some registrations represent the formation of subsidiaries rather than brand new firms. However, these limitations are probably not substantial enough to distort seriously the picture given in table 3.4. The following points from the table should be noted. First, most of the births and deaths occur in services. Secondly, birth and death *rates* vary very substantially across sectors. Two measures of the birth rate have been used: the number of VAT registrations per thousand employees (column 4) and the number of VAT registrations as a percentage of the total registered stock of businesses (column 5). The former is particularly useful if all workers in an industry are regarded as potential founders of businesses in that industry. The first measure shows a low rate in manufacturing and mining and quarrying and a particularly high rate in agriculture, construction and retail distribution. The second measure of the birth rate shows rather less variations across industries. Manufacturing, mining and quarrying has almost as high a birth rate measured in this way as retail distribution. Thirdly, comparisons between columns 2 and 6 show some variations in the net effects of births and deaths on the number of firms. Overall there was a net increase of about 47,000 firms in 1983.

How births and deaths affect industrial structure depends on the impact they have on output. Some births and deaths may simply represent ownership changes. However, they often play a more significant role. For example new firms are known to act as an important channel for certain types of innovation (see chapter 10).

Some indication of the overall importance of births may be obtained from table 3.5 which provides data on employment in new firms in manufacturing in Leicestershire over the period 1947–79. (Similar data are not available for the UK as a whole, or for non-manufacturing industries, or for output changes.) Clearly new firms become more important the longer the time period considered. Firms formed over a 32 year period and surviving to the end of the period accounted for nearly a quarter of all employment at the end date. (Of course the longer the period analysed the nearer the percentage of all manufacturing employment accounted for by new firms would come to 100 per cent.)

Established firms

The second type of mechanism through which changes in industrial structure in the private sector occur concerns the behaviour of existing firms. Such firms may expand or contract their output or employment in any particular industry. They may alter the number of plants that they operate and/or the number of employees in each plant. They may move into other industries for the first time by diversifying, or they may decide to move out completely from an industry in which they are currently operating. An existing firm's behaviour in one industry may be affected

Table 3.4 VAT births and deaths in 1983: by industrial sector (UK)

1 Sector	2 No. of VAT births (000s)	3 % of total VAT births	4 VAT births per 1,000 employees in employment	5 VAT births as % of total registered stock of businesses	6 No. of VAT deaths (000s)	7 % of total VAT deaths	8 VAT deaths as % of total registered stock of businesses
Agriculture	5.8	3.5	16.7	3.2	5.0	4.1	2.7
Manufacturing and mining and quarrying	18.6	11.1	3.1*	13.5	12.1	10.0	8.8
Construction	27.6	16.4	27.2	13.0	14.7	12.1	6.9
Retail distribution	32.2	19.1	15.5	12.1	30.5	25.1	11.4
Wholesale distribution	15.3	9.1	13.2	14.0	10.4	8.6	9.5
Transport	7.4	4.4	8.2	12.8	5.5	4.5	9.5
Financial, property, professional services	10.6	6.3	} 14.8†	11.7	6.5	5.4	7.2
Catering	16.1	9.6		13.3	13.8	11.4	11.4
Motor trades	9.1	5.4		12.4	7.0	5.8	9.5
Other services	25.6	15.2		16.5	15.8	13.0	10.2
Total‡	168.4	100.0	10.8	12.0	121.2	100.0	8.6

*Excludes energy supplies.
†Excludes public administration, postal services and communications and medical and other health services.
‡Figures subject to rounding errors.
Source: *Monthly Digest of Statistics* September 1984, table 3.2; *British Business*, 18 May 1984.

Table 3.5   Employment in new firms in manufacturing, Leicestershire, 1947–79

Year	Cumulative employment in post-1947 new firms	As a percentage of manufacturing employment
1947	0	0
1956	6,100	3.8
1968	14,800	4.8
1975	27,600	17.0
1979	36,000	23.0

Source: Fothergill and Gudgin, 1979, p. 7.

by, and affect, its behaviour in another industry. For example, it may decide that in order to find resources to enter market *A* it has to withdraw from market *B*.

Components of Change

In recent years some efforts have been made to assess the relative importance of births and deaths and of established firms in employment change through components of change analysis. Such analysis decomposes employment change in a given period into a number of categories. A highly simplified example of this kind of approach is given in table 3.6. The data refer to employment in manufacturing in the East Midlands for the period 1968–75. From the table it can be seen that established firms accounted for 83 per cent of gross job gains and 87 per cent of gross job losses. The extent to which the changes were accompanied by a change in product mix is not known.

Components of change analysis must be treated cautiously for at least two reasons. First, as indicated earlier, the results are likely to be heavily dependent on the time period chosen. The contribution of new firms is likely to grow as this period lengthens. Secondly, the various components are interdependent. For example, the birth of a new firm may lead to expansion, contraction or death of *other* firms. Again, the contraction of one established firm may be directly due to the expansion of another. Thus it is not possible from a perusal of table 3.6 to say what the primary causes of job losses and gains are. Nevertheless, components of change exercises can provide a useful first step in the description of employment change.

Table 3.6   Components of change: manufacturing employment, East Midlands, 1968–75

Source of job gains/losses	Employment 000s
Gross job gains	
Births	+ 23.3*
Established firms	+ 116.9†
Total	+ 140.2
Gross job losses	
Deaths	− 19.1‡
Established firms	− 129.9§
Total	− 149.0
Gross job gains *minus* job losses	− 8.8

*1975 employment in firms born between 1968 and 1975 (and surviving to 1975).
†[1975 employment in new plants opened between 1968 and 1975 (and surviving to 1975) by firms *already in existence in 1968*] *plus* [1975 *minus* 1968 employment in plants of existing firms which were already operating in 1968 and which *expanded* between 1968 and 1975].
‡1968 employment in single plant, independent firms which died between 1968 and 1975.
§[1968 employment in plants closed between 1968 and 1975 by firms which were still open in 1975] *plus* [1968 *minus* 1975 employment in plants of existing firms which were *still in operation in 1975* but which *contracted* between 1968 and 1975].
Source: Adapted from Fothergill and Gudgin, 1979.

3.4 SUMMARY

Some form of industrial classification system is a prerequisite for the analysis of industrial structure. The construction of such a system inevitably involves compromise between conflicting considerations.

The UK's industrial structure has experienced a shift away from manufacturing to services in recent years. This change has been accompanied by growth in the public sector and a shift towards larger sized firms and establishments in a wide range of industries.

Changes in industrial structure in the private sector come about in various ways. Births and deaths play some role, but the evidence suggests that at least in the shorter term it is the behaviour of established firms that has most impact.

4

Market Shares

4.1 TYPES OF MARKET

The primary concern in this chapter is the relationship between the distribution of market shares among firms and their market behaviour.

A monopoly is a market in which one seller supplies 100 per cent of the good or service in question. The monopolist has no rivals, although it may be very much aware of the possibility of new entry. In a perfectly competitive market each firm has only a very small share of the total market. It takes the market price as given, i.e. it is a price taker, and acts independently of all other firms. In this sense the firm in perfect competition also has no rivals. In both monopoly and perfect competition therefore, rivalry is absent, although for different reasons.

The absence of rivalry means that when firms make their decisions they do not take into account the possible reactions of *other* firms. Nor do they find themselves reacting to the decisions of these other firms. There is thus no interdependence between firms. This makes the analysis of firm behaviour in these markets relatively straightforward, and it is hardly surprising that the models of monopoly and perfect competition have tended to dominate textbook treatments of the theory of the firm. Given assumptions of perfect knowledge and profit maximization, fairly precise predictions about behaviour can be made in both cases. Some of these predictions are examined in later chapters.

Unfortunately, few markets can be comfortably described as either monopolistic or perfectly competitive. There are of course some near monopolies. Pilkington's domination of the flat glass industry is one example. It is also true that for a few markets, notably certain parts of agriculture, the perfect competition model may provide useful insights. For example, when the individual farmer takes his pigs to market he has virtually no influence on price. However, in the majority of markets in the private sector, neither model is appropriate. Output is often concentrated in the hands of a few firms. As a result interdependence between firms is an important market characteristic. Chapter 7 considers the nature of this interdependence more fully.

Numerous attempts have been made to model behaviour in markets consisting of only a few firms – oligopolies – but the wide variations in the distribution of market shares among firms and indeed in other market characteristics – for example the possibility of entry – that may prevail create substantial (perhaps insuperable) barriers to the provision of a single model. Furthermore, the fact that a key characteristic of oligopoly, interdependence – is absent in monopoly and perfect competition suggests that oligopoly is unlikely to receive satisfactory analytical treatment if it is regarded simply as some kind of half way house between the other two models.

4.2 THE MEASUREMENT OF MARKET SHARES

Some Measures

Numerous attempts have been made to provide suitable measures of the distribution of market shares among firms. Some of these measures incorporate data on the shares of all firms. One such measure is the Herfindahl index, H, which is the sum of the squares of the market shares of each firm.

Thus $H = \sum\limits_{i=1}^{n} s_i^2$

where s_i is the share of the ith firm, and n is the total number of firms.

$\sum\limits_{i=1}^{n}$ means 'summed over all firms, from firm 1 to firm n'. By squaring each share relatively more weight is given to the bigger firms. The H index varies from one for monopoly to zero for perfect competition. There is no reason why the *squaring* of shares should be favoured more than any other procedure (although it is the one most commonly adopted): any exponent could be chosen. The choice clearly depends on the relative importance attributed by the investigator to small and large shares.

Another measure which requires information on the shares of *all* firms is the Gini coefficient. The calculation of this coefficient is illustrated in figure 4.1. The horizontal axis shows the number of firms, cumulated from the smallest, as a percentage of all firms in the market.

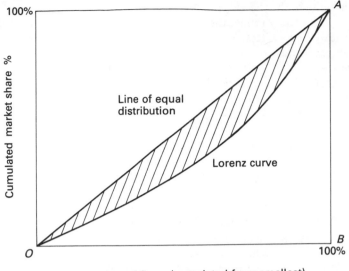

% number of firms (cumulated from smallest)

Figure 4.1   The Lorenz curve and Gini coefficient. The Gini coefficient is calculated as

$$\frac{\text{the shaded area}}{\text{area } OAB} \times 100$$

The vertical axis provides the cumulative market share in percentage terms. The curve which relates these two percentages is known as the Lorenz curve. The diagonal provides the line of equal distribution. At each point on this diagonal, a given percentage of firms accounts for an identical percentage market share. The Gini coefficient is calculated as

$$\frac{\text{the shaded area}}{\text{area } OAB} \times 100$$

For a monopoly, the Gini coefficient is one, and for perfect competition it is zero. It should be noted however that the coefficient is also zero for a market in which there are only two (equal sized) firms, even though these firms may be able to collude and thus act in effect as a monopolist.

Although both the *H* index and the Gini coefficient have the attraction that they reflect the shares of all firms in the market, they are not readily calculated from published industrial statistics. A more widely used measure for which data *are* published is the market concentration ratio (MCR). This measure simply gives the percentage of the market controlled by the *x* largest firms. In the latest *Census of Production*, *x* is set at five. The choice of this number is however rather arbitrary.

Limitations of the MCR

Although it is the most widely used measure in empirical studies of concentration, the MCR has a number of limitations. First, and most fundamentally, it is far from clear how differences in the MCR affect market behaviour. For example, would the output and prices in a market change (and if so to what extent) if the five firm MCR rose from 50 to 60 per cent? What if the MCR increased from 30 to 40 per cent? Would the answers to these questions be any different if three or eight firm concentration ratios were used? The underlying reason for the use of the MCR is a belief that this measure provides some indication of the degree of market power that the firms in the market have. Such power is expressed in the ability of firms to charge higher prices than they would be able to do in a less concentrated market. Higher prices mean that less output is produced. Market power may also make firms less responsive to consumer demands, and less receptive to technological change. Some of these arguments are examined in chapter 12.

The higher the MCR, the less likely it is (so the argument runs) that firms will compete as independent units. Instead they may engage in implicit or explicit collusion, i.e. co-ordination of policies, so that they can achieve for themselves the benefit of market power (Collusion is more fully considered in chapter 7.) Such collusion becomes more feasible as the number of firms falls; it may also become more attractive as the degree of interdependence increases. Both the number of firms and the degree of interdependence may be related (negatively and positively respectively) to the MCR. Unfortunately it is difficult to translate these arguments into hypotheses relating to specific MCRs. Ultimately the relationship between a particular MCR and behaviour (and hence performance) must be an empirical matter.

Secondly, markets may be ranked differently depending on the number of firms to which the MCR relates. For example industry *A* may appear more concentrated than industry *B* when the five firm MCR is used, but the reverse may be so with an MCR based on a larger number of firms.

Thirdly, it must be realized that the MCR refers only to the selling side of the market. The behaviour of sellers may, however, be affected by the structure of the buying side of the market. For example, if there is only one buyer (a monopsonist) the behaviour of sellers, even in a highly concentrated market, may be heavily constrained.

Finally the MCR does not provide information on the links between businesses. These links may stop short of parent-subsidiary relationships but they may nevertheless be very strong. One common form of link is the interlocking directorate in which two or more companies have a common director on their boards. A recent study of directorates in UK industry showed that in manufacturing, 55 per cent of the largest 118 companies had at least one interlock with other manufacturing companies (Johnson and Apps, 1979).

The case against using the MCR may seem fairly strong from the above. However, as long as its possible shortcomings are acknowledged, it can nevertheless provide a useful initial basis for the analysis of market power across industries.

4.3 MARKET CONCENTRATION IN THE UK

The analysis of concentration in the UK has focused almost exclusively on manufacturing. Published data on concentration outside manufacturing are very sparse. The discussion in the remaining part of this chapter focuses primarily on this sector, although much of the discussion is of relevance to other parts of industry.

Post-War Trends in Manufacturing

Changes to the Standard Industrial Classification (in 1958, 1968 and 1980) limit the scope for comparisons over a long period of time to those industries – used here as approximations to markets – which have been defined in the same way throughout. Hart and Clarke (1980) provide three firm employment MCRs for 42 comparable manufacturing industries for the period 1951–73. *Census of Production* data may be used to provide further data for the five firm employment MCRs for 1973 and 1979 for 131 comparable industries. The number of comparable industries is much higher for this later period because the same SIC applied in both years. These data are given in table 4.1. The figures show a clear rise in the level of concentration in UK manufacturing for the post-war period, although since 1968 there has been some stabilization in this level. It may even have declined very slightly in the 1970s. The rise in market concentration in the UK in the 1950s and 1960s is in marked

Table 4.1   Average (unweighted) employment MCRs in manufacturing industry, 1951–79

Year	42 comparable industries (3 firm)	131 comparable industries (5 firm)
1951	29.3	
1958	32.4	
1963	37.4	
1968	41.0	
1970	41.2	
1973	42.2	49.3
1979		48.2

Source: Hart and Clarke, 1980, p. 27; *Censuses of Production*, 1973 and 1979.

contrast to trends in the US, which show only a very slight increase (Hart and Clarke, 1980, p. 27).

The data in table 4.1 must be treated cautiously for the following reasons. First, it cannot be assumed that the industries included in the table are representative of all manufacturing. However, there are no obvious grounds for supposing that they are not. Secondly, the extent of concentration changes have varied considerably among the industries included in the table. Furthermore rapid increases in concentration in one industry in one period do not necessarily mean that such increases are continued in the subsequent period.

Thirdly, the data do not take account of the fact that some firms may produce for export markets and that such production should be ignored when MCRs for domestic markets are calculated. Nor do they allow for the presence of importers in domestic markets. Utton (1982a) has shown that adjustments for the presence of exports and imports can have an important impact on the measurement of trends in MCRs. For example he suggests (on the basis of sample data) that the adjusted level of concentration in 1975 was *below* that in 1963.

Finally, each industry is likely to cover a multitude of different activities and firms assigned to them may vary substantially in the types of product they produce. Not all firms in the same industry are likely to be direct competitors.

There is some disagreement among investigators about the importance of merger activity as the vehicle through which increased market concentration has occurred. However, it would probably not be unreasonable to assign about half of the increase in concentration in the late 1950s and early 1960s to mergers. (HMSO, 1978b, p. 99).

Concentration in Manufacturing in 1981

Table 4.2 provides summary data on market concentration at Group level in manufacturing in 1981. In nearly 40 per cent of industries, the five firm employment MCR was 50 per cent or more. These figures are, however, subject to all the qualifications expressed earlier. (Similar data are not available for non-manufacturing.)

Table 4.2   Five firm employment MCRs in manufacturing, 1981

MCR *range* *(%)*	*Number of* *industries*	*% of total*
less than 10	none	—
10–19	18	17.5
20–29	14	13.6
30–39	16	15.5
40–49	14	13.6
50–59	14	13.6
60–69	11	10.7
70–79	7	6.8
80–89	6	5.8
more than 90	3	2.9
Total	103	100.0

Source: *Census of Production*, 1981.

4.4 MARKET CONCENTRATION AND EFFICIENCY

The Long Run Average Cost Curve

It may of course be necessary for a firm to have a substantial share of the market if it is to operate in an efficient way. To examine this issue it is helpful to consider first the simple example of a single product firm. We can construct a long run average cost (LAC) curve for such a firm. This curve shows the minimum unit costs of production at different levels of

output. The curve is 'long run' in the sense that it describes the
behaviour of unit costs after all possible adjustments in input quantities
have been made. Thus each point on the curve is cost efficient (see p.
11). The curve is constructed on the assumption that the technology of
production and factor prices are constant and that perfect information is
available. One such curve is illustrated in figure 4.2. Economies of scale
are said to exist up to output Q_1, with diseconomies of scale thereafter.
Sometimes the curve may have a horizontal section; over such sections

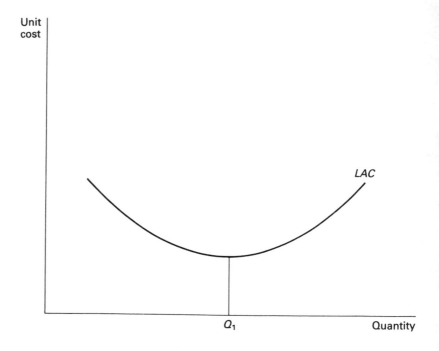

Figure 4.2   The long run average cost curve
The firm's *LAC* curve shows the minimum unit costs of production at different
levels of output. Each point on the curve is cost efficient. Economies of scale are
said to exist up to Q_1 and diseconomies of scale thereafter. Q_1 is the minimum
efficient scale.

there are no economies or diseconomies of scale. Q_1 may be referred to as the minimum efficient scale (mes). At this level of output, the firm may be said to be scale efficient.

Sources of Scale Economies

Economies of scale may derive from numerous sources of which the following are probably the most important. First, there may be indivisibilities in production so that there are some costs which remain the same whatever the level of output. For example, total design and research and development costs of a product are 'once for all' costs and do not increase as the output of that product increases. Thus *average* design and research and development costs fall as output increases. Where these initial costs are very high – such as in computers and aircraft production – the scale of output becomes a crucial determinant of a firm's average costs, and hence competitiveness. Capital equipment is often indivisible. Certain types of machinery can only be built with large capacities. Consequently the more fully such machinery is used, the lower the average capital cost. Secondly, economies of increased dimensions may arise. Such economies derive from the fact that for many types of equipment, capacity increases more rapidly than capital costs. For example, in the case of tanks, the cost of capacity increases roughly in proportion to surface area, whereas capacity rises in proportion to cubic capacity. The engineer's well known '0.6' rule of thumb – whereby it is assumed that on average a 100 per cent rise in capacity causes costs to increase by only 60 per cent – is a reflection of these economies of increased dimensions. (These economies are, of course, only operative over a certain *range* of output.)

Thirdly, large output may permit greater specialization of labour. Specialization by individuals in particular operations may lead to higher productivity. Such specialization may not be possible with low levels of output.

Fourthly, economies of massed reserves may be obtained as output increases. For example, as the number of identical machines increases, so the number of machines that have to be held in reserve to cope with breakdowns increases less than proportionately. A firm with only one machine may find that it has to keep one 'spare' if production is not to be interrupted by a breakdown. However, if it runs two machines, it does not also have to double the number of machines held in reserve, because the probability of both breaking down *at the same time* is very low (unless of course the causes of the breakdowns are related).

Finally, a larger scale of output may permit the firm to introduce other methods of organization which lower unit costs. For example, a firm may switch from batch to flow production.

Diseconomies of Scale

A U-shaped *LAC* curve of the type given in figure 4.2 does, of course, imply that at some stage diseconomies of scale prevail. Many of the economies referred to earlier are eventually exhausted. For example, it is unlikely that economies of increased dimensions can always be obtained as output rises to progressively greater levels. Capacity cannot be increased indefinitely without some strengthening and/or design changes to the structures involved becoming necessary. It may also be necessary to change the materials used. These changes may eventually cause average costs to rise as output increases. Again, too much specialization by labour may generate industrial relations problems as a result of the jobs involved becoming repetitive and divorced from the end product. There is evidence to show that the incidence and duration of strikes rises with the size of plant in UK manufacturing (see p. 96). This finding cannot be attributed to any single cause; however, it is likely to be related in part at least, to the higher level of labour specialization involved in the mass production techniques of the larger plants. Most discussion of diseconomies of scale has, however, centred on the greater complexities of managing a larger firm. As the chain of command grows, it is argued, so information is lost or distorted as it flows up and down this chain. Problems of co-ordination and leadership increase. New organizational forms have been developed to reduce management problems in the large firm, but it is not clear how effective such innovations have been in coping with these problems.

Efficient Scale and Market Concentration

Some limitations of the mes concept

With a knowledge of the single product firm's *LAC* curve it is possible to say how much of the relevant market it requires to achieve mes. It is also possible to make estimates of the unit cost penalty that would be incurred if such a firm were restricted to a size *below* the mes. An *LAC* curve which is saucer shaped implies lower penalties than one whose sides are steeply sloped.

The above discussion of *LAC* for the single product firm does, however, have a number of limitations when it comes to examining the relationship between the most efficient scale of operation in its widest sense and market concentration. First, it provides no information on the most efficient size for technological change. While Q_1 in figure 4.2 may be the most efficient size for a *given* technology, it may not necessarily be optimal for inducing technological *change*. Thus, in this sense, there may be a trade off between efficiency in a *static* sense and the capacity of a firm to innovate. Q_1 may not be the most efficient point when the latter is taken into account. For example, the size of firm implied by Q_1 may imply a management framework which impedes the flow of new products and processes. The relationship between size and invention and innovation is considered in chapter 10.

Secondly, the position and shape of the *LAC* curve may be influenced by a learning effect. This effect arises largely as the result of a labour force gaining greater familiarity with its production technology, and is reflected in average costs falling over time as the cumulated total of output increases. For example, it has been estimated that doubling cumulative airframe output is accompanied by an average reduction in average labour requirements of about 20 per cent (study quoted in HMSO, 1978b, p. 82). The learning effect causes the whole curve to shift downwards over time. Thus a firm producing Q_1 in a period which immediately follows the launch of a new product or process may find that its average costs are far higher than those for an identical output many periods later. There is no guarantee that the mes output level and the shape of the curve will remain intact as these shifts occur. One way round this problem is to define the time period to which the *LAC* curve relates as the total life of the product under study.

Thirdly, the relationship between size and uncertainty has been ignored. The mes in figure 4.2 is defined for a world of complete certainty. However, such a size may reduce the firm's ability to cope with unexpected changes in either demand or supply conditions. The presence of uncertainty may in fact lead a firm to use or develop a technology which gives rise to a flat bottomed *LAC* curve since the latter will permit changes in output in response to changing circumstances without any cost penalty being incurred.

Finally, many large firms have a multi-product character. (One reason for this is that it may be cheaper to produce both x of good A and y of good B in one firm, than to produce x and y *separately* in two single product firms. If this is the case, economies of scope are said to exist.) Where a firm has diversified into several markets, the concept of an efficient scale for that firm in any one market may not be clearly defined since the different parts of its operations are interdependent. Allocation of common costs can only be undertaken on an arbitrary basis.

Empirical studies of economies of scale

Empirical studies of economies of scale have used a variety of methodologies. The types of cost included in these studies have also varied. Some studies consider economies of scale at plant level only (and have ignored those costs which in a multi-plant firm are not allocable to individual plants); others have tried to estimate economies of scale at the firm level.

The most comprehensive study of economies of scale in the UK is still that by Pratten (1971). Some of his results are shown in table 4.3. His study was based largely on engineering type estimates of economies of scale and relates mostly to *plants*, rather than to firms. The engineering approach uses existing design cost and performance standards to estimate costs for different (hypothetical) output levels. The estimates in table 4.3 vary in the types of cost they include (although they *all* exclude marketing and distribution costs) but these variations are unlikely to affect the basic picture. The mes is calculated for 'a narrow range of products' (Pratten, 1971, p. 268) rather than for a single product. The former is a more appropriate frame of reference because very few plants produce only a single product. A 'narrow range of products' means a group of products made on the same machinery (for example footwear of a single style or a number of styles involving small variations). The third column of the table expresses the mes as a percentage of the relevant market size in 1969. For some products the market is defined on both a UK and a narrower geographical basis.

Of course the table may not provide a representative picture of economies of scale in UK manufacturing industry. It might be argued that the markets were *chosen* for investigation precisely because it was thought likely that economies of scale would be extensive. Furthermore many of the estimates are now rather dated and technology may have changed. However, on the assumption that the general picture has not changed dramatically from that outlined in the table, it is clear that if mes is to be achieved in many markets, defined at UK level, a fairly high degree of concentration is necessary. Sixteen of the products mentioned required a quarter or more of the UK market to reach mes.

The relationship between market concentration and economies of scale at the plant level has been systematically explored in numerous studies. (See the survey in Curry and George, 1982.) Most have used a measure of mes which has involved some aspect of the observed distribution of plant sizes. There seems to be general agreement in these studies that mes at this level does exercise an important positive effect on market concentration. However, it is also evident that there are other factors which play a part. For example the initial capital expenditure required to set up a plant has also been shown to exercise a positive effect. Firms may be deterred from entering an industry if they have to incur substantial capital costs to do so. As a result there may be fewer firms in the market as the effect on concentration of mergers between firms already established in the industry may not then be offset by entry.

It also seems clear from the evidence that plant economies do not explain *very* high levels of concentration. In this context, it is interesting to note that many of the largest firms operate *several* plants in a market. The implication of this is that economies at plant level are not a sufficient explanation of the size of these firms. If the existence of multi-plant economies is slight – and the evidence points this way – it seems that other explanations of high concentration levels must be found. The most obvious possibility here is that firms are seeking market power. By growing beyond the mes they may not be suffering cost advantages, but neither may average costs be *increasing*. Salaried managers may also, to some extent, have some freedom to pursue their *own* objectives. These objectives which may not be those of shareholders, may sometimes be satisfied by the firm growing beyond its most efficient size. This issue is considered further in chapter 7.

Some economists have argued that the current high level of market concentration may have another cause. The heart of their argument is that it is the result of pure chance. Scherer (1980, pp. 145–6) has illustrated this argument with a simple computer simulation. The starting point for his simulation was an industry composed of 50 firms, each with a 2 per cent market share. He then examined what would happen to concentration in the industry over time given the following assumption about the growth rates of the firms. Each firm's growth rate in any year was determined by random sampling from the same distribution of possible growth rates. (In effect, each firm's growth rate in each year was drawn from a hat, containing a range of growth rates. Each firm drew from the same hat.) Scherer found that the larger the number of years over which the simulation was run, the higher the level of concentration became. Thus although firms all face equal chances of achieving any given growth rates, nevertheless some climb ahead in market share terms. This counter intuitive result arises simply because these firms enjoy a run of luck. The evidence on the extent to which this 'law of proportionate effect' provides an adequate explanation of trends in concentration is rather mixed. However, it would be difficult to avoid the conclusion that chance factors do have some role to play in determining firm growth. To the extent that they do, they will affect the level of concentration.

4.5 MARKET CONCENTRATION AND PROFITABILITY

Numerous studies have investigated the relationship between market concentration and profitability. (For useful surveys see Scherer, 1980, pp. 276–85, and Clarke, 1984.)

Profitability may be measured in various ways. One of the most frequently used measures is the rate of return on capital which is defined

Table 4.3   Some estimates of economies of scale

1 *Product etc.*	*2* *mes* (physical output)*	*3* *mes* as % of:*	
		(a) *UK* *market* *in 1969*	*(b)* *Sub-market†* *(as shown)*
1 *Oil* general purpose refinery	10 million tons p.a.	10	40 (regional mkt.)
2 *Chemicals* (a) ethylene plant	300,000 tons p.a.	25	100 (regional mkt.)
(b) Sulphuric acid	1 million tons p.a.	30	100 (regional mkt.)
(c) plant – individual dye	(large)	100	—
3 *Synthetic Fibres* (a) polymer plant	80,000 tons p.a.	33	66 (nylon)
(b) plant for filament yarn extrusion	40,000 tons p.a.	16	33 (nylon)
4 *Beer* – brewery	at least 1 million barrels p.a.	3	6 (regional mkt.)

5 Bread – bakery	throughput of 30 sacks of flour per hour	1	33 (city with 1 million population)
6 Detergents – plant	70,000 tons p.a.	20	—
7 Cement – portland cement works	2 million tons p.a.	10	40 (regional mkt.)
8 Bricks – works making non-Fletton bricks	25 million bricks p.a.	0.5	5 (regional mkt.)
9 Steel – steel production—blast furnace and LD route	9 million tons p.a.	33	—
10 Iron foundry – making cylinder blocks	50,000 tons p.a.	1	30 (car cylinder blocks)
11 Cars (a) one model and its variants	500,000 cars p.a.	25	50 (cars of about 1200 cc)
(b) a range of models	1 million cars p.a.	50	—
12 Aircraft – one type of aircraft	> 50 aircraft	>100	—
13 Bicycles – a range of models	< 100,000 p.a.	4	—
14 Machine tools (a) one type	(varies with type)	>100	—
(b) factories	300 employees	0.5	—

cont'd. overleaf

Table 4.3 (cont'd.) Some estimates of economies of scale

1	2	3	
		mes* as % of:	
Product etc.	mes* (physical output)	(a) UK market in 1969	(b) Sub-market† (as shown)
15 *Diesel engines* – models in range 1–100 h.p.	100,000 units p.a.	10	100 or more (individual size)
16 *Turbo generators* – one design	4 p.a.	100	—
17 *Electric motors* – range of models (1–100 h.p.)	£10 million p.a. (1969 prices)	60	—
18 *Domestic Electrical Appliances* – range of 10 appliances	500,000 p.a.	20	50 (refrigerators or washing machines)
19 *Electronic capital goods* (a) one product (e.g. computer or radar equipment)	1,000 units p.a.	100	—
(b) range of products	£200 million p.a.	100	—
20 *Cotton textiles* (a) spinning mills	< 60,000 spindles	<2	(much higher for individual product)
(b) weaving mills	< 1,000 looms		

21 *Warp knitting*	< 100 knitting machines	<3	(much higher for individual products)
22 *Footwear* factories	300,000 pairs p.a.	0.2	(much higher for individual groups of products)
23 *Newspapers*	(circulation equivalent to highest reached in UK i.e. popular Sunday paper)	30	100 (one class of newspaper)
24 *Books* (a) one title	10,000 copies	100 (hard-backs)	
(b) firms	(small)	2	—
25 *Plastic products* (a) one product	(large)	100	—
(b) firms making range of products	(small)	1	—

*This is the minimum scale above which any possible doubling in scale would reduce total average unit costs by less than 5 per cent and above which any possible subsequent doubling in scale would reduce value added (defined here as total costs less the cost of bought out materials, services and components) per unit by less than 10 per cent: Pratten, 1971, p. 26.
†Where applicable, i.e. regional market for trades where transport costs are important, and markets for important individual products for trades making a range of products.
Source: Adapted from Silberston's (1972) presentation of Pratten, 1971, table 30.1.

for a given accounting period (usually a year) as

$$\frac{\text{Profits (i.e. revenue less costs)}}{\text{Value of assets}} \times 100$$

Assets represent the capital employed in the business. There are numerous empirical problems associated with the calculation of this ratio which cannot be analysed here. However, the following should be noted. First, the numerator is a flow, while the denominator refers to a stock, usually calculated for the end of the accounting period. Secondly, both the numerator and denominator are affected by depreciation. Depreciation is a 'cost'; it also reduces the value of the assets.

The results of the concentration–profitability studies have been mixed. The reasons for this diversity are not difficult to identify. First, a wide variety of both concentration and profitability measures have been utilized. Some studies have examined levels, others changes in levels. It is also important to remember that profitability, whatever the particular measures used, refers to *reported* profitability. In some cases, however, 'profits' may be reported as costs. For example, salaried managers may be able to increase their perquisites (such as company cars, lavish office accommodation) at the expense of reported 'profits'. Such perquisites are of course recorded in the accounts as costs. Again, it may be possible for managers to opt for a quieter life thereby allowing costs to eat into profits. If managers' ability to appropriate profits in this way is systematically related to market concentration, then the relationship between concentration and reported profitability may not be very strong, while the relationship between concentration and 'real' profits may be much stronger.

Secondly, the studies relate to many different time periods. These periods often differ substantially in their economic characteristics.

Thirdly, studies have varied in the extent to which they have considered other possible influence on profitability. There may also be statistical problems of separating out the effects of those influences that *are* considered.

Despite the mixed nature of the results, there is some support (particularly in the US) for a positive though weak relationship between concentration and profitability (Scherer, 1980, pp. 278–9). Furthermore there is evidence, again mainly from US studies, to suggest that this relationship is discontinuous, i.e. that there is a critical level of concentration, at which profitability shows a particularly noticeable increase. For example, a study of the US food industry (Dalton and Penn, 1976) suggested a critical level for the four firm MCR of 45 per cent. This may suggest that the pressures and opportunities for implicit or explicit collusion between the largest sellers become particularly intense at this level. The influences of concentration on profitability seems weaker in intermediate goods industries than in final goods industries. The former industries, by definition, supply firms who often have professional buyers. The scope for the exercise of market power in these industries may as a consequence be relatively less.

The identification of a positive relationship between concentration and profitability does not of course give any clue as to whether this relationship arises because increased concentration generates lower unit costs (through, for example, the achievement of more economies of scale), greater market power, or both. For the US, the data suggest that the market shares of the largest firms tend to be larger than that required to achieve mes. This in turn suggests that at least some of the explanation for higher profitability comes from the greater market power associated with higher levels of concentration.

4.6 SUMMARY

There are numerous ways of measuring the distribution of market shares. The most common is the market concentration ratio (MCR) although this measure has a number of important limitations. The evidence suggests some increase in market concentration in UK manufacturing in the post-war period and in many industries, the five employment MCR is now over 50 per cent. A number of studies suggest that profitability increases with concentration although the precise relationship between these two variables is far from clear. The higher profitability may in part be explained by the lower unit costs that greater concentration brings. However the increased market power reflected in the latter is also likely to be an important explanatory factor.

5

The Largest Firms

5.1 INTRODUCTION

The previous chapter examined firm size primarily in terms of market share. This chapter broadens the discussion by considering size in absolute terms.

The Importance of Large Firms in the UK

Table 5.1 gives details of the six largest, privately owned UK companies ranked by their total employment size. Companies whose primary activities are financial and/or commercial services are excluded. The employment figures include overseas employment. Although the businesses in the table are clearly major employers, they are dwarfed by General Motors, the *world's* largest business, which has nearly three-quarters of a million people on its payroll.

It should be noted that the companies in table 5.1 are ranked by their employment. Different size criteria would provide different rankings. For example, British Petroleum is by far the largest company ranked by turnover; ICI is the biggest exporter.

The influence of the largest companies is pervasive. For example Utton (1979, p. 38) has shown that in manufacturing in the early 1970s the 200 largest enterprises were active in all of the 120 industries for which data were available. Some companies are spread over a very wide range of activities. For example, the Lonrho Group comprises over 850 companies and its activities – apart from those given in table 5.1 – cover such diverse industries as brewing, motor vehicle distribution and assembly, printing and publishing, and hotels. On the other hand, most large companies in manufacturing operate in only a few industries and these industries are usually closely related to the area in which their primary interests lie (Utton, 1979, p. 28).

Table 5.1 The largest privately owned UK companies

Company	Principal industries	Total number of employees
General Electric	Electrical engineering	188,802
BAT Industries	Tobacco, retailing, paper, packaging, etc.	178,000
Lonrho Group	Mining, agriculture, textile, construction, etc.	150,000
British Petroleum	Oil	145,150
Grand Metropolitan	Hotels, milk products, brewers	129,454
Imperial Chemical Industries	Chemicals, fibres, paint	123,800

Source: *The Times 1,000 1983–1984: The World's Top Companies,* Times Books Ltd, 1983, London.

The extent to which employment in different industries is concentrated in the hands of the largest firms varies substantially. For example in 1980, 60 per cent of employment in electrical and electronic engineering was accounted for by firms who were among the 100 largest manufacturing businesses whereas in timber and wooden furniture, the percentage was only 8 per cent.

Large Firms: The Issues

The existence of a number of very large companies raises at least two important issues. The first concerns the political power that such businesses may acquire simply as a result of the sheer scale of their activities. The decisions they make can affect, directly or indirectly, the lives of many hundreds of thousands of people. They may also be relatively more able, through their access to funds and their ability to achieve economies of scale in political lobbying, to influence the political decision-making process. This issue is outside the scope of this book, although clearly it is an important one.

The second issue relates to the connection between the total size of a business, and its ability to exercise market power. Two questions are relevant in this context. First, to what extent are the largest companies also leaders in each of the individual markets in which they operate? It is of course possible for a very large firm to be involved in a number of markets without having a substantial share in any one of them. The evidence on this score is thin but in half of a random sample of 30 manufacturing industries Utton (1974a) found that at least one of the 100 largest manufacturing firms was among the three leaders. Secondly, does size itself confer any market power? Is a firm in a stronger market position – whether or not it is a market leader – if it also operates elsewhere? Before these issues are considered on pp. 72–4, changes in the importance of large firms are considered.

5.2 AGGREGATE CONCENTRATION

Trends in the Post-War Period

The measure most commonly used to indicate the importance of large firms is the aggregate concentration ratio (ACR). The ACR measures the extent to which productive activity in the economy as a whole, or a substantial segment of it – for example manufacturing – is in the hands of a few firms. The ACR is subject to all the limitations associated with the market concentration ratio outlined in the previous chapter. It is particularly important to remember that the number of firms chosen as the basis for the ACR is quite arbitrary. By far the most detailed data on the ACR relate to manufacturing and attention is therefore largely confined to this sector. Prais (1981a) has provided details of trends in the share of the 100 largest enterprises. The primary measure of size that he uses is net output. This is similar to gross value added (GVA) although unlike GVA it includes the cost of industrial services. Table 5.2 provides the relevant details. There has been a substantial rise in aggregate concentration in the post-war period. This rise is shown in a second measure of the importance of large enterprises used by Prais: the number of largest enterprises accounting for 50 per cent of net output. This number fell from 420 in 1958 to 140 in 1970 (Prais, 1981a, p. 7). (Later data on this second measure are not available.)

However, table 5.2 suggests that the level of aggregate concentration stopped rising in the 1970s. There was also a pause in the growth of concentration during the Second World War. Although prior to the 1950s, the level of aggregate concentration in manufacturing was lower in the UK than in the US it is now much greater. Utton (1982b, p. 22) suggests that the UK now has one of the most highly concentrated manufacturing sectors in the world.

The second row of table 5.2 gives data on the share of the 100 largest *plants* in manufacturing net output. This share remained relatively

Table 5.2   The percentage share of the 100 largest enterprises and plants in UK manufacturing net output, 1948–79

	1948	1949	1953	1954	1958	1963	1968	1976	1979
Share of largest enterprises		22	27		32	37*	41	43‡	43‡
Share of largest plants	9.0			10.1	10.5†	11.1	10.8		

*Includes steel companies.
†Share of sales.
‡These figures have been adjusted to make them comparable with the previous figures: see Prais, 1981a, p. xviii, fn. 2.
Source: Prais, 1981a, tables 1.1 and 3.1 and p. xviii, fn. 2; *Census of Production*, 1979.

stable throughout the period, 1958 to 1968. (Unfortunately later data are not available.) These data suggest that very little increase in the ACR in this period was necessary to accommodate increases in plant size. It is not therefore surprising to find that the average number of plants owned by the 100 largest enterprises (ranked by employment) increased from 27 in 1958 to 72 in 1972 and the average employment size of plant fell over the same period from 750 to 430. (Prais, 1981a, p. 62). Evidence from *Census of Production* sources suggests that this trend towards larger numbers of plants and smaller average sizes of plants has continued since 1972. Other explanations for the rise in ACR apart from increases in plant size are clearly necessary. Prais attributes a substantial part of this rise to the operation at the aggregate level of the law of proportionate effect (see p. 61). He also suggests that other causes include the rise of large financial institutions, which have a predisposition towards larger client firms (partly because there are economies of scale in dealing with such firms) and the growth in the power of managers relative to shareholders. The latter factor may have permitted managers to pursue greater size as an objective irrespective of whether such an objective enhanced profitability.

Although the rise in the ACR in manufacturing has been accompanied by a rise in market concentration ratios (see pp. 53–4) there is no necessary link between the two. An increase in the ACR may occur solely as a result of greater diversification across markets. The evidence suggests, however, that at least for that part of the post-war period for which data are available, aggregate concentration increased primarily as the result of increases in market concentration rather than in diversification (Clarke and Davies, 1983). It should be noted that both aggregate and market concentration in this particular study are measured by the Herfindahl index (see p. 50).

Data on aggregate concentration outside manufacturing are sparse. It is likely, however, that concentration in other major sectors of the economy has also been upward in the post-war period.

The Effects of Diversification

Market power implications

Concern over the market power implications of the operations of very large companies has centred on four main issues. The relevance of each of these issues for any particular company will vary according to the extent of their diversification and to their share in any particular market. (1) *Cross subsidization* Profits in one market may be used to cross subsidize activities in another. For example a firm may be in a relatively stronger position in market *A* than in market *B*. Using finance from the former it may endeavour to strengthen its market position in the latter by forcing competitors to leave the market or to adapt their behaviour. The cross subsidizer may attempt to reduce competition in market *B* by a variety of means: deliberate price cutting, heavy advertising or substantial capacity expansion. (The last mentioned may force prices below the level at which competitors can remain in business.) Once the competition has been reduced, the cross subsidizer may then be able to reap the returns to his strategy through the higher prices made possible by the absence of competition.

One example of cross subsidization is the involvement of the British Gas Corporation in the sale of domestic appliances. A recent report (HMSO, 1980c, pp. 98–9) suggested that the Corporation had subsidized the latter activity from its sale of gas. For example, in its accounts, the Corporation charged up *all* its advertising to the sale of gas, despite the fact that appliances featured prominently in the advertisements. This cross subsidization made it difficult for private retailers to compete unless they were also able to cross subsidize their activities from other sources. Another well documented instance comes from the US (Mueller, 1982): it concerns the entry of Philip Morris, the second largest cigarette manufacturer, into the brewing industry. In 1969–70 the company took over the Miller Brewing Company, then the eighth largest company in the US beer business. Very substantial sums were poured into the Miller company to finance a massive expansion in plant and advertising. Between 1971 and 1975, Miller incurred losses and made only modest profits in the following two years. Since then its profits have risen each year. It is now in second place in the beer industry. Other areas of cross subsidization have involved price cutting in markets where competition has been particularly strong (Scherer, 1980, p. 337). Cross subsidization designed to reduce competition will only be profitable where the short run costs that arise as a result of such a policy can be recouped by the long run gains in profitability that may be made *after* competition is diminished. If however competitors re-enter (or expand) once the diversified firm ceases to cross subsidize, such gains will be small or non-existent. Whether or not competitors come back in this way will depend on their expectations regarding post-re-entry behaviour by conglomerates and on the costs of such re-entry (and of possible exit). The more likely and rapid re-entry is, the less profitable a policy of cross subsidization will be.

(2) *Full line forcing* This practice occurs when a firm requires its customers, as a condition of sale in one market, also to buy its goods or services in other markets. Most instances of such policies concern fairly closely related products. For example, in the mid-1960s, the UK petrol

supply industry was investigated by the Monopolies and Mergers Commission because of the practice of suppliers to require petrol retailers also to sell their lubricants, other petroleum products and anti-freeze preparations. This practice may be used by a firm, strong in one market, to improve its position in a more competitive market.

(3) *Competitive forbearance* Such forbearance is based on a recognition by diversified firms of the extent to which their activities in different markets are interrelated. This in turn may lead to a reduction in the extent of competition between them.

One example of such forbearance (again from the US) concerned a large conglomerate food manufacturer and retailer, Consolidated Foods Corporation, and a large multi-market food retailer, the National Tea Corporation (Mueller, 1982). Both companies met each other not only as competitors in the retail market but also as supplier and buyer respectively in the food products market. In the mid-1960s, Consolidated Foods initiated an extensive price cutting campaign. National responded by threatening to reduce its purchases of the products of Consolidated Foods. In response the latter dropped its price cutting campaign.

Another way in which competitive forebearance may be exercised is through reciprocal dealing. In this case firm A buys from firm B in one market while firm B undertakes to buy from A in another. New entrants may find it difficult to break into markets where such relationships exist.

(4) *Availability of finance* Very large firms may be able simply by virtue of their overall size to raise finance more cheaply than small firms. They may therefore be in a better position to finance policies designed to eliminate or reduce competition.

Some gains from diversification

Considerable care should be taken in making any assessment of the effects of the practices described in the preceding paragraphs for the following reasons. First, the entry of a diversified firm into a particular market may sometimes make competitors *more* evenly matched in that market if other diversified firms are already operating there. If for example a 'single market' firm is competing against a division of a conglomerate, the former's market strength may be considerably enhanced if it is taken over by another conglomerate. Secondly, diversification may provide an opportunity for a firm to gain certain cost advantages. It may permit the fuller use of centralized facilities and resources and it may allow 'surprise' results of research and development to be more readily utilized.

Some of the specific practices mentioned earlier may have some justification in these terms. For example, reciprocal dealing may lead to savings in transactions costs. Long standing relationships with suppliers and buyers often mean that the parties to the contract already know the quality of the good or service involved. As a result, they do not constantly have to be seeking information on this issue. Cost considerations may also go some of the way towards explaining why finance may be cheaper to a conglomerate than to a smaller single market firm. There may be economies of scale in the vetting of applications for finance. Again, the risk associated with putting money into a conglomerate with interests in many fields may be lower.

Whether the behaviour of a diversified firm in any particular market should be interpreted simply as the use of industrial muscle designed to eliminate competition or as an attempt to obtain gains in efficiency will depend on the particular circumstances of the case.

5.3 MULTINATIONALS

Multinationals in the UK

Many very large private companies operate not only in the UK but also in other countries. Such companies are referred to as multinational (or transnational) corporations. Some multinationals operating in the UK are also ultimately controlled from here (UK based multinationals). For example, ICI whose headquarters are in London has nearly 300 overseas subsidiary companies. Its interests range from major manufacturing concerns in continental Europe, the Americas, Australasia, India and South Africa, to comparatively small selling companies located in many parts of the world. Other multinationals have their headquarters abroad especially in the US ('foreign based' multinationals). Foreign involvement in some sectors of UK manufacturing is substantial. In 1981, overseas companies accounted for 34 per cent of sales in chemicals, 23 per cent in electrical and electronic machinery, 25 per cent in rubber and plastics, and 46 per cent in motor vehicles and parts.

The Effects of Multinationals

The spread of a company's operations across several countries is similar in many respects to the spread of a company's activities across product markets in the same country. Thus many of the issues raised in respect of diversification in the previous section are more or less relevant in the study of multinationals and are not therefore discussed again here. However, there are a number of wider issues associated with multinational operations that also need to be considered. This is done below.

Transfer pricing

Such a practice relates to the determination of prices at which transactions take place internally, i.e. within the multinational. Countries differ in the tax liabilities they impose on companies' earnings. They also differ in the stringency with which their governments scrutinize profits as evidence of abuse of market power. A multinational may therefore find it to its advantage to ensure that profits generated by production in one country are taxed in another. How it can do this is illustrated by the following example. Assume that a multinational operates two divisions, one in country A (Division A) and one in country B (Division B). Assume also that Division A buys various inputs from Division B. Now if country A has a higher profits tax than country B, it will pay the multinational to instruct Division B to charge much higher prices for its supplies to A, for whom such prices are treated as costs, which are not taxable. Thus profits are transferred as 'costs' from country A to country B, and are then taxed in the latter.

One well documented example of transfer pricing was the practice adopted by the Swiss based Roche Group in its sale from Switzerland of the active ingredients of its two tranquillizers, Librium and Valium to its UK manufacturing subsidiary, Roche Products (HMSO, 1973a). In 1970 the parent was selling these ingredients at a price of £407 per kilo for Librium and £1,014 per kilo for Valium. Yet the same ingredients could be obtained from Italian manufacturers for £9 and £20 per kilo respectively. These latter costs were presumably a closer reflection of the true production costs. It is not entirely clear however what Roche's motives for this pricing system were.

Whether or not the UK benefits from transfer pricing does of course depend in part on its relative attractiveness as a country in which to declare profits.

The balance of payments

The most obvious impact of multinational operations on the balance of payments is likely to be on capital and profit flows. However, there may also be more subtle effects. For example if a UK based multinational already operates overseas, it may find exports of its UK produced goods easier, especially if those exports represent inputs for overseas operations. Again, foreign based multinationals may require shipping and financial services for their operations in the UK. If these services are paid for by foreign headquarters, they are classified as exports.

Impact on domestic production

The impact of a foreign multinational on domestic production may not be easy to assess. On the one hand, a foreign based multinational may provide expertise, technology and capital that would not otherwise be available. On the other, its UK activities may attract resources away from domestic producers. The implications of such deprivation of domestic producers would then require closer examination.

Economic sovereignty

It has sometimes been argued that foreign based multinationals operating in the UK may represent a loss of economic sovereignty for the UK in that such firms may not be so sensitive to economic policy as domestic firms. Decisions on key areas such as investment, purchasing and marketing are taken in the context of the *overall* objectives of the multinational. The ability of governments to influence such decisions through their economic policies may thereby be reduced. Although such loss of 'sovereignty' for the UK may be regarded unambiguously as a cost, it must be examined in the context of the alternatives; the absence of a multinational may mean that output overall is correspondingly less.

5.4 THE NATIONALIZED INDUSTRIES

For analytical purposes, nationalized industries may be conveniently regarded as 'firms', even though they do not take any of the legal forms that private sector firms may adopt in the UK (see pp. 21–4).

Some Employment Data

In table 2.1 figures on total employment in the nationalized industries were provided. Table 5.3 gives details for the ten largest nationalized industries (by employment) for the early 1980s. Most of the industries covered in table 5.3 are also in public ownership in other Western European countries. It is perhaps worth noting that four of these organizations are larger than the largest private UK employer, General Electric (see table 5.1).

The Markets of Nationalized Industries

On a very narrow definition of a market, many nationalized industries may be regarded as near monopolies. For example, British Rail faces virtually no competing suppliers of rail travel. (Private railways do not play a significant role in the UK.)

Again, the National Coal Board is the principal provider of UK coal although a few private pits exist. Even where private firms have a not insignificant share of the particular (narrowly defined) market in which

Table 5.3　The ten largest nationalized industries by employment

Corporation	Commencing or vesting date	Employment at 31 March 1983
British Telecom**	1981	245,882†
Post Office	1961	227,886‡
National Coal Board	1947	212,843†
British Railways Board*	1963	212,722§
Electricity Council	1958	141,385
British Gas Corporation	1973	101,225
British Steel Corporation	1967	81,100
British Shipbuilders	1977	66,600†
National Bus Company*	1969	51,951†
British Airways Board*	1974	37,517
Total		1,379,111

*These succeed corporations existing previously.
**Privatized in 1984
†31 March 1982.
‡31 March 1981.
§31 December 1982.
Source: *Economic Trends*, February 1983; annual reports of the corporations.

the nationalized corporation operates, that corporation usually has by far the largest share. For example in UK domestic air services, British Airways is surrounded by numerous independent operators; it is responsible, however, for over 80 per cent of the total number of scheduled passengers carried.

Broader definitions of markets indicate more satisfactorily the level of competition – often intense – faced by some nationalized industries. For example, British Rail faces substantial competition from providers of coach and air services. Again, the National Coal Board sells only one type of fuel. As these examples also illustrate, nationalized industries also compete among themselves in some areas. Furthermore many nationalized industries compete in international markets. British Shipbuilders and British Airways are obvious examples.

However, not all nationalized industries face substantial competition. For example the supply of domestic electricity for lighting is almost exclusively in the hands of the Central Electricity Generating Board: gas provides no competition in this area. Similarly the Post Office has had (until recently) a statutory monopoly in the letter post. Even though the

British Telecommunications Act, 1981, now gives the Secretary of State powers to license other carriers of letters, the bulk of the letter service is still reserved for the Post Office. For these reasons some form of regulation may be necessary to ensure that these industries do not exploit their market power. High prices may not be the only way in which such exploitation occurs. Costs may be allowed to rise. The management of a corporation does not of course have an ownership stake in its assets. This may cause them to seek objectives other than those which would lead to maximum efficiency.

Labour may also take advantage of the 'public' character of the corporation to seek higher wages than it would obtain in the private sector. There are two other reasons why external regulation of nationalized industries may be desirable even when competitive pressures exist. First, many nationalized industries are charged (by statute) with certain non-commercial functions (for example the supply of services to rural areas). The performance of these functions cannot therefore be assessed against normal commercial criteria. Secondly, as was pointed out in chapter 2, since nationalized industries have access to public funds, they can incur losses without being forced into liquidation. Thus the ultimate commercial sanction of closure is weakened if not eliminated altogether.

Public Accountability

Public influence and control over the nationalized industries are exercised in a number of ways. First, Parliament subjects each industry to periodic detailed review through its system of Select Committees. For example, in 1983 the prospects for the British Steel Corporation were reviewed by the House of Commons Industry and Trade Committee. Secondly, the government involves itself in various ways in the activities of the industries. It appoints their Chairmen and Board members. It sets financial and performance objectives and has in the past set guidelines on pricing and investment appraisal procedures. (For pricing guidelines, see p. 190.) It also vets investment programmes although the treatment of nationalized industries in this respect differs substantially (Pryke, 1981, p. 250). The government may require an industry to follow certain policies, for example in relation to pay settlements, which are consistent with its own economic strategy. In the last resort the government may issue a directive. Thirdly, most nationalized industries have statutory consumer watchdogs. For example the Post Office is required to consult the Post Office Users' National Council (POUNC) on all major proposals relating to its main services, such as tariff changes. Finally, the Monopolies and Mergers Commission has had the power (since 1980) to investigate aspects of the operations of nationalized industries. The work of the Commission in this area is considered in more detail in chapter 13.

Nationalization: The Arguments For and Against

Numerous arguments have been advanced for the nationalization of industrial activity. Some of these have been primarily ideological or political in character. For example, it has been argued that nationalization stops the development of unacceptable inequalities of wealth or income that would otherwise arise through private ownership, and that it introduces an essential element of public accountability over the use of the nation's productive resources.

Other arguments have had a stronger *economic* focus. One of the earliest reasons put forward for public ownership was that it enabled the state to control the 'commanding heights' of the economy and thereby to facilitate better macroeconomic management. Nationalized industries have also been seen as a direct channel for the implementation of economic policies. Another economic argument is that nationalized industries can use social rather than private costs and benefits as their criteria in decision making. They might thus be expected to undertake certain non commercial functions, such as the provision of lossmaking services to rural areas.

How valid these economic arguments are is a matter of debate. For example the 'commanding heights' argument has been attacked on the grounds that it assumes that governments are better planners and coordinators than the market mechanism. This may not be the case, especially where government involvement is responsive to short run political considerations. Again, it is sometimes suggested that the use of social rather than private cost-benefit criteria simply provides an open ended justification for virtually any activity of a nationalized industry because social costs and benefits are often extremely difficult to quantify and value.

One issue which has attracted a good deal of attention is the efficiency of the nationalized industries. On the one hand it is suggested that public ownership enables an industry which is a natural monopoly to operate efficiently by restricting production to only one firm. It also provides a mechanism (government monitoring) for ensuring that the industry is properly managed. On the other hand, inefficiency is said to arise from two main sources. First, the strong market position of many nationalized industries reduces competitive pressures to minimise costs; and secondly, the very fact of public ownership means that the ultimate commercial pressure of closure is absent. Additional public funds can always be provided. As suggested earlier, management may follow its own objectives – which may conflict with the maximization of efficiency – because it knows that in the last resort government will bail the industry out. For the same reasons management may be reluctant to undertake programmes of rationalization or innovation because the sanctions for not doing so are weak. It was also suggested that labour, too, may be able, by virtue of its employment in the public sector, to negotiate wages that are higher than it would otherwise obtain. Public ownership may in addition bring a degree of government involvement in the management of industries which impedes effective management.

A number of attempts have been made to make technical and cost efficiency comparisons between the operations of some nationalized industries and those of privately owned firms engaged in similar activities. These comparisons are fraught with difficulty, but the recent evidence does seem to suggest that, despite (or perhaps because of) the public accountability of nationalized industries, at least some of their activities are characterised by lower efficiency. For example, Pryke (1980) points out that in 1980, British Airways' planes averaged 6.8 flying hours per day whereas those of British Caledonian, the main private competitor of British Airways, flew for 8.2 hours. He also shows that in the same year, turnover per employee in the privately owned European Ferries was 24 per cent higher than in its (then) nationalized counterpart, Sealink. There is also evidence to show that in some nationalized industries there is clear scope for increases in efficiency. For example, a recent report on the Inner London letter post suggested it would be reasonable to reduce the labour requirement in man hours by over 20 per cent in three years (HMSO, 1980e, p. 60). In British Rail, less than a quarter of the potential manpower savings thought possible by the Board over a six year period starting in 1976 had been achieved after four years (HMSO, 1980b, p. 98).

In interpreting these findings on efficiency it is important to keep at least three issues in mind. First, it is not at all clear how far any inefficiencies are due to public ownership itself and how far they arise from the strong market positions of many nationalized industries. Secondly, the evidence is not all one way. For example, Pryke has pointed out that many of the weaknesses of UK nationalized industries have been exhibited by the same industries under private ownership abroad (Pryke, 1981, pp. 265–6). Furthermore it must be remembered that some UK private companies have been taken into public ownership in recent years precisely because they were too inefficient to survive as private entities. Finally, even if it could be shown conclusively that nationalized industries are relatively inefficient, it might still be argued by some that this is a price worth paying for the political benefits of the public ownership of productive assets. The essence of this argument is that the criteria that are appropriate for evaluating privately owned firms may not be suitable for the assessment of the nationalized industries.

Privatization

It is the present Conservative government's view that both public ownership itself and over protection of the nationalized industries from the disciplines of market forces have generated unacceptable levels of inefficiency. It has therefore followed a policy of privatization.

Privatization is a wide ranging term and may be seen as having four main aspects, not all of which are directly relevant for the nationalized industries. However, for the sake of completeness, all four are enumerated below. (This classification broadly follows that provided by Heald, 1984.)

(1) The introduction of charges for goods and services produced by the public sector which were formerly provided 'free'.

(2) The contracting out to the private sector of work formerly undertaken in the public sector.

(3) The selling off to private individuals and organizations of publicly owned enterprises.

(4) The relaxation of statutory monopolies and licensing arrangements which stop private sector firms from competing in markets previously exclusively supplied by the private sector.

It is primarily types (3) and (4) that are of relevance to the nationalized industries. As far as (3) is concerned, the early 1980s have seen the introduction of a substantial element of private ownership in some of the nationalized industries. The normal procedure has been the conversion of a statutory corporation (or part of it) into a public limited liability company and the sale of some of the shares of the new company to the public. The government has usually retained a significant shareholding. In some cases it also has the power to appoint directors. However, as Steel (1984) has pointed out, the precise nature of the government's involvement in the new 'hybrid' companies has varied from case to case and does not appear to reflect a consistent view of the part that the state should play in such operations.

Industries that have been privatized in this way include British Aerospace (1981); the National Freight Corporation, sold off to its managers and employees (1982); the oil and gas exploration and production activities of the British National Oil Corporation (1982) and the British Transport Docks Board (1983). Between 1981 and 1983, British Rail sold off its hotel interests and this was followed in 1984 by the sale of its Sealink subsidiary. At the time of writing (November 1984), British Telecom was in the process of being sold, and plans were well advanced for the sale of British Airways and parts of British Shipbuilders.

Alongside such privatization of the nationalized industries has been the sale of some government shareholdings in limited liability companies which have never had the status of nationalized industries (see pp. 26–7). Cable and Wireless, Amersham International and British Petroleum have all had their government shareholdings reduced. It is also the government's intention eventually to give the private sector a substantial stake in BL (Jaguar has already been sold off).

Under type (4) privatization, several of the markets in which nationalized industries operate have been opened up to more vigorous competition from the private sector. The relaxation of the Post Office's letter monopoly has already been mentioned. The government has also made it easier for private businesses to supply electricity and gas. And British Airways has had to face increasing competition from the independent airlines as the Civil Aviation Authority has relaxed its route licensing policy.

It is too early to say what effects this policy of privatization will have on the operations of the industries concerned. Partial ownership changes of themselves may not substantially increase efficiency. If the new companies have statutory protection from competition, their operations may be little different from corporations which are wholly under public ownership. Extensive regulation in some form, with all its attendant costs, would still be necessary, especially where the newly privatized businesses are charged with certain non-commercial functions. The need for such regulation has been recognized in the government's plan for the privatization of British Telecom. Under the 1984 Telecommunications Act, the Office of Telecommunications (OFTEL) has been set up to provide an independent means of supervising the affairs of an industry in which the new British Telecom plc will still have the dominant position.

A further problem over the privatization programme arises over the hybrid nature of the new companies. Governments may be unable, under political pressure, to resist the temptation to use their ownership status and other powers to become extensively involved in the operation of these companies.

However, where privatization leads to a change in the structure of the industry with more organizations competing with each other and with greater freedom of entry, substantial increases in efficiency may result. Beesley and Littlechild (1983) argue that 'appropriately designed' privatization schemes covering four-fifths of the nationalized sector could yield benefits to consumers. However, it remains to be seen how far such schemes could in practice be implemented.

5.5 SUMMARY

Some UK companies are now very large. The largest UK companies in manufacturing have a presence in most industries and they are often market leaders. Aggregate concentration has grown substantially in the post-war period and cannot be adequately explained in terms of the search for greater cost efficiency.

A large diversified business may be able to use the strength it derives from its overall size to reduce competition in individual markets. Diversification may, however, enable certain economies to be obtained. Multinational operation may in some respects be regarded as another form of diversification although it raises much wider issues. Many nationalized industries are larger than the largest private (UK) company. These industries often have substantial market power. The efficiency record of some nationalized industries is not good. However, it remains to be seen how far privatization will alter this picture; changes of ownership alone may not ensure that the full potential for efficiency gains are realised.

So far in this book no attempt has been made to compare the industrial experience of the UK with that of other countries. This is the subject of the next chapter.

6

Some International Comparisons

6.1 INTRODUCTION

Much effort in recent years has been devoted to comparisons of the UK's industrial performance with that of other industrialized countries. Attention in these comparisons has ranged over a number of issues. In this chapter, however, the discussion is focused on three key variables: output, productivity and competitiveness. Before comparative data are examined, two preliminary points on these variables should be made. First, it is important to distinguish between changes in a variable *over time* and the level of that variable *at a given point in time*. It is quite possible, for example, for a country's productivity to be growing relatively rapidly over some time period and for its level still to be relatively low at the end of that period. Secondly, it should be remembered that the variables may be related. For example, it is known that growth of output is positively associated with growth of labour productivity. Which way the causation runs is a matter of debate. On the one hand, increases in output may increase productivity by making certain economies of scale possible. Growth of output may also encourage more investment which may ensure that the most productive equipment and machinery is utilized. On the other hand, increases in productivity may lead to increases in output if the former leads to a reduction in the price of output and thereby causes an expansion in quantity demanded. Both views have some validity. Productivity change is also likely to be closely related to trends in competitiveness.

How international comparisons on output, productivity and competitiveness are interpreted ultimately depends on how *desirable* measured output is considered to be (both productivity and competitiveness require some form of output measurement). At the aggregate level, output figures are largely based on national accounts data. To what extent can such data be regarded as an indicator of all the 'standard of living'? This issue cannot be fully explored here since, in the last analysis, it raises the complex issue of the determinants of human happiness. Different groups in society are likely to take different views on whether particular types of output included in the national accounts represent a positive contribution to such happiness. Members of the Campaign for Nuclear Disarmament for example, would regard 'output' associated with the production and maintenance of a nuclear deterrent as *reducing* happiness. Again, some religious groups might regard material standards of living as being a relatively unimportant component of overall happiness. Despite these difficulties most people would agree on two obvious shortcomings in national accounts data as conventionally calculated (apart from the ones mentioned in chapter 1): first, these data ignore leisure as a component in the standard of living; and, secondly, they do not take full account of all the costs of productive activity, notably pollution and congestion.

In this chapter, the issue of the desirability of output is not considered explicitly. It is not necessary to reach a decision on this issue in order to describe and explain differences across countries in changes in, and levels of output, productivity and competitiveness. Such analyses can provide important insights. For example, Denison (1967, pp. 344–5) in his massive study of growth rates in Western economies, has argued that the very much slower output growth rates in the US in the period 1950–62 were mostly a reflection of that country's already higher level of output per person employed, and that the opportunities for further growth were consequently less. Denison concluded that it would not have been *possible* for the US to match the growth rates of continental countries.

6.2 OUTPUT

Post-War Trends

Table 6.1 shows the growth of output, in total and per head of population, for the UK and its main competitors for a number of sub-periods since 1960. The years 1960, 1968, 1973 and 1979 are all years which mark similar points in the economic cycle. All countries experienced a substantial slowdown in growth after 1973. However, in each of the sub-periods given in the table, the UK's growth of output and of output per head were lower than those of most of the other countries mentioned. The only exceptions which all relate to output per head, occurred in the sub-periods 1968–73, and 1979–82: in the former, UK growth was more rapid than that in the US; and in the latter, output per head *declined* more rapidly in the US and Italy than it did in the UK.

Table 6.1 Output: annual percentage growth rates, selected countries, 1960–82*

	Total				Per head of population			
	1960–68	1968–73	1973–9	1979–82	1960–8	1968–73	1973–9	1979–82
US	4.5	3.3	2.6	0.1	3.2	2.2	1.6	−0.9
Japan	10.5	8.8	3.6	4.1	9.4	7.3	2.5	3.3
West Germany	4.2	4.9	2.4	0.2	3.3	4.0	2.6	0.1
France	5.4	5.9	3.1	1.0	4.2	5.0	2.7	0.5
UK	3.1	3.1	1.4	−0.5	2.5	2.8	1.4	−0.6
Italy	5.7	4.6	2.6	1.2	5.0	4.0	2.1	−0.9

*Output is defined in this table as real Gross Domestic Product.
Source: OECD *Historical Statistics 1960–1982*, OECD, Paris, 1984, tables 3.1 and 3.2.

Two factors should be borne in mind in any interpretation of the UK's record on the growth of output and output per head. First, relative to its own past record in peace time, the UK has experienced *more* rapid growth for at least a substantial part of the post-war period. This is shown in table 6.2 which is based on a comprehensive recent study of British economic growth by Matthews, Feinstein and Odling-Smee (1982). Clearly, growth over the period 1951 to 1973 was at an historically very high level.

Secondly, and notwithstanding the first point, the UK's growth relative to that experienced in other industrialized countries has been low for a very long period. Thus 1960–82, the period covered in table 6.1, does not portray a new development as far as UK relative growth is concerned.

Table 6.2   Output: annual percentage growth rates, UK, 1856–73*

Period	Total	Per head of population
1856–73	2.2	1.4
1873–1913	1.8	0.9
1924–37	2.2	1.8
1951–73	2.8	2.3

*Output is defined in this table as real Gross Domestic Product.
Source: Matthews et al., 1982, table 16.1.

The long history of the UK's relatively low growth in output and output per head is particularly clearly brought out in the study published by Maddison (1980). He provided data on both measures for 16 industrialized nations for the period 1870 to 1976. In *all* four sub-periods he considered (1870–1913; 1913–50; 1950–70 and 1970–6) the UK's growth in both respects was lower, often substantially so, than the arithmetic average (and the median value) for all 16 countries. In most sub-periods it was very near the bottom of the international league table. The implication of this finding is that although it is possible that the factors which can explain relatively low growth in the post-war period are peculiar to that period, it is more likely that more fundamental longer term factors are at work. It is important therefore to retain an historical perspective in any analysis of the UK's performance in the post-war period.

The figures in table 6.1 do of course cover a wide variety of activities including non-marketed goods and services. However, disaggregation of the data by broad sector suggests that the experience of relatively slow growth has been widespread (Morgan, 1982, p. 23). This is not to say, however, that some individual firms and industries have not gone against the general trend.

Levels of Output per Head

Comparisons of absolute levels of output per head are more difficult to make than trend comparisons which are made with reference to some base year in each of the countries involved. However, there can be little doubt that UK output per head is now substantially lower than that in her main competitors. In 1982, for example, output per head of population in the US, Japan, West Germany and France was 54, 5, 25 and 19 per cent higher respectively. Only Italy, at 72 per cent of the UK level, had a lower figure. These comparisons are based on gross domestic product, valued (at official exchange rates) in US dollars.

6.3 PRODUCTIVITY

Post-War Trends

The growth of total output can be decomposed into two main elements. The first is the growth in the quantity of inputs that goes into the productive process. The second is the growth in the productivity of these inputs. Denison has shown (1967, chapter 12) that in most European countries, the second accounted for a very substantial part of total output growth in the period he studied (1950–62). See also Matthews et al. (1982, p. 501).

The most commonly employed measure of productivity growth is that which relates to labour productivity. Such productivity may be measured in various ways, one of which, output per person employed, is used in table 6.3. This measure must be used with care, for the reason given on p. 10 and because it makes no allowance for changes in the number of hours worked or in the skill or occupational mix of the labour force.

Table 6.3 provides data on productivity growth rates for a number of sub-periods between 1960 and 1982. The UK's post-war record on labour productivity is similar to that on output in that it compares very favourably with earlier periods (Matthews et al., 1982, table 2.1). It is also the case that relative to other industrialized nations the UK's labour productivity growth has been low for a very long period (Matthews et al., 1982, table 2.5). In this latter respect the UK's record is also similar to that on output growth.

Table 6.3 Labour productivity: annual percentage growth rates: selected countries, 1960–82*

	1960–68	*1968–73*	*1973–79*	*1979–82*
US	2.6	1.2	0.2	−0.1
Japan	8.9	7.7	2.9	3.1
West Germany	4.3	4.1	3.0	0.7
France	4.9	4.8	2.9	1.2
UK	2.7	3.0	1.2	1.4
Italy	6.3	4.9	1.6	0.7

*Labour productivity is defined in this table as real Gross Domestic Product per person employed.
Source: OECD *Historical Statistics 1960–1982*, OECD Paris, 1984, table 3.7.

The sub-period, 1979–82, during which UK labour productivity grew faster than between 1973 and 1979, is unusual in that the UK showed faster growth than any of the other countries mentioned in table 6.3 apart from Japan. Between 1981 and 1982 the UK's productivity growth even exceeded the Japanese figure.

This recent rapid growth in UK productivity almost certainly reflects greater competitive pressures on businesses and labour, and the stronger commitment to the operation of free markets by the present Conservative government (see p. 212). There can be little doubt that the ability of labour at all levels to inhibit changes that might raise productivity has been substantially reduced. It remains to be seen however whether this represents the beginning of long term change of a fundamental kind or whether it is a consequence primarily of the severe pressures arising from the depths of the recession. On this latter view productivity gains may become very much less once recovery occurs.

It must be remembered that the relatively rapid increase in productivity between 1979 and 1982 occurred when output was falling (see table 6.1). These two trends can of course only be reconciled by a rise in unemployment.

How a relatively slow growth in labour productivity affects the behaviour of relative unit costs of output is a complex issue. Much depends on capital:labour ratios and on the relative behaviour of wage rates and salaries. The evidence suggests that at least in manufacturing, unit labour costs – usually a good guide to total costs – have tended to rise more rapidly over the past 20 years in the UK than in other competing countries. (See OECD *Historical Statistics 1960–1984*, OECD Paris, table 9.10.)

Levels of Productivity

Numerous comparative studies have been undertaken in recent years of productivity levels in particular industries or sectors. For example, a recent study of agriculture, the extractive industries (mining and quarrying), manufacturing, construction, public utilities (gas, electricity and water) and transport showed that, overall, US labour productivity in 1977 was 2.66 times higher than that in the UK. In West Germany it was 1.43 times higher (Smith, Hitchens and Davies, 1982, p. 5). US productivity was higher in each of the six sectors. Only in agriculture was West German productivity lower.

It is of course helpful to know what part differences in the amount of capital employed play in explaining these variations. The study by Smith et al. suggests that differences in capital intensity indeed go some way towards explaining labour productivity differences. For example, in the extractive industries, in which the UK's relative productivity was at its lowest, relative capital intensity was also at its lowest. However, it is also clear from this study that capital is far from providing the *whole* explanation for the differences in labour productivity.

Another study which looked, *inter alia*, at how far differences in capital explain international differences in labour productivity is that by Pratten, (1976). He examined differences in labour productivity across countries *within* multinational companies and found that productivity in UK plants tended to be much lower than that in the US, West Germany or France, but that differences in plant and equipment accounted for only between 12 and 33 per cent of these differences. Major differences in labour productivity given (roughly) the same amount of capital equipment were clearly identified in an official study of the motor industry (HMSO, 1975c, p. xi). This study found, for the mid-1970s, that the labour requirement for assembling the same car in the UK, given the same production techniques, was nearly double that of continental producers. In engines, it was 50 to 60 per cent more. Although wage rates in the UK were lower, this was insufficient to offset the lower productivity levels.

It is sometimes argued that relatively low productivity *levels* may enhance the scope for relatively fast productivity *growth*. However the limited evidence that exists (Caves, 1980, p. 177), suggests that the reverse is true and that factors favouring levels of productivity may also favour productivity growth as well.

6.4 COMPETITIVENESS

Price and Non-Price Competition

The UK's international competitiveness is defined by how successfully it competes in world markets. Competition between countries is in many ways analogous to competition between firms. As the next part of this book shows, the latter may take many different forms. However, a number of international comparisons of competitiveness (see for example NEDO, 1977) have drawn a basic distinction between price and *non*-price competition. The latter embraces such factors as the quality and technical characteristics of the product, the marketing and distribution activities associated with its sale, delivery dates and after sales service. Kravis and Lipsey (1971, chapter 7) have shown the importance of such non-price factors in the purchase decision in world markets.

Price and non-price competitiveness may of course be closely related. For example where a country exports in a highly competitive market which allows little divergence in prices for similar goods, a relatively low price may indicate a relatively low level of non-price competitiveness. In essence, customers 'get what they pay for'. Stout (NEDO, 1977) has used this kind of reasoning in his comparative study of UK, West German and French exports. In 29 of the 35 manufacturing industries (mainly engineering) in which he was able to compare the prices of exports (measured in terms of value per metric tonne) of the UK and West Germany, he found that the UK had lower prices. The same was true in 23 of the 34 industries in which UK-French comparisons could be made. Stout concluded that although some part of these results might be explicable in terms of lower prices for similar products, or by differences in the product mix, 'the differences in [prices] in many cases are so large and are so widespread as to suggest that they probably reflect differences in product quality between the countries' exports' (NEDO, 1977, p. 26). Stout's view gains support from a number of recent studies which have shown that the UK record on technological progressiveness and innovation is relatively poor (see for example the chapters by Rothwell, Walker and Gardiner, and Aylen in Pavitt, ed., 1980). There are however exceptions (see for example the study by Senker, also in Pavitt, ed., 1980).

The UK's Share of World Exports and Import Penetration

Share of world exports

One commonly used measure of a country's international competitiveness is its share of world exports in value terms. This measure must be used carefully. For example it gives no indication of how profitable a country's exports are (a country may expand its share by unprofitable price cutting). However, it has the strong advantage of representing the outcome of competition in *both* price and non-price dimensions.

Figure 6.1 provides details of the share of the UK in world exports of manufactures over the period 1960–83. Apart from the late 1970s, this

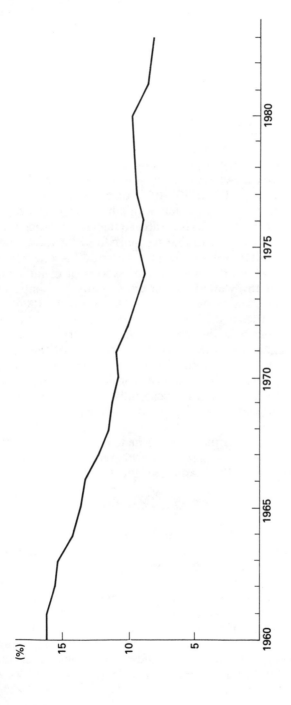

Figure 6.1 UK's share of world exports in manufactures (by value) 1960–83
Source: National Institute *Economic Review*, various years (statistical appendices).

share has shown virtually continuous decline during this period. Although most of the UK's main competitors, excluding Japan, have also experienced a declining share, the drop has been more substantial for the UK. Experience has of course varied among industries. For example, chemicals and food have done rather better than average, while engineering and metal manufacturing have performed rather worse. This variation is also shown in current *levels* of export shares.

The decline in the UK's share of world trade in manufactures has been linked to a decline in the UK's non-price competitiveness (NEDO, 1980). Of course the latter need not *necessarily* lead to a declining share of exports: customers may *prefer* a mix which lowers price at the expense of non-price characteristics such as quality or after sales service. However, Stout has argued (NEDO, 1977) that the income elasticity of demand in world markets for products with a higher non-price element is greater. Thus as world incomes increase, so demand for such products rises relatively more rapidly than that for more 'down market' items. In Stout's view, this difference in income elasticities is one important reason behind the fall in the UK's share of exports of manufactures.

Some support for the view that non-price factors are important in world trade comes from a recent study by NEDO (1984) of 12 manufacturing industries in the UK. This study suggested that a positive relationship exists between the change in an industry's share of new foreign patents taken out in the US – one measure of the industry's relative involvement in generating new, 'non-price' elements in its products – and changes in its share of world exports. While such a relationship must be interpreted very carefully, it is certainly consistent with the view that non-price factors are significant in determining patterns of world trade.

As far as non-manufacturing is concerned, Brown and Sheriff have shown (1979) that the UK's share of world trade in services has also fallen substantially since 1960, although the fall has been rather less severe.

Import penetration

Another indicator of trends in competitiveness which reflects both price and non-price elements is based on the degree of import penetration in UK domestic markets. Such penetration may be measured in various ways (Hewer, 1980). One measure frequently used is the ratio of imports to home demand, where the latter is the sum of sales by firms plus imports minus exports. Over the period 1971 to 1982 this ratio (for manufacturing) increased from 17 per cent to 29 per cent. Other competing countries also faced greater import penetration although for much of the period, the UK experienced a more substantial increase (NEDO, 1984). The increase in import penetration in the UK was felt across a wide range of industries although there were a few exceptions: in the food and drink industries for example, the ratio *fell* (rather erratically) from 17 per cent to 15 per cent. Increased import penetration may of course be the direct result of greater specialization by countries. Increased imports may be matched by increased exports. Over the period 1971 to 1982 the increase in import penetration in UK markets for manufactures was largely matched by the increase in the export sales to total sales ratio. However, at least some of this increase has been due to the relatively slow growth in output rather than to any autonomous increase in exports (Brown and Sheriff, 1979).

In non-manufacturing, for which there are much less data available, the evidence suggests that the increase in import penetration has been less (Sargent, 1979).

Deindustrialization

Its nature

The decrease in the UK's share of world exports of manufactures and rising import penetration in domestic markets in this sector has sometimes been referred to as de-industrialization (Cairncross, 1979). The issue of deindustrialization has attracted considerable interest because of its possible implications for the financing of essential UK imports of raw materials and food. It may however be argued that deindustrialization is of little consequence since the UK's comparative advantage now lies in services. Whether or not this is the case – and the arguments here are complex – it nevertheless remains true that the expansion of exports in services required to compensate for even a small fall in the UK share of world exports of manufactures would be very substantial. For example in 1982, a one percentage point fall in the UK's share of world exports of manufactures would have required an increase of over 25 per cent in the UK's exports of private services (sea transport, civil aviation, travel, financial and 'other' services).

Some possible causes

Numerous different explanations have been put forward for the UK's deindustrialization. These explanations continue to be the subject of considerable debate. Some of the main arguments are briefly outlined below.

First, it has been argued that UK manpower at both managerial and shop floor levels has been less able or willing to exploit new opportunities. In a recent study, Swords-Isherwood (1980) has argued that in the UK, management is a less attractive career option for the most able. Managerial personnel also tend to be trained less well for their role. At shop floor level, international comparisons of industrial disputes may provide some indication of the conflict that exists with management. Such comparisons do not, however, suggest that the UK is particularly prone to industrial disputes. For example both the US and Italy had a worse strike record (as measured by the average annual number of working days lost per 1,000 people employed) over the period 1967–1976. However, the UK compares very unfavourably with Japan, West Germany and France (Caves, 1980, p. 109). It must also be remembered that strike statistics may not tell the whole story. Strikes are *overt* expressions of conflict. Trade union opposition to change, expressed for example through restrictive practices, may be so effective that management may decide that to pursue a policy that would result in a strike would be counter-productive.

A number of possible reasons have been put forward for the international differences in the quality of manpower. In particular it has been argued that the educational system has given relatively less emphasis to technological subjects. One expression of this is the relatively low status assigned to engineers in industry (Albu, 1980; HMSO, 1980d, chapter 2). A more rigid class system which perpetuates conflict in industry, a greater commitment to established values, practices and institutions, and a rather less enthusiastic attitude towards money making have all been suggested as further reasons.

It is known that the incidence of strikes increases with the size of plant and that this relationship is stronger in the UK than in West Germany and the US (Prais, 1981b, p. 262). This may in turn mean that UK firms are less able to take advantage of economies of scale as output increases because of this stronger relationship. Competitive strength may thereby be reduced.

Secondly, it is suggested that the UK's capacity to produce new and improved goods and services has been relatively low. Freeman (1979) has argued that although the UK spent relatively more on research and development (R & D) in the first 20 years or so of the post-war period than its competitors apart from the US, most of the expenditure was concentrated on areas in which the UK had relatively little to gain in terms of competitiveness in world trade. The industries which were important in world trade terms – for example, machinery, vehicles, metals and metal products – received relatively little R & D input. The UK now ranks among the lowest R & D spenders among the advanced countries. There is also tentative evidence to suggest that the industrial R & D that *is* carried out in the UK is relatively less productive (NEDO, 1984).

Thirdly, the expansion of the public sector has been regarded by some economists as a factor inhibiting increased competitiveness. One of the arguments here is that the growth of this sector has reduced the capital and labour services available for the private sector. There is relatively little supporting evidence for such a 'crowding out' hypothesis. For example, there seems to be no strong grounds for arguing that funds for capital investment are in short supply, except possibly in certain clearly defined areas such as small firms (see p. 180); rather a major problem seems to be securing the most productive use of the funds that *are* invested and the identification of future profitable opportunities (Mueller, 1977). It is also worth pointing out that many faster growing economies have had larger public sectors than the UK (Phelps-Brown, 1977).

The government has of course been extensively involved in productive activity through its industrial policies (see chapter 13). It is sometimes argued (HMSO, 1975a) that frequent changes in such policies and the uncertainties such changes have generated, have not been conducive to a rapid growth of productivity. While this may well be the case, it is not at all clear how far the UK's record in this respect compares with that in other countries.

Fourthly, official report for an over-valued exchange rate up to 1967 has been seen as initiating a process of cumulative decline in which the resulting low competitiveness led to low profitability and hence low investment (see for example George, 1974). Low investment then reduces the scope for productivity increases. While there is some validity in this proposition, it is unlikely to be the *sole* factor behind deindustrialization.

6.5 SUMMARY

The UK has experienced relatively slow growth in output and labour productivity since 1960. However, it must be remembered that the UK's post-war record in these respects compares very favourably with that in earlier periods. It must also be remembered that historically, the UK's performance, relative to that of other industrialized nations has been poor for a very long time. As far as *levels* of output and labour productivity are concerned, there is evidence to suggest that the UK now ranks well down in the international league table. How such findings are interpreted does of course ultimately depend on how desirable output is considered to be.

The UK's share of world trade in manufactures has declined almost continuously over the past two decades and has been accompanied by increasing import penetration. Such deindustrialization has attracted a good deal of attention in recent years, although its causes are clearly complex. Services have fared rather better than manufacturing, although the expansion in the export in services needed to compensate for even a small further drop in the share of the world export of manufactures would be very substantial.

PART II
Competition in Industry

7

The Nature of Competition

In the first part of this book various changes in the structure of UK industry were described. Particular attention was focused on changes in the patterns of industry, the relative importance of firms of different sizes, concentration at both market and aggregate levels, and the relative position of UK industry in an international context. These changes may all be regarded, in part at least, as the outcome of competitive forces in the economic system at both national and international levels. These forces lead to the strong growing at the expense of the weak. Some of the reasons why certain firms, industries or nations are stronger than others, and some of the ways in which strength may be expressed have been briefly explored in part I. Little attention, however, was given to the precise nature of competition. The present part therefore focuses on this issue.

7.1 COMPETITIVE ACTIVITY

The Sources of Competition

Competition or rivalry between firms in product markets arises because consumers' purchasing power is not unlimited: consumers have to *choose* between the goods and services of different firms. Competing firms are thus striving for what are essentially mutually incompatible positions (Scherer, 1980, p. 10). Success is achieved by 'giving more than one's rivals give in proportion to what one asks in return, or by making the public think so, or by making them at least act as if they thought so to the extent of buying one's goods in preference to those of one's rivals' (Clark, 1926, p. 149). Firms may see themselves as competing not only with other existing firms but also with potential entrants, i.e. those firms that might set up in production.

The intensity with which any given set of firms competes depends in part on the degree to which potential customers see these firms' products as substitutes. Customers' views on substitutability between firms' goods and services is in turn determined by a whole range of factors. These include the prices of the products in question; how (in the customer's view) they compare on characteristics and quality; the location of the relevant sales outlets (a haircut offered in Aberdeen is no substitute for one offered in Plymouth); the degree of loyalty to a particular product generated by advertising and other promotion techniques; and the (perceived) quality of the after sales service (if any).

As a rule the greater the degree of substitutability, the more intense the competition is. This may not always be the case. For example, firms selling close substitutes may (by various means) restrict the degree of rivalry among themselves in order more effectively to meet a common threat from firms operating outside the market in question or to achieve greater market power than they would otherwise have. Again, as indicated in chapter 4, firms operating in a perfectly competitive market, and hence by definition selling homogeneous products, are so small that they do not see themselves as competing with one another in the sense that each is able to sell as much as it wishes at the going market price. Thus for the individual firm, consumer purchasing power appears unlimited at that price. However, even in these markets competition can always emerge from a firm, new or established, which has exclusive (or better) access to new or improved products and processes. It was also pointed out in chapter 4 that a monopolist by definition has no rivals in the particular market in which he is operating. Again, however, the monopolist may eventually face a challenge to his position from firms who are able to circumvent the barriers that gave rise to his monopoly in the first place. It must also be remembered that the monopolist's demand curve is likely to be affected by the behaviour of firms in other markets.

Most markets lie somewhere between the polar cases of perfect competition and monopoly. Rivalry between existing firms in a market is therefore widespread. Most firms would of course prefer to be monopolists. Indeed it may be argued that for the individual firm, a key purpose of its competitive activity is actually to reduce or eliminate competition. However, such an objective is not easily achieved as rival firms are likely to have similar views.

Different Types of Competition

Competition between firms may take a variety of forms. Traditionally economists have concentrated on *price* competition, the subject of chapter 8, but this is altogether too narrow a focus.

The wider nature of competitive activity is illustrated by the recent rivalry between British Airways (BA) and British Midland Airways

(BMA) on the Heathrow–Glasgow route. BMA started flying this route in October 1982 following the granting of a licence by the Civil Aviation Authority. Prior to this date, BA had had the monopoly of the traffic. BA offered a high frequency 'shuttle' service on which tickets could be purchased on board the aircraft and passengers were guaranteed a flight provided they turned up not less than ten minutes before departure. To provide this guarantee BA had to maintain a back-up facility through which an additional aircraft could be laid on at very short notice. No catering service was offered to passengers. The service that BMA launched offered a lower fare (£49.50 compared with £55) and a full hot meals service. However, the frequency of the service was less, and it offered no back-up guarantee. Within a few months BMA had obtained 30 per cent of the market. In July 1983, BA launched its counter-offensive with the introduction of its 'super shuttle'. It abandoned on board purchase of tickets and offered a hot breakfast, more lavish than BMA's, on its early morning flights. It also offered free drinks. BMA responded to this challenge by offering half price drinks and (more recently) by focusing its advertising on the absence of hot *dinners* on BA's evening flights. The two airlines use different aircraft types. Both have been involved in heavy promotional expenditure. BA for example launched its super shuttle by offering trips to Glasgow by Concorde for the ordinary fare. Interestingly BA has explicitly stated that it does not intend to start a price war (*The Times*, 31 August 1983), even though BMA still has a lower price (in May, 1984: £55 compared with £58).

Some non-price dimensions of competition are explored in chapters 9–11. It must of course be remembered that the different dimensions of competition are interrelated. For example, as the BA-BMA rivalry shows, the price of a product can only be meaningfully interpreted in the context of what is offered by the firm for that price. Again, innovation (chapter 10) and investment (chapter 11) are clearly related.

Some forms of competitive activity may be outlawed. For example, firms cannot burn down competitors' premises, nor can they make claims in their advertising that are patently false. Other activities may not be illegal in themselves but may nevertheless be subject to some form of review by the authorities. Some of the practices of firms operating in several markets (see chapter 5) come within this category. The acceptability of different forms of competitive activity are considered further in chapter 12.

The Objectives of Firms

Profit maximization and other objectives

A firm's competitive strategy depends crucially on the objectives of those determining it. Different objectives will usually give rise to different strategies. Traditionally, economists have focused on profit maximization as the goal of businesses. However, in the post-war period, a number of 'managerial' models of firm behaviour based on motives other than profit maximization have been developed, and it is important to consider these when analysing competitive behaviour. (For a useful survey of these models, see Sawyer, 1981, chapter 11.)

The newer models hinge on the separation of ownership and management in the large company. Salaried managers, who typically only have a small percentage, if any, of the total number of shares, are seen as having objectives other than that of profit maximization. The latter is assumed to be the objective of the owners, i.e. the shareholders. Such managers may go for business strategies that (for example) maximize their own salaries, prestige, security or working conditions.

For the manager, good working conditions may include freedom from stress and pressure and may be expressed in organizational slack (see p. 11); it may also be reflected in substantial 'perks' from the job, such as lavish entertaining accounts.

It may sometimes be possible to express these objectives of managers in terms of *other* objectives. For example, Baumol (1967, p. 46) has suggested, on the basis of his contacts as a consultant with American industrialists, that managers may go for maximization of sales revenue, *inter alia*, because managerial salaries are more closely correlated with the size of a business than with its profitability. There is certainly a good deal of evidence to support this proposition (see for example Cosh, 1975). This is not to deny, however, that profitability may also have *some* role in determining executive remuneration (see Meeks and Whittington, 1975).

Management and shareholders' objectives may not always be in conflict with each other. The assumption, for example, that shareholders want profits to be maximized may not always be wholly valid, although for simplicity it is maintained here. Furthermore managerial remuneration may also be substantially affected by profits, where for example executives are also shareholders, or where they receive part of their income in the form of profit bonuses. Thus managers seeking to maximize their salaries may also have an incentive to maximize their firms' profits.

Conditions for managerial freedom

Where conflict in objectives does exist management's freedom to pursue its objectives will be determined by a number of factors. First, management will only be free to pursue objectives which conflict with those of shareholders where the latter are unable to exercise much control over the running of the company they own. Most small shareholders simply do not have the information necessary to make judgements on management performance, nor are they usually able to mobilize sufficient support to make their voice effective. However, the same limitations are less likely to face financial institutions which are taking a growing proportion of shares in UK companies (see p. 23). There is also the possibility that while shareholders may not be able to force the companies they own to maximize profits, they may nevertheless be able to ensure that some *minimum* profit level is attained. (There is presumably some point at which even a highly fragmented group of shareholders would find it worthwhile to co-ordinate their efforts to control the management of a company they own.)

For this reason a number of managerial models incorporate a minimum profit constraint, which managers must satisfy before they can pursue their own objectives. This constraint is that amount of profit which is necessary to keep shareholders 'happy', i.e. dormant.

Secondly, only where markets are not highly competitive will managers be able to pursue objectives other than profit maximization. The latter is necessary for survival in competitive markets.

Thirdly, managers' freedom to pursue their own objectives depends on the degree to which their activities are likely to attract take-over bids from profit maximizing companies. Such take-overs may lead to unwelcome management redundancies. The limited evidence to date suggests, however, that beyond a certain level of profitability, even higher profitability does not reduce the chances of take-over (Singh, 1975).

Finally, the way in which a company is organized internally may have implications for the kinds of objectives that management may be able to pursue. Where a firm is organized by function (for example 'personnel', or 'finance'), the scope for objectives other than profit maximization may be greater than where the firm is divided up into semi-autonomous divisions on the basis of products or geography. This latter form of organization based on the multi-divisional firm is becoming much more common among large companies. It provides a more powerful way of controlling the performance of managers since each division is responsible for its own profitability, which is calculated separately, and acts for most purposes as an independent unit.

Some complications

Not all writers accept that the maximization of some objective is an appropriate way to describe managerial motivations. Instead, it has been argued that satisficing – reaching some minimum level of attainment in respect of some objective – more closely describes business behaviour. Furthermore it has been suggested that managers may have many conflicting objectives (sometimes they may not even be aware that they conflict). The process by which the conflicts are resolved thus becomes an important element in the analysis of business behaviour.

Some examples of the ways in which different objectives may affect competitive behaviour are explored in the following chapters. However, the main assumption in these chapters is that firms profit maximize.

Competition under Uncertainty

Firms compete with each other in conditions of uncertainty. They therefore have to make judgements on how likely different outcomes of their decisions are. On the revenue side a firm has to assess how customers are likely to respond to an initiative such as price cutting, a new advertising campaign, or a new product launch. It also needs to estimate what is likely to happen if it leaves its present policies unchanged. The firm's view of the likely behaviour or rivals and of potential entrants will often be crucial to these judgements.

On the cost side, the firm has to reach a view on what will happen in input markets if it changes its demand for inputs as a result of a change in its output level. It will also need to estimate how the costs that are directly under its control will alter if output changes. Research and development costs may be particularly difficult to estimate. The difficulties involved in this area are perhaps most vividly shown in the successive escalation of the estimates for the development of Concorde. In November 1962, the estimate was put at between £150 and £170 million. By May 1972, it had risen to £970m (HMSO, 1973b, p. xi). Estimates of operating costs of new products may also be wildly out. For example, estimated operating costs for the rubber skirts which are used at the front and back of the rigid sidewall hovercraft developed by Vosper Thorneycroft rose by over 230 per cent between the date of the first launch and the date the vessel was ready for commercial service (Johnson, 1975, p. 281). Even if a firm intends to leave its output and product range unchanged, it still has to come to some view on whether or not factor prices, technology and the general business environment are likely to change, and if so, to what extent and with what implications for its operations. As on the revenue side, the likely behaviour of rival firms and of potential entrants will influence the firm's cost estimates.

The uncertainty surrounding both future revenues and costs is likely to be greater the bigger the departure the firm is planning to make from its existing practices, the more substantial the expected change in the business environment and the longer the time horizon over which planning is undertaken. Firms entering a market for the first time are likely to face greater uncertainty than a firm already in the market; and an entirely new firm is likely to be less well placed than an established firm which is entering the same market from an existing base in another industry.

There are of course ways of reducing uncertainty. For example a firm may gain a good deal of useful information on the likely markets for a new product by test marketing first. It may also undertake market research without attempting such pilot sales. Again, it may seek long term contracts with suppliers and customers. Such contracts can provide greater certainty on costs and prices. However there is no way in which uncertainty over the future can be completely eliminated: a firm will never really know whether a particular strategy will work until it has implemented it.

The degree of sophistication with which assessments of alternative strategies are made varies from firm to firm. Some businesses, particularly small ones, may make no explicit evaluation at all. Certainly this seems to be the case with many investments by small firms: see pp. 176–7. The owner's 'instincts' may be the primary guiding force for business action. Others may attempt a much more formal examination of possible outcomes. The bigger the financial resources involved, the more detailed is the scrutiny likely to be.

Firms may sometimes be able to reduce the amount of uncertainty they face by taking out insurance. However, insurance will normally only be available if a large number of businesses seek insurance for a similar category of uncertainty, if the risks faced by each firm are substantially independent, and if the insurer can calculate reasonably accurately the scale of the losses that are likely to be incurred among the insured businesses taken as a whole. Many of the uncertainties that arise from business decisions, do not satisfy these conditions.

Entrepreneurship and Competition

The testing out of new initiatives, the development of the successful ones and the discarding of the unsuccessful ones in a world of uncertainty lies at the heart of the competitive process. It is in this context that Kirzner's concept of entrepreneurship referred to in chapter 1 comes into its own. He saw entrepreneurship as consisting essentially in alertness to new market opportunities which might arise in any area of business activity. Such alertness is not shared by everyone; it can therefore be exercised only where there is imperfect information.

Business histories abound with examples of alertness. Michael Marks, one of the founders of Marks and Spencer saw a large untapped market among the working classes of the late nineteenth century for low priced domestic items. The slogan on his market stalls 'Don't ask the price, it's a penny' thus proved to be highly successful. The fixed price of a penny came eventually to apply to a large variety of goods including hatpins and paintbrushes (Rees, 1969, p. 7). William Lever, whose company eventually grew into Unilever, realized that these same people would become increasingly willing to buy more soap as their incomes rose. The essence of Lever's alertness was to see a huge market for the marketing of high quality soaps in wrapped tablets under a heavily advertised brand name, 'Sunlight' (Wilson, 1954, chapter III). In America, Henry Ford's conviction that there was a vast market for a mass produced car made to a standard design at prices that would lead the majority of American families to abandon the family horse in favour of the family car, is of course a classic case of entrepreneurial awareness. His views on car production methods were, for his time, hardly conventional: 'The way to make automobiles is to make one automobile like another automobile, to make all alike, to make them come through the factory just alike; just as one pin is like another pin when it comes from a pin factory ...' (quoted in Nevins, 1976, p. 276). Marks, Lever and Ford all saw opportunities that no one else (or few others) perceived at the same time. In their view they possessed information on market opportunities that others did not have. Of course, once they had proved their success others tried to follow.

Unfortunately conventional analyses of firm behaviour assume that everyone has perfect (or near perfect) information; consequently there is no room for a competitive process involving alertness. (The central preoccupation of such analyses is with equilibrium positions and not with the mechanisms by which markets *move towards* equilibria.)

Some firms may think that they can see an opportunity to advance their market position, or to defend it more effectively, but their projections turn out to be incorrect. The reasons for such unanticipated outcomes may be varied. For example, a new product launch may not fulfil expectations because of over-optimistic forecasts in relation to the effects of advertising, costs, consumer reaction, the response of rival firms or the business environment. The consequences of a wrong forecast may vary from a small loss which the firm is able to sustain, to a financial disaster which leads to the firm, and possibly some of its customers and suppliers going out of business. The collapse of Laker (p. 9) provides an example of such a disaster.

Data on the extent to which firms make wrong forecasts are rather sparse. However, it is known that substantial numbers of new products fail. For example in food manufacturing, up to 60 per cent of new products are withdrawn from sale within five years (Maunder, 1980, p. 91). There is also evidence to suggest that substantial numbers of new businesses close down within a few years of formation. Of the businesses that registered for VAT in the UK in 1974 and 1975, about 25 per cent had deregistered within two years. Within six years 59 per cent had deregistered. Even when the limitations of the VAT data are taken into account (see pp. 43–4), it is difficult to avoid the conclusion that a significant proportion of businesses last only a few years. Of course, some business founders may only *intend* to be in business for a short period; the majority, however, are likely to have had a much longer business life in view.

Some businesses may find that their expectations are more or less fulfilled. Others may experience substantially better results than anticipated. The accuracy with which a firm predicts its successfulness (measured, say, in profitability terms) may not be positively related to the level of success it actually achieves. For example a firm may accurately predict a low level of profitability, or even loss or liquidation. It may be unable to take remedial action. Again, a firm that underestimates its future profitability may obtain a low or a high actual level of profitability.

If a firm finds that it is successful (whether or not it predicted that this would be the case) it will rarely have any incentive to disclose that success, or its source to other firms, unless it knows that the latter are prevented from following its lead. Some of the signs of success such as high reported profits may be apparent to others, but the less information that the successful firm has to give away, the better its competitive position will usually be. It may even have an incentive to distort information flows.

7.2 INTERDEPENDENCE BETWEEN FIRMS

As chapter 3 suggested, one factor which a firm is likely to take into account in deciding on its competitive strategy is the probably reactions of other firms. How are rival firms going to respond to an initiative? The answer to this question could have a major impact on the firm's forecasts. The issue may be most simply illustrated with reference to price changes. In figure 7.1 two demand curves are drawn for the firm contemplating a price change from the existing price of P_1. DD is its demand curve if *all* rivals in the market match a price cut or a rise. The less steeply sloped demand curve, dd, shows demand when the firm's price change is *not* copied. It is assumed that both DD and dd are known to the firm. Now if the firm is contemplating a price decline from P_1 to P_2, the outcome in revenue terms could be either $P_2 \times Q_1$ or $P_2 \times Q_2$ depending on whether all rivals match the price cut or no one does. Clearly what rivals are expected to do will have important implications for the firm's forecasts and its decisions.

The above example considered different price responses of rivals to a price cut. In some cases, however, such a cut may induce a non-price response. Conversely, a non-price initiative may provoke a price response.

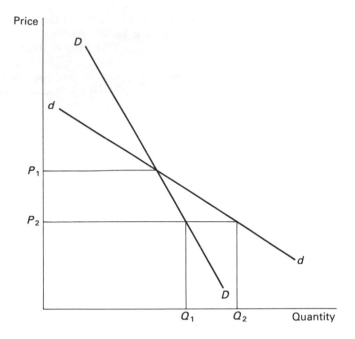

Figure 7.1   The effects of a price cut

The existing price is P_1. *DD* is the firm's demand curve if *all* rivals in the market match a price cut or rise; *dd* is the demand curve when the firm's price change is not copied. If the firm reduces price from P_1 to P_2, the outcome in revenue terms could be either $P_2 \times Q_1$ or $P_2 \times Q_2$ depending on how rivals react.

Collusion

Types of collusion

It may sometimes be possible for rivals to collude on their policies. This may become easier as the number of firms in a market falls: see chapter 4. Such collusion may be either explicit or implicit. The former involves agreements often of a written form and may cover a wide range of issues including pricing, advertising, new product development and investment. An example of explicit collusion is provided by UK ready-made concrete producers. Up to 1977 they had agreements over the allocation of contracts. In most cases the main element in these agreements related to the selection of a 'preferred tenderer' who would quote the lowest price, with the other companies agreeing to quote higher prices (HMSO, 1981, p. 29). The scope for explicit collusion in the UK is now severely restricted. As chapter 12 points out certain types of agreement are now illegal, and most of the remainder have failed to meet the now very strict criteria that have to be satisfied if an agreement is to survive.

Implicit collusion arises when firms develop an unwritten code of 'acceptable' behaviour amongst themselves without any formal agreement. For example one firm may become accepted as a price leader so that when this leader changes its price, it is normal practice for the other firms to follow suit. The price leader may have this position because it is the most efficient producer, or because it is the most powerful. Historical factors and personalities may also play a part. The identity of the leader may change over time. Price leadership may range from collusive price leadership through which joint maximization of monopoly profits is attained to barometric price leadership, through which competitive prices and outputs emerge. In this latter case, the leader simply acts as the 'eyes and ears' of the firms in the market. There is evidence to show that price leadership has been in operation for at least part of the post-war period among UK producers of bread, electric lamps, gramophone records, petrol and tyres (HMSO, 1973c). The firm with the largest market share has usually been the leader.

Implicit collusion may also be assisted by the existence of focal points. These are factors which facilitate co-ordination between firms. There may be certain customary pricing practices to which most firms adhere. Traditionally, price changes may be made when a new wage agreement has been made in the market, or when government changes a price control ceiling. Again, it may be accepted practice that firms round up to the nearest pound in their pricing.

Implicit collusion is perhaps more difficult to achieve than its explicit counterpart. One reason for this is that there are no agreed penalties by which delinquent firms may be disciplined.

Collusion, of whatever kind, does of course affect the competitive activities of the firms involved. If it is effective, it reduces the degree of rivalry in the areas to which it relates. However, it may increase rivalry in the areas that it does *not* cover. For example, collusion on price may lead to greater competition in advertising.

Collusion or independence?

A firm has to decide whether its objectives are most likely to be met through some form of collusion with rival firms, or through following an independent line. One advantage of collusion is that if it is effective it reduces the likelihood that any one firm will unilaterally set off a process which eventually places all firms in a worse position than they would otherwise have been in. For example collusion on prices avoids the possibility of a price cutting war whose ultimate effect is to reduce everyone's profits.

A firm may, however, decide to follow an independent line for several reasons. First, it may have little alternative: for legal or other reasons effective collusion may not be an option. Secondly, even if collusion were possible the firm may *wish* to spark off reactions among rivals. For example, a general realignment of prices in a market may be to its advantage. Thirdly, the firm may think that other firms will not follow its initiative. Lack of response may be due to rivals knowing about the initiative but for various reasons not wishing (or being able) to follow it. But it may also result from ignorance on the part of rivals. Some decisions – for example to launch a new advertising campaign or a new product – are clearly observable. However, price cutting which leaves list prices unchanged, but which uses secret discounts may be far less easy to detect. A firm may even attempt to follow such a policy while overtly adhering to some form of collusion. Rival firms may pick up some signals about the activities of the price cutter by unexplained movements in their sales. Sales figures are however affected by a whole range of factors and it may be difficult to pinpoint the precise reason why they are changing. The collaboration of customers is required if secret price discounts are to remain secret. If customers are unable to resist the temptation to play one firm off against another the secrecy may be shortlived.

Market structure and collusion

Both the incentive for and the feasibility of collusion are likely to vary with market structure. Other things being equal, collusion is much less likely in a market which consists of a large number of firms each with only a small part of the market than in a market in which only a handful of firms (of roughly equal size) operate. In the latter, firms are likely to be much more aware of their independence and of the dangers of sparking off retaliatory action. And there are fewer interests to be taken into account in any attempt at co-ordination. Collusive arrangements are also easier to maintain. However, it is extremely difficult to go beyond these broad generalizations about the relationship between collusion and market structure. As chapter 4 suggests, empirical investigation must ultimately provide the crucial test.

Competition as a Game

Competition between interdependent firms has sometimes been likened to the playing of a competitive game. The development of game theory

Table 7.1   A pay-off matrix

		Profit outcome (A's outcome given first)		
		B's strategies		
		New advertising campaign	Price rise	New product launch
A's strategies	New advertising campaign	−50, −50	+200, −100	−100, +210
	Price rise	−100, +200	+300, +300	−150, +250
	New product launch	+210, −100	+250, −150	+230, +230

in the post-war period has given a number of insights into oligopolistic behaviour.

Some of the basic ideas behind the game theory approach can be illustrated with a simple example. Suppose that there are only two firms, *A* and *B* in the market, each of whom has the objective of maximizing its profits. It is assumed that both firm *A* and firm *B* must simultaneously select one of three mutually exclusive competitive strategies: a new advertising campaign, a price rise or a new product launch. It is also assumed that although neither knows what strategy the other will adopt, both are aware of what the profit outcome from any pair of strategies will be. These outcomes may be arranged in a pay-off matrix of the kind illustrated in table 7.1. Which strategy will the firms choose? One possibility is for them to be cautious and for them each to choose a 'maximin' approach. They first identify the minimum profits for each of the three strategies. For both firms these minima are −100 (new advertising campaign), −150 (price rise), and +210 (new product launch). They then select the strategy which gives them the maximum of these minima. Thus both firms select the new product launch as their strategy, and both gain 230. It is important to note, however, that profits could have been *further* increased by each firm selecting the price rise strategy. However, this strategy is not selected because neither firm knows for certain that the other firm will also adopt such a strategy. Collusion of some kind could however bring such a solution about.

Clearly the above example is highly simplified. It does, however, bring out the impact that collusion can have on competitive strategy.

7.3 ENTRY

Types of Entry

A firm may face competition not only from established firms currently producing similar products but also from other sources. These sources may be of three basic kinds. First, firms and individuals who previously bought in the market may undertake self-supply. For example, a firm may decide to make its own components. Similarly, final customers may decide to produce for themselves. (Cat and dog food manufacturers are very conscious of the competition they face from home-made 'scraps': see HMSO, 1977a.) Secondly an entirely new firm may be set up. This is referred to as new entry. Thirdly a firm operating in another market may enter. Such entry by diversification is referred to as cross entry.

The following discussion considers only new and cross entry, although some of the analysis may also be appropriate for self-supply. The new or cross entrant has to form expectations about its post-entry position. These expectations in turn partly depend on how it thinks established firms will behave after it enters. For their part established firms have to form expectations about the likelihood of entry given different policies, and about the effects of such entry on their post-entry positions.

Barriers to Entry

Established firms may sometimes have certain advantages over the potential entrant. These advantages are often referred to as barriers to entry, with the implication that they act to impede entry. Three types of barrier are usually identified.

Types of barrier

(1) *Higher costs* An established firm may have lower unit costs at some or all levels of output than a potential entrant. It may have access to cheaper techniques of production, finance and raw materials. It may have a superior location. This advantage may be obtained (and maintained) by a variety of means. Production techniques may be protected by patents or industry secrecy. Cheaper finance may arise because the established firm has a track record which the entrant does not have. The disadvantage may be less for the cross entrant than for the new entrant since the former does at least have a history of operating in another market. The established firm's access to raw materials may be protected by normal property rights: it may have bought up all the locations of the best deposits of a particular mineral.

In some cases potential entrants may not simply be at a cost disadvantage in the production of a particular good or service; they may not be able to produce *at all*, because of the established firm's exclusive rights. If it is to compete the entrant may therefore be forced to produce a rather different product and incur additional costs in order to compete effectively with the established firm. For example, firms providing catering facilities on motorway service stations have exclusive legal rights; no entrant may come in during the life of the tenancy agreement. However, a new rival may open a cafe or restaurant off the motorway itself. In order to attract custom, however, it has to incur additional costs of promotion and signposting. Sometimes entry may be inhibited by the behaviour of suppliers. For example Raleigh refuses to supply certain retailers with bicycles bearing the 'Raleigh' name. Such retailers have therefore to find other sources and this may involve them in higher costs.

(2) *Customer loyalty* Established firms may enjoy customer loyalty to their products that an entrant has to challenge if it is to compete. Such loyalty may arise for a variety of reasons, including effective advertising and marketing. Once again the cross entrant may be at less of a disadvantage than a new entrant. Customers of the former may already be aware of, and attached to, the firm's products in *other* markets. Thus the firm may find it relatively easy to generate customer loyalty on the basis of its record in other markets, especially if customers are attached to its business name (which is not usually product specific). Marks and Spencer for example has undoubtedly been able to build on existing customer loyalty to its 'St Michael' label when it has moved into new markets.

The existence of greater consumer loyalty towards the established firm's products may of course be interpreted as another type of cost disadvantage: The entrant has to incur higher costs in order to sell a given output. However, customer loyalty as a barrier to entry is usually given separate treatment in the literature. Strictly speaking, an entrant only faces a customer loyalty 'barrier to entry' where the attachment to the products of established firms is greater than that which the latter faced *when they entered*. However, it is often helpful to assess the disadvantage that a particular entrant faces at the time of entry.

(3) *Scale economies* The argument that the presence of scale economies creates an entry barrier takes several different forms of which one is illustrated in figure 7.2. This figure assumes that market demand (D_m) and long run average costs (LAC) intersect where the latter is falling. The implication of this is that the whole market is most efficiently supplied by *only one firm*. Such a situation is known as a natural monopoly. If another firm were to come in so that at each price the two firms shared the available market equally, the individual firm demand curve would shift to $D_m/2$ in figure 7.2. *Neither* firm would be able to operate profitably as the LAC curve would everywhere be above the demand (average revenue) curve.

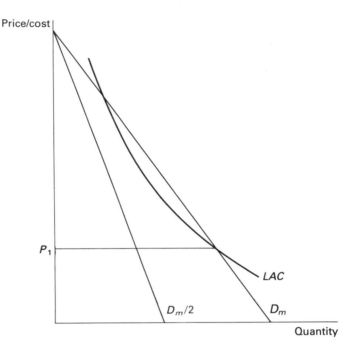

Figure 7.2 Natural monopoly
Market demand, D_m, and LAC intersect where the latter is falling. The whole market is therefore most efficiently supplied by one firm. Such a situation is known as a natural monopoly. (If the market were divided between two equally sized firms, each with a demand curve of $D_m/2$ neither would be able to cover costs.) If the natural monopolist raises price above P_1 an entrant could supply the whole market at a lower price, and still be profitable.

Entry to a natural monopoly is therefore in effect barred. Note however that if the single firm charged any price above P_1, a new entrant could come in and supply the whole market at a lower price and still be profitable.

Barriers and the entry decision

Some element of uncertainty is bound to surround the presence and scale of entry barriers. However, even if they are known with accuracy, it is not clear how they would affect the competitive behaviour of established or entrant firms. The standard argument has usually been that these barriers give established firms greater freedom to charge higher prices than would otherwise be possible. Even if they deliberately follow a pricing policy which *attracts* entry because they know they can reap short run profits before entry actually occurs, the prices they can charge in the short run will be higher than in the absence of entry barriers. There are two points to be made here.

First, as was shown earlier, the scale economies barrier of the type described in figure 7.2 does not of itself provide greater freedom to charge prices above P_1. Secondly, the existence of barriers may be irrelevant to the entry decision if the potential entrant considers that after entry, established firms may engage in price cutting or other predatory practices to force it out. If the entrant believes this, and that it could not survive such an attack, it will not enter *whatever* the *pre*-entry price. Even in the natural monopoly case, a price above P_1 might not attract entry if the potential entrant thinks that the established firm would drop its prices below that level for a while if any entrant came in. Established firms may of course have different views among themselves about the desirability of entry, and have different expectations regarding the likely behaviour of potential entrants. In such circumstances, it may be difficult to agree a co-ordinated policy. In some industries, however, there may be a sufficiently common view to enable collusion to occur. The relationship between entry barriers and prices are considered more fully in the next chapter.

Some economists have argued that no firm or group of firms can ultimately be protected from entrants. Even the barriers described earlier provide no protection against the new product or process. Very many firms have thought they enjoyed a strong competitive position only to find, to their surprise, that it has been eroded by an innovator. The role of innovation in the competitive process is examined in chapter 10.

Contestable Markets

In recent years, the analysis of entry has received a new impetus from the development of the concept of market contestability. A perfectly contestable market is one 'into which entry is absolutely free and exit is absolutely costless' (Baumol, 1982). Entry is free in the sense that the entrant is at no disadvantage relative to established firms. Exit is costless in the sense that any firm can leave 'without impediment and in the process of departure can recoup any costs incurred in the entry process' (Baumol, 1982). The key characteristic of such a market is that a potential entrant can come in at any time and for any period to take advantage of profitable opportunities. Potential entrants are not deterred by the possibility of post-entry predatory price cutting as they can always leave without penalty. A perfectly contestable market may be perfectly competitive, but it need not be. For example, a natural monopoly of the type illustrated in figure 7.2 may qualify as perfectly contestable. In practice of course few markets if any are likely to qualify for this description.

The concept of contestability is attractive in that it can be applied to *any* market structure, irrespective of how many firms there are or of how the market is shared out between them. Furthermore, how contestable a market is has important implications for allocative efficiency, (see p. 191).

7.4 SUMMARY

Competition between firms arises because consumer purchasing power is limited. Competitive activity takes many forms, and occurs under conditions of uncertainty. It is in these conditions that entrepreneurship has a key role to play. The competitive strategy that a firm adopts will depend on its objectives. This has traditionally been seen as one of profit maximization, although in the post-war period, several 'managerial' models of firm behaviour based on other motivations have been developed.

Firms may decide to collude either explicitly or implicitly rather than to pursue an independent line. Markets with only a few firms of similar size are particularly likely to show evidence of collusive activity. Potential entry provides another source of competition for established firms. Various barriers may act to impede the entry of newcomers although, in the long term, no firm is likely to be secure from the entrant who has a new product or process. In recent years the analysis of entry has received a greater emphasis as a result of the development of the concept of contestability. This chapter has considered the nature of the competitive process in general. The next four chapters examine specific aspects of this process.

8

Pricing

In the previous chapter it was argued that firms compete in a whole range of areas apart from pricing, on which most treatments of the theory of the firm tend to concentrate. However, pricing nevertheless remains a very important component of competitive activity. This chapter is therefore devoted to it. The first section considers the nature of price. The second section looks at the way in which prices may be arrived at by firms. The final section examines the practice that some firms are able to adopt of discriminating between customers in the prices that they charge.

8.1 THE NATURE OF PRICE

Prices and Exchange

The price of a good or service is the payment the buyer makes to the seller. In return for that payment the seller transfers certain rights over the product to the buyer. In some cases all property rights are transferred. Thus the purchaser of a tin of baked beans becomes, by virtue of his payment, the legal owner of the tin and its contents. When someone rents a holiday cottage, it does not become the property of the leasee, but the latter is given some rights, often of an exclusive nature, over the cottage, and its use, for the period of the rental. In the case of services, payment is made in return for the seller undertaking a particular task or tasks on the buyer's behalf. Prices are of course attached to both final and intermediate output. They may be defined before or after taxes and subsidies. In this chapter, price will be defined as that which the customer pays.

Comparisons of Prices

Comparisons of price across firms is not always a straightforward matter for the following reasons. First, the *list* or published price may be different from the *actual* price that is agreed between the buyer and seller. Customers may be given discounts on the former. A recent survey by the Motor Agents Association (*Financial Times*, 17 May 1984) reported that three out of four car dealers were offering a substantial discount on a new car's list price without even being asked for one. The extent of discounting may vary from seller to seller and from transaction to transaction in which the same seller is involved. Secondly, in markets where customers trade-in an old item for a new (or newer) replacement, the actual payment that the customer makes for the item he is buying is affected by the allowance he is given for the trade-in. These allowances may be of two kinds. Customers may be offered a fixed allowance whatever the condition of the trade-in. This kind of offer will usually attract many trade-ins whose market value is well below the allowance offered. In some cases the trade-in may have virtually no market value, in which case the fixed allowance differs little from a straight price discount. The variable allowance on the other hand is the subject of negotiation between the buyer and the seller. If firms differ in the allowances they offer on similar trade-ins, comparisons of their list prices will be misleading. Thirdly, although a group of firms may be in the business of selling what is basically an identical product, they may vary in what they include for the price of that product. In new car sales for example a wide range of extras is often offered. These extras may include cheap hire purchase, extended guarantees, holiday vouchers, entry into competitions, and 'free' accessories such as radios. Firms selling identical models may differ in the particular packages that they offer. Comparisons of car prices alone without regard to these other items will be misleading. Furthermore, it must be remembered that customers are often involved in the purchase of several products in one transaction. For example, the typical payment at a supermarket check-out is for a substantial number of goods. To compare the retail price of any one good, such as bread, across supermarkets would not be very meaningful as it is the *total* package which is bought that is important for both buyer and seller. Indeed, some shops may deliberately sell certain goods at a loss in order to attract customers into the shop where they will then buy several products. Such goods are known as loss leaders.

This last point raises a more general issue. Even where customers are seeking to make a single purchase – a car, a book, a loaf of bread, a haircut – they are not usually buying a good or a service which is defined by some narrow technical specification. They are also 'buying' such factors as pleasant and helpful services from sales staff, availability, congenial surroundings, geographical location, ease of parking, delivery and after sales service. Thus the two litre tin of Dulux Brilliant White gloss bought at the local hardware store (usually) comes with more personalized service and geographical convenience than when it is purchased from an out-of-town hypermarket. The purchase from the local shop may even provide the customer with the additional satisfaction that he has supported local industry. Valid comparisons of prices in the two stores require these factors to be taken into account.

Single Product Firms

Throughout this chapter it is assumed that the firm sells only one product or one 'package' consisting of fixed proportions of different products. Multi-product operations present a number of analytical complications. For example, on the demand side particular problems arise when the firm sells a range of products to the *same* customer, since the demand schedules for the products are often interdependent: the price of one will affect the amount demanded of the others.

8.2 PRICE FORMATION

Most firms are not pure price takers (see p. 49). They usually have some freedom to determine their own prices. This freedom arises as a result of imperfect information among customers (they do not always know which firm is selling the cheapest product), and/or some differentiation among the firms' products.

Average Cost Pricing

Given this element of freedom, which is likely to vary from firm to firm and market to market, how do firms set their prices in practice? A number of studies have shown that many firms build up their prices from average cost (see the references in Silberston, 1970). This approach is often called cost plus pricing. Because it is a widespread practice, it is considered in detail below.

The mechanics of average cost pricing

One variant of this approach is based on an estimate of short run average variable cost ($SAVC$) for some appropriate level of output. Variable costs are those costs which, as their name implies, vary as the firm's level of output in a given period changes. They may be distinguished from fixed costs, or 'overheads' as they are often called, which do not change as that output level changes. The distinction between variable and fixed costs is only valid for the short run, the period in which at least one factor of production is in fixed supply to the firm. In the long run, all costs are variable. Most firms include expenditure on materials and components and the wages of production workers under the variable cost heading. The salaries of management, interest payable on debts, and rates are usually regarded as fixed costs. (There is no hard and fast system of classification here; it all depends on how the firm chooses to define its 'short run'.)

$SAVC$ at each output level is obtained by dividing total variable costs by output. Similarly, short run average fixed cost ($SAFC$) is total fixed cost, which by definition remains unchanged whatever the output level, divided by output.

To its estimate of $SAVC$, the firm adds a percentage gross margin which is intended to cover its estimated $SAFC$ for the relevant output level and to generate profit. The outcome of these calculations is the average cost price.

This procedure is illustrated in figure 8.1. It is assumed that the price calculations are based on an anticipated output of Q_1, which may be regarded as full capacity. (It is 'full' in the sense that after Q_1, $SAVC$ rises rapidly.) It is also assumed, for reasons that will become apparent later, that $SAVC$ is constant prior to Q_1. $SAFC$ does of course decline as output increases since the same total fixed costs are spread progressively more thinly over larger outputs. The short run average total cost ($SATC$) curve is obtained by aggregating $SAVC$ and $SAFC$ at each level of output.

At Q_1, $SAVC$ is represented by z. The firm then adds a percentage, $(y/z) \times 100$, to cover $SAFC$ for that output (this percentage would of course be different if an output other than Q_1 were chosen as a basis for calculating price) and then a further percentage $(x/z) \times 100$ for profits. This latter percentage is known as the net margin. The gross margin is $((x + y)/z) \times 100$, and the average cost price is P_1. If the firm sticks to this price, and sells all that the market wants and the firm's capacity can provide at that price, then the amount of profit it makes will depend on how much it *actually* sells. If it only sells Q_2 for example, it would make no profit at all because the gross margin would be swallowed up by fixed costs. If it sells Q_3, the price would cover only $SAVC$.

The gross margin and the firm's objectives

So far a crucial question has been ignored: what determines the size of the gross margin? A key factor here is the firm's objectives. Some possible objectives are considered below. For analytical simplicity, the firm considered in (1) and (2) below is assumed to be a monopolist. This enables the analysis to abstract from some of the complexities which

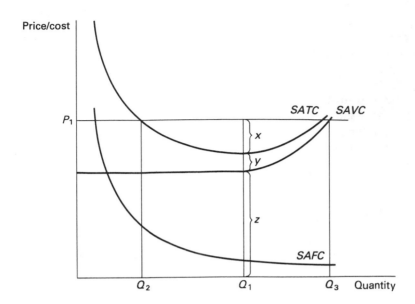

Figure 8.1   Average cost pricing
The firm is assumed to base its price calculations on output Q_1. At this output,
SAVC are represented by z. The firm adds a percentage, $(y/z) \times 100$ to cover
SAFC for that output, and a further percentage, $(x/z) \times 100$, for profits. The
gross margin is $((x + y)/z) \times 100$. If it *actually* sells only Q_2, it makes neither a
profit nor a loss. If it sells Q_3, the price covers only *SAVC*.

arise from oligopolistic interdependence and which were discussed in
the previous chapter. The analysis in (1) and (2) also assumes that the
firm has short run objectives. This latter assumption permits even
further simplification as it means that the firm does not consider the
possibility of entry in its pricing. (Entry is necessarily a long run
phenomenon.)
(1) *Short run profit maximization* In the conventional theory of the firm
the short run profit maximizer sells that output at which short run
marginal cost (*SMC*) – the addition to total cost of producing one more

unit given that at least one factor is fixed – is equal to marginal revenue
(MR) – the addition to total revenue of selling that last unit. (It is
assumed that average revenue (AR) exceeds $SAVC$ at this output.) Thus
for the monopolist illustrated in figure 8.2 the profit maximizing output
and price are Q_1 and P_1 respectively. It is assumed that the $SAVC$ curve
is identical to that shown in figure 8.1. Up to output Q_2, SMC is also
horizontal and equal to $SAVC$. The conventional theory thus sees the
firm as relying on marginal concepts for determining its profit maximizing output and hence its price. However, it is not difficult to show that

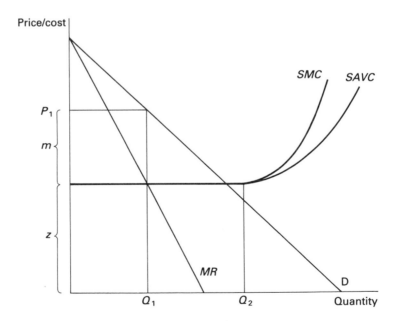

Figure 8.2   Average cost pricing and profit maximization
Up to output Q_2, SMC is horizontal and equal to $SAVC$. The short run profit
maximizing monopolist using cost plus pricing applies a gross margin of (m/z) ×
100. Price is P_1 and output Q_1.

the same profit maximizing price and output can be obtained through a form of average cost pricing.

It should be noted that the short run profit maximizing firm can ignore fixed costs in its calculations, as there is nothing it can do about them anyway: the same amount has to be paid (in the long run) whatever output level is chosen. The firm simply wishes to apply that *gross* margin which maximizes the difference between total variable costs and total revenue. In figure 8.2 it does this by setting a gross margin on its (constant) *SAVC* of $(m/z) \times 100$. Thus although the firm does not explicitly use marginal cost and revenue concepts in its pricing, it may nevertheless be achieving profit maximization. It acts *as if* it is equating *SMC* and *MR*. It should be noted that the application of the same (percentage) gross margin to *SAVC* yields the same average cost price up to output Q_2, because *SAVC* is constant up to this level. Provided the firm knows that it will not be selling beyond that output level, it does not have to select any particular output level before calculating its gross margin.

It is interesting to see the link between the gross margin and the price elasticity of the firm's elasticity of demand. It can easily be shown (see appendix to this chapter) that

$$MR = P\left(1 - \frac{1}{|e|}\right) \tag{8.1}$$

where $|e|$ is the absolute value of the firm's price elasticity of demand. Now since the short run profit maximizer equates *SMC* with *MR*, and since $SMC = SAVC$ where *SAVC* is constant, (8.1) becomes

$$SAVC = P\left(1 - \frac{1}{|e|}\right) \tag{8.2}$$

Rearranging, (8.2) becomes

$$\frac{P - SAVC}{P} = \frac{1}{|e|} \tag{8.3}$$

Thus if the gross margin as a proportion of the price is equal to the reciprocal of the absolute value of the price of the firm's demand, average cost pricing generates a profit maximizing outcome.

(2) *Short run sales maximization* In the previous chapter, Baumol's (1967) hypothesis that managers may seek to maximise sales revenue was briefly considered (p. 104). Here it is assumed that managers pursue such an objective in the short run, subject to the condition that they satisfy a minimum profit constraint (see p. 105). The following analysis

should be considered in the light of some of the qualifications that are associated with the newer 'managerial' theories (see p. 105).

The firm's total revenue is maximized at the output where MR is zero since at this output, increasing sales by one unit through a reduction in price adds nothing to *total* revenue. (As can be seen from equation (8.1) above, the price elasticity of demand at this output must be one.) Thus in figure 8.3 output would be Q_1 and price, P_1.

The firm using average cost pricing can arrive at this outcome by adding a gross margin of $(m/z) \times 100$ on its (constant) $SAVC$. This outcome does of course assume that the profits made (the shaded area

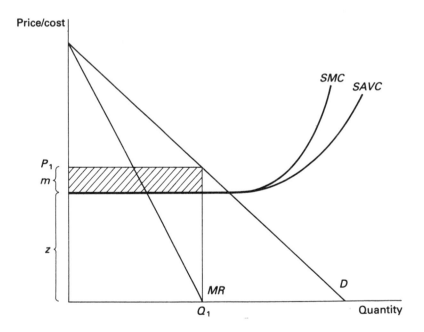

Figure 8.3   Average cost pricing and sales maximization
A gross margin of $(m/z) \times 100$ yields the appropriate price (P_1) for the sales maximizing firm which sells Q_1. At Q_1, MR is zero, and the absolute value of the elasticity of demand is one.

less total fixed costs) are sufficient to meet the minimum profit constraint laid down by the owners. If this were not the case, the managers would have to adjust their pricing policies. They would do this by increasing the gross margin and shifting the average cost price up. This would reduce the output sold, but total profits would rise. This process could continue until the firm reached its profit maximizing output where $SMC = MR$. (Beyond this point, any increase in the gross margin would generate a reduction in total profits.)

(3) *Other pricing objectives* The objectives considered above do of course represent only two among numerous possibilities. Firms may for example seek long run rather than short run sales or profit maximization. Where long run objectives are important, the firm may have to take the possibility of entry into account in deciding on its pricing policy (see p. 117). Firms may also go for some of the other kinds of objective mentioned in the previous chapter. (The pricing implications of these objectives are not however clear: Wildsmith, 1973, p. 125.) Or they may be content with a gross margin that generates a 'satisfactory' level of profit.

It is very difficult to establish what the precise objectives of a firm using average cost pricing are. For example it might be expected that a short run profit maximizer would adjust its gross margin and hence its price every time cost and demand conditions changed. Certainly one of the earliest studies to show that average cost pricing was widespread in industry (Hall and Hitch, 1939) also showed that many firms applied it very flexibly and amended their margins in the light of business conditions. However, even rigid adherence to an average cost price in times of frequent cost and demand changes (as followed by some firms in the Hall and Hitch study) does not *necessarily* rule out profit maximization since such adherence may be the best rule of thumb for achieving this objective in conditions of considerable uncertainty. It must also be remembered that the alteration of prices may involve substantial costs (for example as a result of the reprinting of price lists and sales literature).

Interdependence and pricing

Pricing behaviour may become much more complex where the implications of interdependence among rivals are taken into account. For example rivals selling similar products and using cost plus pricing may have different price preferences. These differences may arise for a variety of reasons. Firms may have different objectives. There may also be differences across firms in demand and cost conditions. Again, firms may vary in their views on the likelihood and desirability of entry at different prices and on future trends in the industry and its environment.

Although the firms may have preferences which differ substantially, the scope for substantially different prices in the market place may be very limited given the similarity of the products involved. Whose price preference will prevail?

It will usually be that of the firm seeking the lowest price although this may not always be the case: for example the firm with the lowest price preference may not be the strongest financially and the other firms may be able, by some means, to persuade or coerce it into raising its price. Where price settles – if it settles at all – will depend on the relative strengths of the oligopolists.

Where a firm's pricing freedom is heavily constrained by the preferences of other rivals it may, if it wishes to preserve a given gross margin on costs, adopt a form of price minus costing. This procedure may be illustrated with respect to a firm with short run objectives. The appropriate price becomes the starting point. The firm deducts from this price the relevant profit and average fixed cost margin and thereby arrives at an acceptable *SAVC*. This *SAVC* then determines the nature and quality of the output produced. There is evidence to suggest that this procedure has been common among motor manufacturers (Smyth, 1967).

Once price stability has been achieved in an oligopolistic market, firms may be very reluctant, because of all the uncertainties involved, to upset the established pattern, even though changes in demand and cost conditions may lead (given constant prices) to a change in both the gross and net margins. However, reluctance to change prices may be less where the market has established an orderly mechanism for such change, for example through price leadership (see p. 111).

8.3 PRICE DISCRIMINATION

Price discrimination occurs when two varieties of a good or service are sold by the same seller to two buyers at different net prices, the net price being the price paid by the buyer corrected for the cost associated with any form of differentiation (Phlips, 1983, p. 6). Such discrimination may occur therefore when actual prices do not differ if the costs of producing the good or service are different. Conversely, differences in price may not indicate any discrimination if these differences simply reflect differences in cost. The most obvious case of price discrimination occurs when prices differ but where the differences cannot be attributed, to any substantial extent, to cost differences. One example of such discrimination is the charging of different rail fares for different categories of rail traveller. Discrimination is only possible where customers who are being charged different prices do not (or cannot) trade with one another. Otherwise, the customers paying the cheaper price may be able to resell to the customers who are being charged the higher prices. Separation of consumers may be achieved in various ways. It may be implicit in the nature of the product. Private medical consultations for example cannot be sold between clients. Thus the consultants may have some scope for charging different prices to different types of customer. Various restrictions may be imposed on the good or service. For example, certain rail tickets are only valid at specified times or on specified trains.

The term 'price discrimination' is also applied to instances where the *same* customer is charged different prices for the same product depending on how much is bought. For example many fairground operators charge lower prices for a second 'go'.

Why does it pay the firm to discriminate? The answer to this question (for the short run profit maximizing firm) is illustrated in figure 8.4. It is assumed that the firm has two groups of consumers A and B and their respective demands are D_A and D_B. The horizontal aggregation of these demand curves is given in figure (iii) as D_{A+B}. Since this aggregate demand curve is kinked, the corresponding MR curve is $ABCDE$ and is discontinuous over CD. The short run profit maximizing firm unable to price discriminate produces that output where SMC equals MR, i.e. Q_M, and charges P_1 in both markets. Thus Q_{1A} and Q_{1B} are sold in markets A and B respectively. If the firm is able to discriminate the relevant MR concept for the firm's decision is the *horizontal sum* of the MR_A and MR_B curves. This 'aggregate' MR curve (ABE in figure (iii)) has no discontinuity. It simply shows the total output that is sold when marginal revenues are equalized in both markets. If they were not so equalized it would pay the firm to move output from the market where MR is lower to the market where it is higher. By this means the firm would raise total revenue. The firm's output level is again Q_M where $MR_A + MR_B$ equals SMC. The prices charged in each market are those associated with that MR level, i.e. P_{2A} and P_{2B} respectively. Output is Q_{2A} and Q_{2B} respectively. (It should be noted that it is not necessary to construct D_{A+B} in the discrimination case.)

In both the non-discrimination and discrimination case, output is Q_M. Total costs, as measured by the sum of the marginal costs are the same in both cases, but total revenues, as measured by the *sum* of the marginal revenues, differ between the two cases. In the non-discrimination case, total revenue is given by the area bounded by $ABCDFQ_M$. In the discrimination case, it is the area bounded by $ABDFQ_M$. Thus the triangle BCD represents the increase in profits that results from discrimination. Of course where the demand curves of the two groups are identical, price discrimination will not be profitable.

Price discrimination may sometimes lead to more being supplied than would be the case if no discrimination were possible. If the SMC curve

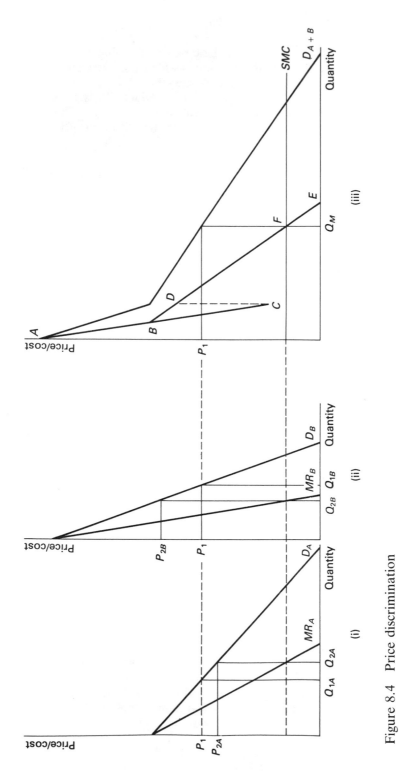

Figure 8.4 Price discrimination

A firm faces two groups of consumers A and B. Their respective demand curves are D_A and D_B. The firm that is unable to discriminate charges P_1 in both markets. The discriminating firm charges P_{2A} to group A and P_{2B} to group B. BCD in (iii) represents the increase in profits from discrimination.

were to pass through the discontinuous portion of the *MR* curve derived from D_{A+B}, *CD* in figure 8.4, it might pay the non-discriminating firm to choose that output level where *SMC* intersects the portion *AC* of the *MR* curve rather than to expand output to the point where *SMC* intersects the portion *DE* of the *MR* curve. (By so expanding it might add more to costs than to revenues.) Thus no consumer in market *B* would be supplied, as the (common) price would be above the kink on the aggregate demand curve. However, it would always pay the discriminating monopolist to expand output to the point where *SMC* intersects the *DE* portion of the aggregate *MR* curve. As a consequence, output is higher in this case under discrimination and both markets are served.

8.4 SUMMARY

The 'price' of a good or service is not always easy to define and price comparisons across firms must be approached with care. Most firms have some freedom to determine their own prices. They often build these prices up from average cost, an approach which is compatible with more than one objective. The price preferences of firms in an oligopolistic market may vary. Where, however, the scope for actual price differences is limited, it will usually be the lowest price preference that prevails in the market.

If a firm is able to separate groups of customers with differing demands so that they cannot trade among themselves, it can increase its profits by discriminating in price between them. Such discrimination may even lead to an expansion in output.

8.5 APPENDIX: THE RELATIONSHIP BETWEEN MARGINAL REVENUE, PRICE (AVERAGE REVENUE) AND THE ELASTICITY OF DEMAND

Let *MR*, *P*, *Q*, *TR* and *e* be the firm's marginal revenue, price, quantity, total revenue and the price elasticity of demand respectively.

Then

$$MR = \frac{\partial TR}{\partial Q} = \frac{\partial (PQ)}{\partial Q}$$

$$= \frac{\partial P}{\partial Q} Q + P \qquad (8A.1)$$

Rearranging and multiplying through by $\frac{P}{P}$

$$MR = P\left(1 + \frac{\partial P}{\partial Q}\frac{Q}{P}\right)$$

$$= P\left(1 + \frac{1}{e}\right) \qquad\qquad (8.A2)$$

On the assumption that e is negative (because $\dfrac{\partial Q}{\partial P}$ is negative), (8.A2) is frequently expressed as

$$P\left(1 - \frac{1}{|e|}\right)$$

where $|e|$ is the *absolute* value of the elasticity of demand.

9
Advertising

Firms selling similar products frequently seek to differentiate their products. The purpose of such differentiation is to give a product a distinctiveness which places the firms producing it in a stronger market position. Differentiation may be achieved in three main ways. First, the product itself may be differentiated. For example, car models differ in their technical specifications and in the accessories included in the basic price. Brands of toothpaste vary in their colour and taste. Secondly, the selling process may be differentiated. The quality of the sales staff, the geographical location of the seller, and the availability of special finance for purchasing for example may all vary across firms. Thirdly, a company may attempt to alter the image of the product to give it a distinctiveness of its own.

All these forms of differentiation are likely to have some influence on the consumer's purchasing decision. In this chapter attention is focused exclusively on the role of advertising in differentiation primarily through its effect on product image. Advertising may be defined as 'mass paid communication, the ultimate purpose of which is to impart information, develop attitudes and induce action beneficial to the advertiser ...' (Colley, quoted in Doyle, 1968). It is important to realize that advertising is only one part of the total differentiation 'package', and that, for reasons outlined later in the chapter its role will vary from industry to industry.

9.1 THE NATURE OF ADVERTISING

Informative vs Persuasive Advertising

A distinction is sometimes made between informative and persuasive advertising. The former is seen simply as imparting information on the product: for example its technical specifications and its availability. The 'small ads' in newspapers and periodicals are frequently cited as an example. Persuasive advertising is designed more directly to influence consumers' views on a product and thereby to affect purchasing decisions in a way favourable to the advertiser. Most television advertising is usually placed in this category. Both types of advertising are seen as affecting the product image, although this is more obviously the case with persuasive advertising.

The distinction between these two types of advertising is not, however, clear cut. Much information is provided to persuade the receiver of that information to adopt one course of action rather than another. The 'small ad' which describes the characteristics of an item that is for sale is placed to persuade someone to respond. Because of this objective the information is often couched in terms that are designed to 'win over' the customer. Conversely some persuasive advertising contains information on the product (for example advertisements for breakfast cereals sometimes include details of vitamin content). At the very least, an advertisement informs the customer that the product is available. Without the advertising a demand curve may simply not exist. Because of the interrelated nature of the 'informative' and 'persuasive' elements in advertising, the distinction is not a particularly useful one.

In a perfectly competitive world, in which both firms and customers are fully informed about all possible opportunities there is of course no role for advertising.

Advertising as a Capital Good

An advertising campaign may affect not only current purchasing decisions but also those in the future. People who are not contemplating a purchase of the advertised product during a particular campaign because for example they had acquired enough of the product *prior* to the campaign to meet their needs *during* the campaign may nevertheless become buyers at some later date. Current advertising may have some impact on that future decision.

Advertising may also be cumulative in its impact. While one campaign may not cause some people to purchase, a second, which reinforces the message of the first, may do so. With some potential customers it may take several messages before they are persuaded to buy. There may also be 'bandwagon' effects which are triggered off by an initial advertising campaign but which are only felt over several periods of time. The initial advertising persuades some of the more adventurous customers to buy and their purchases encourage others to buy. This second group of purchases may stimulate further sales and so on. This process may take place without further advertising.

In these cases any evaluation of the impact of an advertising campaign which considered immediate purchases only would be misleading. It may therefore be appropriate to treat advertising more as a form of investment, rather than as a current expense. Such a treatment requires estimates to be made of the rate at which the effects of advertising on purchasing decisions declines over time. In other words the rate of advertising depreciation has to be estimated. (Even the effects mentioned in the previous two paragraphs do not continue for ever.)

The depreciation rate will depend on numerous factors including the nature of the product and frequency of purchase. It is hardly surprising therefore to find that a wide range of depreciation rates have been estimated. However, there is a fair amount of empirical support for very high annual depreciation rates: a number of studies have suggested that it is near to 100 per cent (see Comanor and Wilson, 1979). These authors have also argued that since much advertising is defensive and is designed to protect market positions it should be treated as equivalent to maintenance costs for machinery and equipment rather than be seen as being subject to depreciation.

9.2 ADVERTISING IN THE UK

No official statistics on advertising expenditure are published. The two main sources of data are the Advertising Association (a body financed by the industry) which provides the only complete survey of annual expenditure levels and Media Expenditure Analysis Ltd., which produces data down to the level of individual brand advertising. According to Advertising Association data (Waterson, 1983) advertising expenditure in the UK was £3,126m in 1982, equivalent to just under 2 per cent of total consumers' expenditure.

Table 9.1 provides a breakdown of this figure by media. Newspapers and television accounted for about 70 per cent of the total in 1982. Comparisons with 1960 must be treated very cautiously because of variations in methods of data collection. However, it would be difficult to avoid the (not surprising) conclusion that there has been a substantial increase in the relative importance of television and radio, mostly at the expense of magazines and periodicals.

In the first two columns of table 9.2, advertising expenditure is broken down by broad industrial sector. The great majority of advertising is clearly devoted to the promotion of *final* goods and services. (Most advertising from the nationalized industries, the retail trade, and the

Table 9.1   Total UK advertising expenditure by media (% of total)

Media	1960	1982
National newspapers	19.8	16.5
Regional newspapers	23.8	23.6
Magazines and periodicals	12.4	6.7
Trade and technical	9.6	7.9
Directories	0.6	4.0
Press production costs	4.6	4.9
Total, Press*	70.9	63.5
Television	22.3	29.7
Poster and transport	5.0	4.0
Cinema	1.5	0.6
Radio	0.3	2.2
Total*	100.0	100.0

*Figures subject to rounding errors.
Source: Waterson, 1983, pp. 159–68; details of definitions and coverage are
given in this article.

savings and financial institutions comes within this category, as does
much of the classified advertising.)

The reasons for the emphasis on consumer goods are not difficult to
find. The buyer of an intermediate product, such as a machine tool, is
likely to be less influenced by a television advertisement. However, he
might respond more readily to a comprehensive discussion of the merits
of a machine and to detailed technical literature. Furthermore, television or newspaper advertising which, by its nature, is directed at a mass
audience, may be less cost effective at reaching the customer for an
intermediate product than a direct approach.

The absolute level of advertising expenditure by industry (or sector)
does not of course provide a basis for comparisons of the importance of
advertising across industries because the latter differ in size. For
comparative purposes, it is necessary to relate the advertising expenditure in an industry to some measure of that industry's size. The resulting
ratio is usually referred to as the industry's advertising intensity. The
most frequently used measure of an industry's size in such calculations is
its total sales. There are of course other ways of measuring an industry's
size, but sales data are the most readily available. The last two columns
of table 9.2 provide some estimates on advertising:sales ratios for 1969
and 1981 by broad industrial sector. The data must be treated very

Table 9.2 Advertising expenditure and advertising: sales ratios in the UK

Product group	Advertising expenditure, 1981		Advertising: sales ratios (%)	
	£m	% of total	1969	1981
Manufacturers' consumer advertising*				
Food	256	9.1	1.06	1.06
Clothing and footwear	31	1.1	0.52	0.31
Automotives	138	4.9	0.92	0.95
Drink and tobacco	204	7.2	1.18	1.20
Toiletries and medical	119	4.2	7.32	5.06
Household and leisure	302	10.7	1.97	2.01
Publishing, books	51†	1.8	2.23	2.30
Tourism, entertainment Foreign	107†	3.8	0.89	0.78
Total, manufacturers' consumer advertising‡	1,208	42.9	1.27	1.23
Remainder of media expenditure				
Nationalized industries, government	114	4.1	0.36	0.28
Retail trade	487	17.3	0.38	0.76
Savings, financial	156	5.5	1.09	0.67
Industrial	310	11.0	0.5	0.6
Charity, education and classified	543	19.3	—	—
Total, remainder‡	1,610	57.1	0.47	0.60
Total, overall‡	2,818	100.00	na	na

*Manufacturers' consumer advertising is advertising from the private sector aimed at the general public and this excludes all government, charity and industrial advertising
†All advertising expenditure in this product group has been counted as manufacturers' consumer advertising.
‡Figures subject to rounding errors.
Source: Waterson, 1982, pp. 53–5; Waterson, 1983, pp. 159–68; Media Expenditure Analysis Ltd; further details of definition and coverage are given in these articles.

cautiously for at least two reasons. First, it is simply not possible to estimate 'sales' on a consistent basis across all sectors. Secondly, the level of aggregation disguises very substantial differences across more finely defined product groupings. Table 9.3 provides some indication of the variations that exist *within* the 'Food' and 'Toiletries and medical' product groups. Similar variations may be found in some of the other groups listed in table 9.2. Despite these difficulties, table 9.2 provides some useful insights into advertising intensities in the UK. First, the 1969 and 1981 ratios, particularly for manufacturers' consumer advertising, are fairly similar; secondly, by far and away the most advertising intensive sector is toiletries and medical products; and thirdly, the most rapid increase in intensity has been among retailers. This last development reflects the growth of large scale retailing operations (see p. 41) which can take advantage of economies of scale in advertising.

One reason why advertising intensities vary across markets may be the structure of the industry. (The effects of market structure are considered in section 9.4.) But there may be other reasons. The differences between final and intermediate products have already been considered (see p. 136). But within the final goods sector as a whole, however, there may be differences across industries in the effectiveness of a given level of advertising expenditure.

Table 9.3   Some examples of advertising sales ratios in the 'Food' and 'Toiletries and medical' product groups

Product group	Product	Advertising: sales ratio 1980 (%)
Food	Meat and vegetable extracts	15.5
	Cakes and pastry mixes	9.5
	Fresh and frozen meat/poultry	0.2
	Fresh fruit and vegetables	0.1
Toiletries and medical	Hair dressing and setting lotion	51.9
	Oral hygiene	24.1
	Muscular and rheumatic remedies	3.3
	Disinfectants	0.8

Source: Media Expenditure Analysis Ltd.

For example products which customers find difficult to evaluate for themselves provide more scope for advertising. Frequency of purchase may also affect returns to advertising. Consumers are less likely to forget advertising where that frequency is higher. It might be expected therefore that, *ceteris paribus*, the intensity will be higher, the lower the frequency of purchase.

9.3 OPTIMAL EXPENDITURE ON ADVERTISING

To simplify the analysis it is necessary to assume that the effects of advertising are dissipated in the current period, and that firms are perfectly informed. The first of these assumptions is probably not too far removed from reality and the second is briefly considered at the end of this section.

Advertising affects *both* costs and revenues. This dual effect is illustrated in figure 9.1, in which it is assumed that the firm can choose one of two levels of advertising. Expenditure $A1$ gives rise to $SATC_{A1}$ and demand schedule D_{A1}, with its associated MR curve, MR_{A1}. Expenditure $A2$ leads to $SATC_{A2}$, D_{A2}, and MR_{A2}. SMC is the same in both cases. Before analysing the figure further, it is important to note that it assumes that comparisons of different advertising levels may be undertaken on the *same* diagram, where the horizontal axis measures quantity *in the same units* in each case. Not all economists would accept that this is permissible. They would argue – see for example, Kirzner (1973), pp. 137–40 – that advertising does not simply shift the demand curve for a given product but that it actually *alters the product itself*. For example, advertising may attach certain attributes to a good that were not previously there. Although this criticism has some force and is important when it comes to the analysis of the welfare effects of advertising (see p. 147) the single diagram is retained here as it is adequate to illustrate the basic comparisons that are being made.

The strategy the firm adopts depends on its objectives. The short run profit maximizing firm produces at the point where SMC and MR are equal and hence chooses output Q_{A1} and price P_{A1} or output Q_{A2} and price P_{A2}. The sales revenue maximizer produces the output at which MR is zero, and hence selects either Q'_{A1} and P'_{A1} or Q'_{A2} and P'_{A2}, assuming that the profit constraint is not binding in either case. In the example illustrated in figure 9.1, it is clear (from inspection) that the profit maximizer would go for Q_{A2} and P_{A2} and the sales maximizer for Q'_{A2} and P'_{A2}.

The short run profit maximizing position may be explored further. The firm will advertise up to the point where the marginal unit of expenditure on advertising, ΔA, is equal to the marginal revenue from

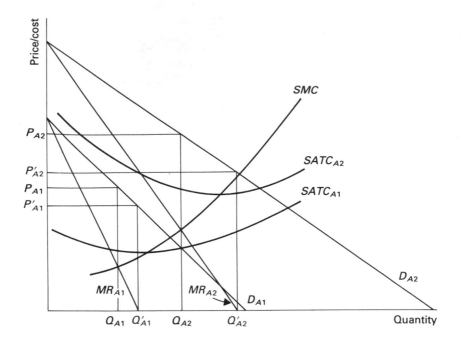

Figure 9.1   Optimal advertising expenditure
It is assumed that the firm can choose one of two levels of advertising, $A1$ and
$A2$. $A1$ gives rise to $SATC_{A1}$, D_{A1} and MR_{A1}, while $A2$ generates $SATC_{A2}$, D_{A2}
and MR_{A2}. The short run profit maximizer can thus choose output Q_{A1} and price
P_{A1}, or Q_{A2} and P_{A2}. The sales revenue maximizer can choose either Q'_{A1} and
P'_{A1} or Q'_{A2} and P'_{A2}. In this example it is clear (from inspection) that the
former chooses Q_{A2} and P_{A2}, and the latter Q'_{A2} and P'_{A2}.

advertising. Assume that both *SMC* and price are constant (price may
be fixed by oligopolistic agreement). Thus the profit maximizing position is

$$\Delta A = \Delta Q \ (P - SMC) \tag{9.1}$$

where ΔQ is the change in output that results from ΔA and P is price.
    It can be shown (see for example Koutsoyiannis, 1982, pp. 82–3) that

the above equation implies that the firm will set its advertising:sales intensity equal to the following ratio:

$$\frac{\text{Advertising elasticity of demand}}{\text{Price elasticity of demand}}$$

The numerator of the ratio measures the responsiveness of demand to a change in the firm's advertising and is given by:

$$\frac{\%\text{ change in the firm's demand}}{\%\text{ change in the firm's advertising expenditure}}$$

(*Price* elasticity of course measures the percentage change in demand over the percentage change in *price*).

Some investigators have examined the extent to which advertising: sales ratios in different industries have reflected the estimated elasticity ratio. The results have been mixed. Cowling et al. (1975, p. 60ff) for example found that for the two durable products they studied, the ratios showed little similarity whereas for at least two of the three non-durable products examined, they were reasonably close.

The above analysis sidestepped consideration of rivals' reactions to a firm's advertising. An advertising campaign by one firm may however trigger off a response from other firms anxious to maintain their market position. The calculation of the advertising elasticity of demand for any one firm may thus involve estimating how other firms are likely to respond. In some cases the firms themselves may try to reach an agreement that avoids such competitive duplication of advertising. For example in the early 1960s, Unilever and Proctor and Gamble reached an agreement for a short period on advertising and sales promotion of heavy duty laundry brands (HMSO, 1966, p. 16). The analysis also ignored the implications of imperfect information. In practice, firms are likely to have great difficulty in estimating the likely impact of any advertising. They may, as a result, resort to 'rules of thumb' that past experience has shown work reasonably well. A recent study (Gentry and Rodger, 1978) of advertising by large and medium size companies selling mostly intermediate products found that factors such as 'intuition', 'hunch' and 'feel' played an important part in determining budgets. A few firms used a fixed percentage of (current or past) sales as their rule of thumb.

9.4 ADVERTISING AND MARKET STRUCTURE

The relationship between market structure and advertising intensity (usually measured by the advertising:sales ratio) has been extensively studied. Although a two-way relationship almost certainly exists, most studies have concentrated on one direction of causation only.

The Effects of Market Structure on Advertising

Most attention has been focused on the impact of concentration, usually measured by the concentration ratio, on advertising. What relationship would be expected here? Sutton (1974) has argued that advertising intensity is likely to be relatively low in both unconcentrated and highly concentrated industries, and at its highest in *moderately* concentrated industries. Graphically, the relationship between advertising intensity (on the vertical axis) and concentration (on the horizontal axis) would therefore be depicted as an inverted *U*. Key elements in Sutton's argument (which all relate to the determinants of the advertising elasticity of demand) are as follows. First, the gains from advertising obtained by *diverting* sales from competitors depend on the firm's ability to maintain an above average advertising intensity and/or on economies of scale in advertising which give an advantage to larger firms. Such gains are most likely where there are relatively large differences between the sales volumes and/or financial resources of firms in an industry. Such disparities (in Sutton's view) occur most frequently in moderately concentrated industries. In unconcentrated industries, firms may be unable to finance a greater commitment to advertising than other firms, and in near monopolies, there are no significant gains to be obtained from diverted sales anyway. Secondly, the role of advertising as an entry barrier is likely to be most effective in moderately concentrated industries (such barriers may enable profit margins to be raised). In such industries according to Sutton there will usually be greater disparity between the sizes of established and potential entrant firms, with the latter less able to challenge the former. In unconcentrated industries where the disparity is likely to be less, the new entrants will more easily be able to match the advertising of the existing firms. In very highly concentrated industries, the barriers are likely to be high anyway. Finally, if product innovation is at its highest in relative terms in moderately concentrated industries – and there is some evidence for this: see pp. 162–3 – then there may be greater scope for advertising designed to exploit such innovation.

Sutton found some empirical support for his arguments among the industries producing final goods that he studied. However his work has not gone unchallenged. Reekie (1975) for example failed to find any evidence of an inverted *U* – or indeed a linear relationship – when he used other, more finely classified, data. Rees (1975), using yet another data set, found some evidence for both an inverted *U* and a linear relationship although the evidence for the former was not as strong as that found by Sutton. Other studies have also produced conflicting results. However, it is probably fair to say that most provide some kind of support for a positive effect of concentration on advertising intensity.

The Effects of Advertising on Market Structure

It was suggested above that one effect of advertising may be to raise entry barriers. It may do this by raising the amount of promotional expenditure a potential entrant would have to incur in order to break into the market. Established firms may have advertised their products for many years. Thus in markets where the advertising depreciation rate is low, the potential entrant has to face substantial *accumulated* effects of past advertising expenditure. Now the entrant may be unable, however much he spends at the time of entry, to challenge these accumulated effects since it may only be *possible* to generate customer loyalty over a long period of time. However, assuming that there is some expenditure level at which a successful challenge could be made, the entrant may still have difficulty in raising the additional funds necessary, or, if it is able to do so, it may have to pay higher interest charges. High advertising expenditures by existing firms may also raise barriers in another way. The potential entrant may have to enter at a large scale in order to ensure that the advertising expenditure per unit of output is low enough to enable him to price competitively. Again the large scale may bring the firm up against financial constraints. Higher barriers may in turn lead to higher concentration as any merger activity that takes place will not be offset by new entry. On the other hand, it may be argued that advertising provides a vehicle for making entry easier (newcomers can inform customers of their presence).

It is hardly surprising to find that studies which have examined the effects of advertising on concentration have thrown up mixed results (compare for example, Telser, 1964, and Mann et al., 1967).

Some Reasons for the Mixed Results

At least part of the reason for the considerable variations in the results obtained in studies of the relationship between advertising and concentration may be found in the following. First, a number of statistical problems arise when attempts are made to examine one aspect only of what is essentially a two-way relationship. Secondly, there are difficulties associated with identifying an appropriate measure both of advertising intensity and concentration. In particular, the choice of 'market' is inevitably arbitrary. Finally, even if it is possible to solve these data problems satisfactorily, it remains unlikely that advertising or concentration are determined by *one* factor only. Some studies have taken other determinants into account, but, again, precisely which variables have been included has varied from study to study.

9.5 ADVERTISING, PRICES AND PROFITABILITY

Prices

It is frequently argued that advertising raises prices. There is certainly some evidence to suggest that branded goods, i.e. those which have a distinctive name of their own, tend to have higher prices than their unbranded 'equivalents'. Advertising usually plays a major role in developing and maintaining a brand image. In food retailing for example it is estimated (Maunder, 1980, p. 90) that retailers' 'own label' products which are not extensively advertised have prices which are typically at least 10 per cent lower than the manufacturers brands which *are* being promoted through advertising. Another industry in which the effect of advertising on prices has attracted much attention is pharmaceuticals: many 'branded' drugs have substantially higher prices than their unbranded or 'generic' equivalents. Table 9.4 provides some comparisons, for particular drugs, between the price of the most expensive branded product and the price of the drug when supplied under the drug tariff. This tariff is based largely on the prices of unbranded generic equivalents. In no case is the branded price differential less than 50 per cent. (The saving to the National Health Service in the year 1982/3 if all the drugs in table 9.4 had been dispensed at the tariff prices was estimated at about £30m: see source to the table.)

The promotion of branded drugs is not of course restricted to advertising. For example, Roche Products spent less than half of its promotion budget for pharmaceutical products on advertising – the rest was on sales staff, samples and promotional material (HMSO, 1973a, p. 16). However, the price differences in table 9.4 do in part at least reflect the higher advertising for the branded products.

The interpretation of the price differential between branded and unbranded 'equivalents' is not straightforward. First, there is the difficulty of establishing what an 'equivalent' unbranded product is. In some cases, the latter may be technically inferior to its branded counterpart. Even if it is not inferior in this sense it may be *regarded* by the customer as being so. Indeed it may be argued that such a view is intentionally generated by the advertising. This then raises the issue of whether, if a customer thinks a product is different, it *is* different. This issue is discussed further in the next section. Secondly, the advertising of the higher priced branded product may affect the sales of the unbranded good. Thus if Kelloggs did not advertise its brand of corn flakes,

Table 9.4 Some comparisons of drug prices (December 1982)

Strength mg	Pack size	Drug	Drug tariff price £	Most expensive branded price £	Most expensive branded price / Drug tariff price
250	1,000	Methyldopa	22.50	49.50	2.2
40	500	Frusemide	4.00	26.91	6.7
5	500	Nitrazepam	5.50	10.45	1.9
250	250	Ampicillin	8.50	21.33	2.5
5	1,000	Diazepam	2.50	14.16	5.7
25	500	Imipramine	2.40	16.25	6.8
25	500	Amitriptyline	3.90	10.40	2.7
25	500	Indomethacin	16.16	27.66	1.7
40	1,000	Propranolol	27.86	42.12	1.5

Source: *Hansard*, written answers, 24 February 1983, col. 515–16.

Sainsburys might find the sales of its similar 'own label' cereal declining. Thirdly – and this may be particularly important with drugs – the very existence of the generic substitutes may have derived from the branded version in the sense that it may only have been in anticipation of the profits from the latter, that the original research and development was undertaken. How valid these arguments are will vary from case to case.

So far consideration has only been given to the price differential between branded and unbranded goods. It may be, however, that the general level of prices in an industry alters as a result of advertising. To investigate this issue it is necessary to know the impact of advertising not only on firms' demand curves but also on their cost schedules. In some cases advertising may lead to greater economies of scale in production being achieved through higher sales – perhaps of *both* branded *and* unbranded goods. This may mean that the resulting prices are lower than those that would have obtained in the absence of advertising even though the latter may generate market power.

One American study which examined the wider impact of advertising was that by Benham (1972) which took advantage of the fact that the laws relating to advertising differ across states for certain products. Benham considered the case of eye glasses. Some states prohibit the advertising of eye glasses while others do not. He found that the prices of eye glasses were higher by 25 per cent to more than 100 per cent in the states where there were advertising restrictions. He also found that these differences were largely due to the advertising restrictions and not to other factors. Nor was there much evidence to suggest that eye glass advertising had a particularly high informational content. Thus advertising lowered the general level of prices. This finding is consistent with the view that the advertising increased consumer information on the availability of alternative products and hence made demand in general more, not less, responsive to price. It may also at the same time have reduced the amount of time customers spent 'searching' for the right product to buy. Thus the true price that they paid was lowered. However, whether advertising affects the general level of prices in any particular industry must in the end remain an empirical matter.

Profitability

The basic argument here is that advertising may raise profitability through reducing competition from existing and potential firms.

Most studies have found that advertising exercises a positive effect on profitability. (This is hardly surprising if firms undertake advertising primarily to increase profits!) As with the advertising–concentration relationship, however, there are difficulties associated with isolating the effects of advertising. The latter may simply be acting as a proxy for product differentiation as a whole. Some investigators – notably Bloch (1974) have also argued that when allowance is made for the *investment* nature of advertising, no effect of the latter on profitability can be discerned. Treatment of advertising as a form of investment affects both the denominator and numerator in the rate of return figure (see p. 66). (Profits may be too *low* because the *whole* of current advertising instead of the relevant depreciation figure only is treated as a cost; and net assets may be too low because they do not include any undepreciated advertising.) This criticism is dependent, however, on *precisely* how any adjustments to the profitability figures are made. Of course if the depreciation rate is high (see p. 135), the criticism loses much of its force.

Profitability may of course have an impact on advertising. High profitability may provide a firm with funds to which it might not otherwise have access.

9.6 SOME WELFARE ASPECTS OF ADVERTISING

It has often been argued that advertising represents a waste of resources. This argument may be illustrated in figure 9.2 which is based on Steiner (1966). The S curve in the figure is the supply curve of advertising. It relates the quantity of advertising messages to the price of those messages. D_c is the demand curve of the buyers of the advertised good while D_s is the demand curve of the sellers. This latter curve is determined (for profit maximizers) by the profitability of advertising. It is assumed that at any given price the amount of advertising demanded by sellers is greater than that demanded by buyers. This may not be unrealistic given the loyalty creating effects of advertising. It is the interaction of the *sellers'* demand curve and the S curve that determines the price and quantity of advertising since the advertising and the good itself are supplied jointly. Consumers cannot restrict advertising to Q_1. At P_e the sellers can pass on to consumers only Q_2. They must absorb the rest $(Q_3 - Q_2)$ themselves. 'Excessive' advertising of $Q_3 - Q_1$ is the result.

The above analysis has been challenged on several grounds (see Telser, 1964). First it is argued that in industries where customers have the choice between advertised and unadvertised goods, they presumably only buy the former if they are willing to pay the cost of the advertising. Secondly, it may be that joint supply of advertising and goods may lead to some savings in resources (for example, payment for advertising does not have to be collected separately). Thirdly, the static framework of

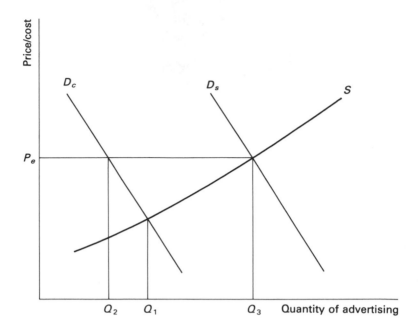

Figure 9.2   The argument for 'excessive' advertising
S is the supply curve of advertising, D_c is the demand curve of the buyers of the
advertised good, and D_s is the demand curve of the sellers of the good. It is the
intersection of S and D_s that determines the equilibrium price, P_e. At this price,
consumers only demand Q_2 of advertising. $Q_3 - Q_1$ represents 'excessive'
advertising.

analysis may be inappropriate. Advertising may exercise a positive
influence on technical progress and new product development. For
example, in so far as advertising raises profits and reduces risk, it may
encourage research and development. It is not clear how far these
criticisms modify or eliminate the 'advertising is wasteful' argument.
One difficulty is that some of these counter-arguments are themselves
open to question. For example the argument that advertising may
encourage technical development in the way postulated simply begs the
question of the desirability of such development. Presumably technical
development is not *by definition* desirable. In any case, as Koutsoyiannis

has pointed out (1982, p. 135), most markets in which the advertising expenditures are heaviest have very little innovation.

Advertising has also been attacked on the grounds that it often stimulates 'unnecessary' consumption, by creating desires that were not previously there. It is argued that if customers had access to all the relevant facts rather than to the advertising only, they would make different consumption decisions. Instead they are 'manipulated' by the advertiser who seeks ever expanding markets for his output. For a good exposition of this view see Galbraith (1958, chapter 11). This condemnation of advertising as wasteful has not however gone unchallenged. Kirzner (1973, p. 173ff.) for example has argued that it implies that the product itself has not been improved by advertising, and that 'without advertising' consumer tastes are somehow superior to those which emerge after advertising. To Kirzner, neither assumption may be valid. Advertising alters the perceived 'package' that the customer buys; and without imposing arbitrary value judgements, it is not possible to say whether one set of consumer tastes is better than another.

The above arguments cannot be explored further here. However, it should be noted that even if the Galbraithian view were to be accepted by policy makers it would not necessarily follow that controls on advertising should be introduced, since such controls might generate even less acceptable forms of competitive activity.

9.7 SUMMARY

A distinction is sometimes made between informative and persuasive advertising, although such a distinction is far from being clear cut. Nor is it likely to be particularly useful. In some industries advertising may be better regarded as a capital good rather than as a current expense. Most advertising in the UK is undertaken through the press and television and is concentrated in the industries producing final goods and services. There are, however, substantial variations in advertising intensities even among these industries. Simple models of profit maximizing behaviour of advertisers must be treated cautiously; they may, however, provide insights into the determination of an industry's advertising intensity.

The relationship between advertising and market structure has been extensively studied. Although it is probably fair to say that concentration has a positive effect on advertising intensity, the relationship is clearly a complex one. This relationship is further complicated by the possibility that advertising may also affect concentration.

Branded products tend to have higher prices than their unbranded counterparts although how this differential should be interpreted is far from clear. How advertising may affect the *general* level of prices in an industry is an issue which in the end can only be resolved by empirical study.

The evidence suggests that profitability is enhanced by advertising; however, the latter may also be increased by the former.

The debate on whether advertising uses any 'excessive' amount of resources remains unsettled. Any attempts to control advertising, however, should consider the implications for firm behaviour of such controls.

10

Innovation

10.1 THE IMPORTANCE OF INNOVATION

Types of Innovation

Innovation – the commercial introduction of new and improved products and processes – is an important dimension of competitive activity. Innovations vary considerably in their nature. Some innovations, such as a new drug or a new electronic component, may be regarded as primarily technological in character. Others, such as fashion changes in clothing or a new brand image for an existing product, may be seen as primarily of a non-technological kind. The latter category also includes changes in the way production is organized and managed, and the development of new markets. These two types of innovation are frequently related. Freeman (1982, p. 217) has pointed out that the introduction by Ford of assembly line production – essentially an organizational innovation – both entailed and stimulated much technological innovation. Conversely technological innovation may lead to organizational change: the advent of the microprocessor for example has led to extensive innovation in office procedures. Innovations also differ in the extent of their newness. Some, such as the introduction of television, are radically new in character. Others represent only minor modifications to existing products and/or processes.

Innovative activity may have major effects in the long term on industrial structure, as new industries displace the old. Perhaps these effects are most simply illustrated by some of the revisions that have been made in the Standard Industrial Classification (SIC) in the post-war period. Synthetic fibre production which was classified as part of a minor category in the 1948 SIC was given its own Class as part of Division 2 in the 1980 SIC. In 1948, no mention was made of nuclear fuel, telecommunications or electronics. All three are now important elements in their respective 1980 SIC Divisions. In view of these effects on industrial structure, it is hardly surprising to find that a number of studies have suggested that technological change of which innovation activities are an important part has made a significant contribution to modern economic growth in Western nations (see Johnson, 1975, pp. 6–15).

Competition in Innovation

Traditional economic analysis between firms has tended to ignore innovative activity, and to concentrate on competition in the context of existing products and processes. Yet innovation may be of major significance for the market positions of firms, particularly in the longer term. In the pharmaceutical industry for example drugs firms are unlikely to survive for very long if their product range remains unchanged. Reekie (1980, p. 114) has pointed out that 96 per cent of the 150 leading drugs by sales value in 1972 were developed after 1947. A further indication of the importance of innovation in this industry is given in table 10.1 which shows that only two of the top ten products in 1980 were in the top ten in 1965. Furthermore, only four of the ten leading *companies* in 1965 were still in that category in 1980. In many other industries – notably aircraft, chemicals, electronics and scientific instruments, the rate of innovation is also high. One of the most spectacular areas of advance has been in computer manufacture. According to one estimate (quoted in Freeman, 1982, p. 71) the cost of 100,000 computations fell from $1.38 in the early 1950s (vacuum tube computers) to $0.04 in the late 1960s (hybrid integrated circuits). In the 1970s and 1980s, there have been further massive reductions in cost as a result of the microprocessor revolution (Stoneman, 1980, p. 156).

Another industry which has experienced rapid development in the twentieth century has been the oil industry: for example Enos (1962, p. 319) has shown that for 100,000 tons of output, labour requirements in 1955 were less than 1 per cent of those in 1913. (For fuel, they were less than 10 per cent.) Any firm in these industries which did not keep up with these developments would experience rapid deterioration in its competitive position. Ultimately it would go out of business. (Some businesses may of course deliberately choose this option rather than remain under constant pressure to change.)

Even in traditional manufacturing industries, such as textiles or shipbuilding, innovation plays an important role in determining competitiveness. *Non*-manufacturing is also constantly affected by – and introducing – new types of product, and new developments in methods of production. The introduction of High Speed Trains on the railways,

Table 10.1   The UK pharmaceutical industry: product and company rankings; 1965 and 1980

Position of 1980's leading ten products in 1965		Position of 1965's leading ten companies in 1980	
1965	*1980*	*1965*	*1980*
—	1	1	2
—	2	2	13
—	3	3	37
10	4	4	12
—	5	5	11
—	6	6	7
4	7	7	24
—	8	8	15
—	9	9	6
—	10	10	4

Note: Ranking is by value of sales.
Source: Association of the British Pharmaceutical Industry, London.

powered roof supports in coal mining, self-service in retailing and package tours in tourism are a few examples.

It was Joseph Schumpeter who perhaps more than any other writer emphasized the central role of innovation in competition.

> ... it is still competition within a rigid pattern of invariant conditions, methods of production and forms of industrial organisation in particular that practically monopolises attention [of economists]. But in capitalist reality as distinguished from its textbook picture, it is not that kind of competition which counts but the competition from the new commodity, the new technology, the new source of supply, the new type of organisation ... competition ... which strikes not at the margins of the profits and the outputs of the existing firms, but at their foundations and their very lives. This kind of competition is as much more effective than the other as a bombardment is in comparison with forcing a door, and so much more important that it becomes a matter of comparative indifference whether competition in the ordinary sense functions more or less promptly 127 (1954, p. 84)

As this quotation shows, Schumpeter's view of innovation was all embracing; to him, innovation extended far beyond the narrow confines of purely technological change. This chapter concentrates on technological innovation, although this emphasis should not be construed as denying the importance of innovations that fall outside this category.

Invention vs Innovation

Schumpeter saw a clear distinction between invention – which may be defined as the creation of an idea and its first reduction to practice in a physical form – and innovation. In his view, the former has no economically relevant effects at all; it is only when an invention is launched commercially that such effects occur. (Probably the majority of inventions do not get launched in this way.) There is much to be said for maintaining this distinction between the two activities; however, they often interact with each other: the very process of innovation sometimes requires further inventive work to enable the original invention to be utilized commercially. It must also be remembered that a firm's ability to obtain a competitive advantage over rivals by its retention of exclusive rights to an innovation may be determined by its property rights in the original invention(s). In principle, a patent if granted confers such rights, subject to certain qualifications, for 20 years. Patents apply to inventions, not to innovations. There has been a good deal of debate over whether the patent system stimulates invention, and hence innovation. One of the few empirical studies of the UK system – by Taylor and Silberston (1973, p. 198) concluded that apart from pharmaceuticals, patents do not act to any major extent to provide a stimulus to invention (as measured by R & D expenditure). Individuals and organizations tend to seek protection in other ways, for example through industrial secrecy or by obtaining a strong technological lead.

Innovation and Imitation

Only the first firm to introduce a product or process change is usually regarded as the innovator. Firms which subsequently adopt the innovation are referred to as imitators. The innovator does of course face certain costs associated with the initial R & D that the imitator may be able to avoid. On the other hand, the former may obtain a technological lead which the latter is unable to challenge. This may be especially true where the innovator can (by various means) impede the pace of imitation by competitors. It may also be the case that imitation involves the payment of licence fees. The relative costs and benefits of innovation and imitation are likely to vary from case to case: a firm that innovates in one instance, may imitate in another. The determinants of the rate of imitation are considered in section 10.4.

10.2 RESEARCH AND DEVELOPMENT

Some Definitions

Most though not all modern technological innovations are the outcome of formally organized research and development (R & D). R & D is usually seen as embracing three types of activity: basic research, applied research, and development. Basic research is work undertaken primarily for the advancement of scientific knowledge and has no application in view at the time of investigation. The work of Shockley and others on solid state physics at the Bell laboratories in the US, which eventually led to the transistor; by Carothers on polymers at Du Pont which eventually led to Nylon; and by Kipping on organo-silicon chemistry at Nottingham University, which ultimately led to the commercial exploitation of silicones, are a few examples of this kind of work. As these examples show, basic research may nevertheless form the basis in the long term for specific commercial developments. Applied research relates to investigations that have a practical application in view. For example once it had been established by Carother's team that molten polymer could be drawn out in the shape of a fibre, a major programme of applied research aimed at identifying commercially useful fibres followed. Development is largely devoted to bringing the results of basic and applied research to commercial fruition. Development frequently involves the construction of prototypes and pilot plants. The development phase is often very expensive. For example £9.5m was spent by Beecham on the development of semi-synthetic penicillins between 1957 and 1966. This excludes the £2.5m spent on investigations leading up to the discovery of the penicillin nucleus (Jewkes et al., 1969, p. 215).

The boundaries between these three activities are not clear cut. Even the most fundamental investigation is likely to have *some* application, albeit a vague and distant one, in view. However, despite difficulties at the margin, some distinction between the terms must be maintained since they are often subject to different constraints and stimuli.

Industrial R & D

Most R & D financed by private firms is concentrated towards the development end of the R & D spectrum. It is also largely directed towards improvements in products and processes, particularly the latter, rather than towards entirely new developments. Relatively little expenditure – probably less than 5 per cent – goes to basic research. The reasons for this limited commitment to basic research are not difficult to find. First, the eventual commercial outcome of basic research is likely to be much less certain. Secondly, any returns from such research are usually much longer term in nature and may accrue well beyond the time horizon that a firm sets itself in its investment appraisals. It may be many decades before findings filter through to commercial applications. Thirdly, because of the nature of basic research it may be more difficult for a firm to obtain exclusive rights to the results that may arise. These results have 'public good' characteristics (see pp. 5–6). It is not usually possible to keep basic research findings secret or to secure property rights in them. They are therefore characterized by 'non-excludability'. Furthermore, there is 'non-rivalness' in their use: the *same* research result can be used by firms other than the firm undertaking and financing the work. The former may therefore obtain a 'free ride' and by so doing obtain a cost advantage. Of course the return from basic research work may still be *sufficient* to induce a firm to provide finance. It may for example anticipate that by being first in the field in this kind of activity, it can also be first in more applied work and ultimately in commercial applications. It may also be sufficiently diversified to take advantage of any surprise results that emerge. Two examples of company financing of basic research have already been given.

It is of course true that some of the difficulties associated with the industrial financing of basic research mentioned above are also present in development work. For example there is often still a good deal of uncertainty at the development stage, and the losses resulting from a wrong decision at this stage may be high: it is estimated that Du Pont lost about $100m on Corfam, their synthetic leather product, before withdrawing it from the market (Freeman, 1982, p. 155). Also, it has already been pointed out (p. 106) that development costs are notoriously difficult to estimate. Nevertheless there can be little doubt that in general companies are much happier working at the development end of the spectrum.

In the UK, as in other Western economies, most basic research is financed from public sources and is undertaken outside industry in universities and independent non-profit making institutions.

R & D Expenditures in 1981

In 1981, total R & D spending amounted to £3,793m, or about 1.8 per cent of Gross Domestic Product. Details on R & D conducted in industry are given in table 10.2. Column 6 in the table provides one measure of R & D intensities. Like advertising intensities, these are calculated to facilitate comparisons across industries of different sizes. The data must be interpreted carefully. In particular it should be stressed that R & D expenditure is an *input* measure; it does not give any indication of the output from such activity. Furthermore the data refer only to officially organized R & D; 'informal' R & D, likely to be important among small firms, is ignored. However, it is probably fair to say that the table provides a good approximation to reality.

The following points should be noted from table 10.2. Firstly R & D is heavily concentrated in just a few industries. As column 3 shows, chemicals (including pharmaceuticals), electrical and electronic engineering (including instrument engineering, office machinery and data processing equipment) and aerospace account for nearly 74 per cent of total R & D spending in all industries (compared with their 19 per cent share of sales). Secondly, industries vary considerably in the proportion of R & D financed by government (column 4). For the majority of industries, the government contribution is under 5 per cent, whereas in aerospace and electrical and electronic engineering it is 68 and 45 per cent respectively. These two industries are of course important for defence; furthermore the kind of R & D they undertake is inherently costly. Finally, government financed R & D is concentrated in a few industries (column 5). Over 90 per cent goes to the two industries already mentioned. Whether this industrial concentration of government finance is optimal is a matter of dispute: see p. 96.

The R & D figure used in the calculation of research intensities is privately financed R & D as it is the private firms' expenditure decisions which are of most interest here. However, such expenditure might not truly reflect the amount of R & D that might be privately financed *in the absence of* government funds because the latter may influence how much industry itself is prepared to spend. For example, government money may induce an industrial recipient to spend less from its *own* sources. In other words the firm may be able to transfer some R & D activity from under the privately financed heading to the government funded heading. Governments may try to ensure that this does not happen, but they are unlikely to be wholly successful. Conversely, the government money may act as a pump primer, inducing the firm to spend *more* than it would otherwise do. Similar conclusions would, however, emerge whatever R & D figure was used: UK industries differ substantially in their commitment to R & D.

What accounts for these differences in R & D intensity across industries? One plausible explanation is that R & D profitability varies across industries. Such variations may arise for several reasons. First, technological opportunity is likely to differ: a given volume of R & D expenditure in one industry may produce much bigger returns than in another. Secondly, the nature of the demand facing different industries varies. In some industries, only the latest product will sell. In more traditional industries being in the vanguard of innovation may not be so important. Thirdly, industries differ in their growth rates. In rapidly

Table 10.2 R & D expenditure in UK industry, 1981

1	2	3	4	5	6
Industry	R & D expenditure (£m)	% of all industrial R & D expenditure	% of expenditure financed by government	% of all government financed R & D in industry	$\dfrac{\text{Privately financed R \& D expenditure*}}{\text{Total sales}} \times 100$
Iron and steel	21.6	0.8	6.6	0.2	0.3
Non-ferrous metals	31.7	0.6	7.4	0.1	0.6
Bricks, cement, glass, etc.	33.1	0.9	3.6	0.1	0.5
Pharmaceutical products	296.1	7.8	—	—	11.3
Chemicals, apart from pharmaceutical products	321.3	8.5	2.3	0.7	2.1
Metal goods	22.7	0.6	2.6	0.1	2.8
Mechanical engineering	234.0	6.2	16.3	3.3	1.0
Office machinery and data processing equipment	202.7	5.3	1.7	0.3	1.2
Electrical and electronic engineering	1,181.1	31.1	44.9	46.6	4.9
Motor vehicles	180.4	4.8	3.8	0.6	1.7

Shipbuilding and repairs	9.5	0.3	8.4	0.1	5.4
Aerospace	762.9	20.2	67.5	45.3	5.2
Instrument engineering	32.7	0.9	7.6	2.2	1.7
Food, drink and tobacco	91.5	2.4	3.4	0.3	0.3
Textiles (other than man-made fibres)	9.7	0.3	9.3	0.1	0.2
Leather, footwear and clothing	4.7	0.1	12.8	0.1	0.1
Timber and furniture	3.6	0.1	33.3	0.1	—
Paper, printing and publishing	18.3	0.5	4.4	0.1	0.1
Rubber and plastics	30.0	0.8	2.7	0.1	0.1
Other manufacturing	24.1	0.6	3.7	0.1	1.1
Construction	15.3	0.4	10.5	0.1	0.1
Manufacturing and construction†	3,527.0	92.9	32.0	99.3	1.3
Other industries†	265.5	7.0	3.2	0.7	na
All industries†	3,792.5	100.0	30.0	100.0	1.3

na = not available
*Includes public corporations.
†Figures subject to rounding errors.
Source: Department of Industry, *Census of Production*, 1981.

growing industries, R & D may be more attractive because the introduction of new products and processes is less likely to upset existing market patterns – and therefore to invoke retaliatory action. The relationship between output growth and R & D intensity is, however, complex and it is likely that causation runs *both* ways. Fourthly, some industries may find it more economic to buy in R & D results, through licences and indeed purchases of capital goods and materials, rather than to engage in R & D itself. Fifthly, the more diversified an industry, the more R & D may be profitable as there will be greater opportunity for the surprise results of R & D to be utilized. (Of course, R & D may also *cause* diversification.)

Finally, market structure may affect R & D profitability. The purpose of industrial R & D is of course some form of innovation. Thus how market structure affects innovation is of crucial importance for analysing how it affects R & D profitability. The former is the subject of the next section.

10.3 MARKET STRUCTURE AND INNOVATION

Firm Size and Innovation

A key issue in the debate on which type of market structure is most conducive to innovation is the relationship between firm size (measured, say, in employment terms) and innovative activity. If it is necessary for firms to be of a certain size before they can innovate, for example because of the costs and risks involved, this fact will have implications, given the overall size of a market, for the market shares of those firms. In the UK, work by Freeman (1982, p. 138) and Townsend et al. (1982, p. 44) have shown that about 12 per cent (by number) of the innovations made between 1945 and 1980 in a wide range of UK industries could be attributed to small firms, i.e. of less than 200 employees. These firms accounted for about 19 per cent of net output and 22 per cent of employment in 1963, a year which is approximately midway between 1945 and 1980. These data suggest that small firms, while making an important contribution to innovation tend to be *relatively* less innovative than the large firms. Of course, the picture varies substantially from industry to industry. In some industries, such as aerospace and motor vehicles and pharmaceuticals small firms make only a small contribution (less than 5 per cent) to innovation. These industries are marked by high capital intensity and/or very large development costs. At the other extreme are industries like scientific instruments in which the contribution of small firms is significantly *greater* than their share of net output.

It should also be noted that small firms' share of R & D (at 3–4 per cent) is lower than their innovative share. One interpretation of this fact is that small firms are relatively more efficient in their R & D, i.e. they produce relatively more innovations for a given amount of expenditure. However, it is possible that there are other explanations: for example the *type* of innovation produced by the small firms may tend to be relatively less R & D intensive anyway. Of course, the vast majority of small firms do not spend any money on R & D, nor could they be classed as innovative.

The above paragraphs have focused on innovation. It does not necessarily follow from the evidence presented that small firms have the small (overall) relative position in inventive activity. There are some grounds for supposing that their contribution here is likely to be greater: invention is usually less costly than innovation; and small firm management, because it may be more flexible and less bureaucratic may be relatively more amenable to the inventive process, and to all the change it implies. There may therefore be a case for arguing that while large companies may be relatively better than small firms at innovating, they may be less good at inventing. Certainly, there are many instances of large firms absorbing the inventions of small firms and individuals and then bringing them to full commercial fruition. The history of Cellophane provides an interesting example of this transfer mechanism. Cellophane was originally invented by a French chemist but its further development and commercial exploitation was taken up first by a large French textile firm and then by one of the largest American chemical companies, Du Pont. This second company has a long history of taking 'outside' inventions to the innovation stage (Mueller, 1962).

Jewkes et al. (1969) have shown that, contrary to what is often supposed, the independent inventor and the small firm continue to play a very important role in invention. Inventions that have come from these sources include air conditioning, the jet engine, radio and the zip fastener. It is interesting to note here that many inventions come from outside the established firms in an industry. For example, the majority of basic inventions associated with the development of radio came from individual inventors who had no connection with established firms in the communications industries or who had worked for, or created new small firms. One reason for this 'outsider' characteristic of invention is that the uncommitted onlooker can often take a fresh and unorthodox view of the relevant technology.

Market Shares and Innovation

Monopoly is sometimes regarded as a market structure that is particularly conducive to innovation. The case for monopoly is made on several grounds. First, monopolies tend to have relatively higher profits and hence are in a better position to finance R & D particularly of the more speculative kind. Secondly, a monopolist generally faces less uncertainty in its market. Pricing is under its control and it does not have to take rivals' actions and reactions into account. This greater certainty in the market may thus enable the monopolist to devote more managerial energy to innovative work, which by its nature generates uncertainty and to adopt rather longer time horizons. Thirdly, a monopoly may provide a greater incentive for inovation, if it enables the firm to capture a greater proportion of the returns. The case *against* monopoly hinges on the relatively lower pressure to innovate that a monopolist experiences and on the fact that, by definition, there is only *one* independent source of ideas within the industry. The arguments for and against monopoly apply to a greater or lesser degree to oligopolies.

It is not difficult to find examples of innovation being apparently both retarded and fostered by strong market positions. An example of the former effect is given in an early study of the electrical industry (Bright and Maclaurin, 1943) which suggested that General Electric's dominant position in the incandescent lamp industry led to a slower development of newer forms of lighting, notably the fluorescent lamp. An example of the latter is Pilkington's development of the float glass process. Yet this evidence is difficult to interpret. In the case of float glass, for example, it might be argued that factors other than market structure were responsible for the innovation. One of these other factors may have been the family nature of the Pilkington business at the time of the innovation. This may have given the firm a greater willingness to risk capital on the project (Layton, 1972, p. 85). In any case, what *might* have happened under an alternative market structure must in the end be a matter for speculation.

More general empirical studies on the relationship between market structure and innovation have yielded mixed results (see the survey by Scherer, 1980, pp. 433–8). This is hardly surprising since different data and concepts have been used. Innovation has been measured both in terms of inputs, for example R & D expenditure on employment, and in terms of output – for example productivity change. (Productivity change is of course a more relevant measure for process, rather than product innovations.)

It is also the case that many factors, other than market structure affect innovation. Of particular importance here is the speed with which other firms can imitate. Innovation may be slowed down if the innovator knows that other firms can 'free ride' quickly and easily. Another factor is the extent of technological opportunity. Despite these difficulties, the evidence does suggest that some market power does stimulate innovation, especially where technological opportunity is low. However, apart from the odd exception very high levels of concentration do not appear to assist the innovative process.

10.4 THE DIFFUSION OF INNOVATION

The Measurement of Diffusion

The spread of an innovation is referred to as its diffusion. The particular type of innovation considered here is that among firms, rather than customers. The pattern of such diffusion may be measured in various ways. Figure 10.1 which illustrates a diffusion curve provides one example. The vertical axis in this figure shows the cumulative adoption percentage. This is calculated for any point in time on the basis of some specified saturation level represented by 100 per cent on the axis. The definition of this saturation level raises at least two questions. First, to which group of firms does it refer? Secondly, on what units of measurement is the saturation level to be based? Different pictures of the diffusion pattern may emerge from the use of different measurement units. For example in a study of the diffusion of special presses in papermaking, it was found that while just under two-thirds of *the number of companies* participating in the study were using the presses in 1968, less than a third of their *output* was involved (Ray, 1969). The diffusion process starts of course with the innovator. Any firms subsequently becoming involved are imitators. Most empirical studies of diffusion have found that some form of *S* curve provides a good description of the pattern of diffusion (see Davies, 1979, p. 34). In the early phases of an innovation, particularly if it is of a radical kind, there may be relatively few firms willing to take it up. Furthermore there may be teething troubles associated with the supply of the innovation which restrict sales. However, once these problems have been eliminated and the innovation has established itself among consumers a 'bandwagon' effect may set in with adoption rising rapidly in consequence. Finally the increase in adoption tails off as saturation is reached, and firms are unable to find further profitable uses for the innovation.

The development of an innovation may of course continue while diffusion takes place. Improvements are often being made long after the original innovation. For example although Pilkington launched its float glass process in 1959, many subsequent developments occurred. Pilkington's licensees alone patented over 100 new developments in just over a decade (Layton, 1972, p. 87). Some developments may extend the range of potential adopters, and thereby alter the diffusion pattern.

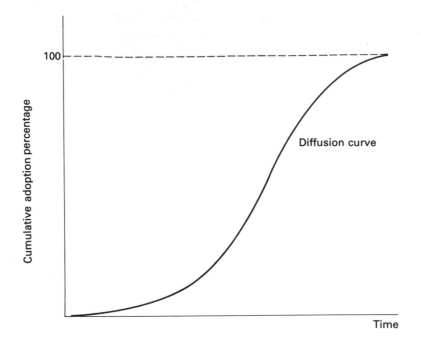

Figure 10.1   The diffusion of innovation
The diffusion curve shows for any point in time the extent to which an
innovation has been adopted. The cumulative adoption percentage on the
vertical axis is measured with respect to some specified saturation level.

Patterns of Diffusion

Even though diffusion may follow *some form* of S shaped pattern for
most innovations, the latter are still likely to differ in the speed with
which they reach saturation. It is not possible here to provide an
exhaustive examination of the determinants of this speed. However, not
surprisingly, studies suggest that the more profitable an innovation for
potential adopters is, the speedier the diffusion. This profitability in turn

depends on many factors, including the nature of the innovation and market structure. The influence of market structure may be varied in character. On the one hand, it may be argued that the more competitive industry is, the more pressure there will be for a firm to take up an innovation, since it will be unable to survive for long if it does not match the efficiency of its competitors; on the other it may be suggested that information on the innovation may travel more slowly in an industry where there are large numbers of firms than in one where only a few firms exist.

There are also some grounds for arguing that, other things being equal, the large firm may find an innovation more profitable to adopt than a smaller firm. First, large firms may be better able to meet the risks associated with adoption, especially if they are already diversified. Secondly, the larger firm may have greater opportunity to utilize a given innovation. At any point in time it is more likely to have machinery that needs replacing. Also, its production operations are likely to experience a greater range of operating conditions. Thus the likelihood of a given innovation being appropriate is greater. Although it might be argued that the larger firm is likely to be more lethargic in its approach to innovation, the available evidence suggest that on average, larger firms *do* adopt more quickly (Davies, 1979, chapter 6). The pricing policies that firms adopt for their new products may influence the diffusion pattern. Some firms may go for very low prices to start with in order to establish a strong position in the market early on. Once established they may then raise their prices. Such a policy, sometimes known as penetration pricing, will lead to a steep start to the diffusion curve. On the other hand, the firm may decide to charge relatively high prices for its newly launched product (in order, for example, to sell to those buyers whose demand elasticity for the product is low, before selling, at a lower price, to those with a higher elasticity). Skimming the market through such a pricing policy may cause a shallower start to the diffusion curve.

10.5 SUMMARY

Innovation, which may take many different forms, and the imitation of innovation may be of vital significance in determining the market positions of firms especially in the long term. Most modern technological innovations emerge from R & D activity. In industry, R & D focuses largely on development work. There are wide variations across industries in research intensities and in the importance of government finance. Furthermore, R & D expenditure is heavily concentrated in a few industries, as is government finance. The expected profitability of R

& D is likely to be an important factor in explaining an industry's commitment to it. Although small firms make a relatively low contribution to innovation, they (together with the independent inventor) continue to be an important source of modern invention. They may also be relatively more efficient in conducting R & D. *Some* market power may stimulate innovative activity, but this argument should not be pushed too far.

The evidence for some kind of *S* shaped diffusion curve among firms is strong, although the precise pattern followed will be influenced by numerous factors. Important influences are likely to be the nature of the innovation, the market structure of the relevant industry, and the pricing policies of the firms concerned.

11

Investment

11.1 CATEGORIES OF INVESTMENT

Fixed Assets

Expenditure by a firm on new buildings, plant and machinery, and vehicles, ships and aircraft is referred to as investment in fixed assets. The adjective 'fixed' is used as such assets are typically located (or based) in one place. The economist usually restricts the term investment to the purchase of newly produced assets. Second-hand purchases, either of individual items or of whole factories, or indeed companies, are excluded on the grounds that they simply represent changes of ownership and no new addition to the flow of assets into the economy. This rather specialized view of investment is largely maintained in this chapter although some consideration is given to the purchase of one business by another on p. 181. To acquiring firms, such purchases may be used as an alternative to investment in new assets.

Investment in fixed assets plays a key role in the competitive process. It is often necessary if expansion of output is to occur and it is almost invariably an integral component of the innovation process. It may also be used (as suggested later) to reduce the threat of entry. *Wrong* investment decisions can be disastrous for the competitive position of the firm. If for example, the firm raises investment funds through fixed interest loans and the expected returns from the investment do not materialize, it may be unable to meet its commitments and be forced out of business. Sale of the assets may offer no solution, as their second-hand value may be low.

Investment in fixed assets, or physical investment as it is sometimes called, may be distinguished from human investment, which describes expenditure by the firm on the enhancement of the skills and abilities of its labour force. The primary concern of this chapter is with physical investment although human investment is briefly considered in section 11.6.

Replacement, Net and Gross Investment

Investment expenditure which is directed towards the replacement of assets that have become worn out or obsolete is called replacement investment. Investment over and above this is net investment. The two types of investment together represent gross investment.

Types of Net Investment

A firm's net investment may take several different forms. An initial distinction may be made between diversifying and non-diversifying investment. The former leads to an increase in the range of goods and services produced by the firm. The latter does not.

Diversifying investment may itself be classified into two main types. Vertical investment occurs when a firm moves into a stage of production which precedes (backward vertical investment) or succeeds (forward vertical investment) the one it is already engaged in. An example of backward investment is the move over the post-war period by ready-mixed concrete companies into the production of aggregates. By 1978, the nine largest companies in this industry held 40 per cent or more of the sand and gravel reserves with planning consent in six of the eight planning regions in England (HMSO, 1981, p. 34). Forward investment is typified by the major petrol wholesalers movement in the 1950s and 1960s into petrol retailing. In 1953, Shell Mex/BP, Esso, Regent Mobil and Petrofina had less than 100 outlets. In 1964, they had over 5,000 (HMSO, 1979b, p. 37). A major motivation behind vertical investment is often the securing of sources of supply and/or markets.

The second type of diversifying investment, conglomerate investment, describes the movement of the firm into the production of goods and/or services not directly connected with its current range. A good example of this type of investment is Imperial Tobacco's move into markets not directly connected with its original tobacco interests. On the surface, there may appear to be no link between a company's existing and new activities. However, a closer examination may reveal significant ties. For example a firm may generate research results that it cannot use in its current range of products or services. Again a business may diversify in order more fully to utilize some existing capacity or expertise which is not specific to its existing range of output.

Net investment may be either capital widening or capital deepening. Capital widening occurs when more capital is used but the capital/labour ratio remains unchanged. For example a firm may expand its capacity simply by replicating the production facilities it already has. Capital deepening on the other hand raises this ratio. The introduction of robots on a car assembly line provides an example of such deepening.

11.2 INVESTMENT IN THE UK

In 1982, gross investment in the UK was £42.1m. This figure includes all forms of fixed investment including that made by individuals – mainly in dwellings – and by government. As a percentage of gross domestic product (at market prices), gross investment declined fairly steadily from 20.2 per cent in 1974 to 15.4 per cent in 1982. Throughout this period the UK percentage has been lower – often substantially so – than that of virtually all the UK's main competitors (see OECD *Historical Statistics* 1960–82, OECD Paris, 1984, table 6.2). UK net investment as a percentage of the gross figure also fell steadily (and dramatically) from 46.7 per cent in 1974 to 21.6 per cent in 1982. Thus over three-quarters of all investment in 1982 was being used for replacement, i.e. maintaining the capital stock.

Table 11.1 provides a breakdown of gross and net investment in 1982 by broad industrial sector. This breakdown is based on ownership rather

Table 11.1   Investment in fixed assets in the UK, 1982

Sector	Gross investment (£m)	Net investment (£m)
Agriculture, forestry and fishing	1,058	−132
Extraction of mineral oil and natural gas	3,081	641
All other energy and water supply	3,819	11
Manufacturing	5,183	−2,096
Construction	404	−215
Distribution, hotels, catering and repairs	3,698	1,519
Transport	1,930	−750
Communication	1,462	23
Financial and leasing services	7,387	4,765
Other Services	5,931	3,064
Dwellings	6,073	2,285
Transfer costs of land and buildings	2,146	
Total	42,172	9,115

Source: *National Income and Expenditure*, 1983.

than on the purpose of the investment. Thus the purchase of machinery and equipment by leasing companies is shown under 'leasing' rather than under the industrial sector in which those assets are used. It is interesting to note that in some industries (agriculture, manufacturing, construction and transport) net investment was negative. Financial and other services, including leasing, accounted for 86 per cent of all net investment.

Negative net investment may be associated with decline or slow growth in output. This is certainly the case in manufacturing and construction (see table 3.1), although it is not easy to say whether low growth in these industries *causes* negative net investment or vice versa. Even if it can be shown that the direction of causation is from growth to net investment, the former is unlikely to be the only factor at work. For example in transport and communication, negative net investment may be a reflection in part at least of public policies in this area which have restricted investment expenditure. (Over the last 20 years this sector has grown fairly rapidly in output terms.) Negative net investment is a fairly new phenomenon: none of the sectors mentioned above had experienced it before 1979. It must be remembered too that the overall figures given in table 11.1 hide significant variations within the sectors.

The public sector undertook about 11 per cent of all net investment in 1982.

11.3 THE INVESTMENT DECISION

The Distinctive Character of the Decision

The timing, scale and form of a firm's investment activity is frequently of crucial significance for its market position. There are three aspects of the investment process which make investment decisions particularly challenging. First, there is often a substantial time lag between the decision to go ahead with an investment and the beginning of its commercial use. (For North Sea investment the typical lag between discovery to first output is five years: Robinson and Rowland, 1980.) This lag means that a firm may have to forecast market trends many years in advance. If it does not do this it may get left behind its competitors. Secondly, the returns to a particular investment once it has been completed may accrue over many years. In commercial vehicle production for example basic designs usually run for 10 to 20 years. Much of the initial investment required to put a new design into production will remain in existence for this period. Finally, once a firm transforms its funds into physical investment, it may not easily be able to reverse the process without incurring a substantial loss. For example a firm may invest several millions in a new plant which, if it were to be sold immediately after construction, would have scrap value only.

Appraisal Techniques

A firm has to consider whether its proposed investment projects will help it to meet its objectives. As suggested in chapter 3, these objectives may be wide ranging. Most of this section, however, is devoted to the implications of an investment for a firm's profits.

The analysis in this section focuses on net investment which takes the form of a single, separately identifiable project, and which adds to the flow of profits that the business receives. It is assumed that this addition is also separately identifiable. Such a project represents an abstraction from the reality of industrial investment in a number of important respects. First, some investments represent the replacement of existing assets. Secondly, projects are often interdependent. A firm may find that if it wishes to invest in new plant, it also has to invest in more transport capacity for its distribution network, or more canteens for its staff.

Thirdly, some investments do not yield returns in the normally accepted sense. For example a firm sometimes has to invest in order to conform with legal requirements. It may also invest in facilities which generate goodwill among employees and customers. Fourthly, some projects may not generate an observable additional return. For example investment by an established firm may be aimed at building up excess capacity in order to deter new entry. The potential entrants know that if they come in this excess capacity will then be used to drive prices to uneconomic levels. It may not ever actually be used and the investment does not result in the current flow of profits being increased. However, the established firm could argue that it maintains profits above the level *at which they would otherwise be* because entry does not occur. In this sense there is an 'addition' to profits caused by the investment. Similar arguments can be applied to other forms of 'strategic' investment. It has already been argued that backward and forward vertical investment may be undertaken for defensive reasons, to ensure continuing sources of supply and outlets respectively. No increase in actual profits is recorded but again they are higher than would otherwise be the case.

These complications present practical difficulties for investment appraisal. However, the basic principles outlined below in respect of the assessment of the simple project with clearly identifiable returns still apply.

Numerous techniques of investment appraisal are employed in industry. Consideration is given below to three that are widely used. For the moment uncertainty is ignored. It is, however, considered later in the chapter.

Payback period

This period is simply the time it takes for the profits from an investment
to equal its costs. Thus if an investment project costs £6m and gives rise
in each of the next five years to £2m profits then the payback period is
three years. For these calculations profits are defined before any
allowance is made for depreciation but after tax. (Depreciation is not
deducted because the firm is interested in the total flow of profits that
the investment generates.) Where the firm faces no constraint on funds
it accepts all projects which 'pay back' within the period that it has laid
down as acceptable. Where financial constraints are operative and there
is more than one project which has an acceptable payback it assigns a
higher ranking to those projects with shorter paybacks. The main
advantages of this method are that it is simple to calculate and
understand, that it emphasizes the relationship over time between the
flow of funds *out* of the business (investment outlays) with those into it
(profits), and that it provides a useful 'rule of thumb' method for
responding to uncertainty (see below).

The main shortcomings of the payback method are twofold. First, it
ignores any profits that accrue after the selected payback period. Thus
in the example given earlier, the £4m profits obtained in years 4 and 5
play no part in the appraisal. It thus favours short run projects.
Secondly, all profits and costs are given equal weight irrespective of
when they occur. This point may also be illustrated by the previous
example which is set out formally in table 11.2. It is assumed that the
investment is made at the *beginning* of year 1, i.e. the end of year 0, and
that the profits accrue in a lump sum at the *end* of each year. (These
assumptions are made purely for expository purposes.)

Now £2m profits received at the end of the first year does not have the
same value to the firm as £2m received at the beginning of that year,

Table 11.2   Illustration of the outlay and profits of an investment
project

Time		Outlays	Profits
end of year	0	6m	nil
"	1	nil	2m
"	2	nil	2m
"	3	nil	2m
"	4	nil	2m
"	5	nil	2m

because the firm could use the latter in some other profitable use. If it is assumed (for simplicity) that the best yield obtainable on the firm's funds in another use is 10 per cent per annum, then £2m profit accruing at the beginning of the year would have an *end* year value of £2.2m, i.e. £2m × (1.0 + 0.1). Conversely, £2m profits at the *end* of the first year would be worth the equivalent of £1.82m (i.e. £2m/(1.0 + 0.1) at the beginning of the year. If the beginning of the first year is defined as the 'present', i.e. the point in time at which the investment is evaluated, this sum of £1.82m represents the *present value* of the £2m profits accruing at the end of the first year. In other words, the firm would be indifferent (given the 10 per cent interest rate) as between receiving £1.82m at the beginning of the year and receiving £2m at the end. The present value of the £2m received at the end of year 2 would be

$$\frac{£2m}{(1.0 + 0.1)} \, / \, (1.0 + 0.1) \text{ or } \frac{£2m}{(1.1)^2}$$

which is equal to £1.65m. The £2m at the end of year 3 would have a present value of $£2m/(1.1)^3$ (or £1.50m) and so on. Present values are obtained by a process of *discounting* with the appropriate rate of interest being used as the discount rate. This interest rate is sometimes referred to as the 'cost of capital' since it shows how much it 'costs' to tie up money in an investment. It is important to stress that discounting does not arise because of the existence of inflation. It would be necessary, given that a firm always has an alternative use for funds, even in the absence of inflation.

No discounting of the investment *outlays* in the example is required as they occur at the point of time defined as the 'present'. However, if such outlays were spread over several years, present value calculations would have to be made to bring them all to a common base.

It should be clear from the above that *after discounting*, the project in the example does *not* 'pay for itself' in three years: (£1.82m + £1.65m + £1.50m) is *less* than £6m. Further implications of discounting for project assessment are discussed later in this section.

Accounting return method

This method simply expresses annual profit after depreciation and tax as a percentage either of the total investment outlay or of some concept of the 'average' value of the investment over its life. This return is then assessed against some target return specified by the business.

The more sophisticated versions of the accounting returns method do take some account of the profits earned by an investment over the whole of its life. However, none allows for the fact that profits (and investment outlays) may not all occur at the same time.

Discounted cash flow (DCF) technique

DCF techniques explicitly take into account differences in the timing of profits and, where relevant, investment outlays. There are two main types of DCF technique.

(1) *Net present value* The example given earlier may be generalized. If profits at the end of year t are denoted by π_t and the annual rate of interest that a firm can earn on its funds by r, then the present value (*PV*) of those profits may be defined as

$$PV \text{ of } \pi_t = \frac{\pi_t}{(1 + r)^t} \tag{11.1}$$

If t runs from 0 to n, then the present value of *all* profits is as follows

$$\sum_{t=0}^{n} (PV \text{ of } \pi_t) = \sum_{t=0}^{n} \frac{\pi_t}{(1 + r)^t} \tag{11.2}$$

Equation (11.2) simply aggregates the present value of the profits in each of the years. Since the calculations are concerned with the full recovery of costs, there is no need to allow for depreciation.

On the investment outlay side a similar exercise is necessary to provide a present value. Thus if investment outlay in time t is denoted by C_t, then

$$\sum_{t=0}^{n} (PV \text{ of } C_t) = \sum_{t=0}^{n} \frac{C_t}{(1 + r)^t} \tag{11.3}$$

In the case of the earlier example all outlays occur at the end of year 0, thus

$$\sum_{t=0}^{n} (PV \text{ of } C_t) = \frac{C_o}{(1 + r)^o} = \frac{C_o}{1} = C_o \tag{11.4}$$

Now the *net* present value (*NPV*) of a project is the difference between the present value of outlays and the present value of profits. Thus,

$$NPV = \sum_{t=0}^{n} \left(\frac{\pi_t}{(1 + r)^t} - \frac{C_t}{(1 + r)^t} \right) \tag{11.5}$$

A positive *NPV* means in effect that at the same time as the firm pays out the investment outlay with one hand, it receives a sum greater than its expenditure with the other. Where there is no financial constraint, firms would accept all projects with a *NPV* greater than zero. Where such a constraint exists, projects would be ranked by their *NPV*s.

(2) *Internal rate of return* (IRR) The *NPV* method takes as given the appropriate rate of interest which it uses as the discount rate. The *IRR* method on the other hand, is that discount rate, or *IRR* as it is called, which gives an *NPV* of *zero*. The *IRR*, which is found by trial and error, is *then* compared with the appropriate interest rate. Thus a knowledge of the firm's cost of capital is required under *both* the *NPV* and *IRR* methods; it is simply used at different stages in the appraisal.

It should be noted that under special circumstances, the *IRR* method may yield more than one solution (see Reekie and Crook, 1982, pp. 273–4, for a good discussion of this issue). This possibility will be ignored here.

Where projects do not have to be ranked, the *NPV* and *IRR* methods give the same answer. However, where ranking is necessary because of financial constraints or because the projects are mutually exclusive the two methods may yield different results depending on which cost of capital is appropriate. Figure 11.1 illustrates this issue. Project *A* is preferred to project *B* on the *IRR* criterion. However at cost of capital *r*, project *B* is preferred to project *A* in terms of *NPV*. At any cost of capital beyond *r**, the two approaches yield the same ranking. This problem arises because of differences in the time pattern of profits in the two projects.

There has been a good deal of debate about the relative merits of the two DCF techniques. Generally, economists tend to favour the *NPV* method in part because it always yields an unambiguous answer. However, discussion of relative merits should not detract from the importance of the principle of discounting itself.

Methods of Appraisal Used in Industry

In the 1960s, a number of surveys of investment appraisal techniques in British industry reported that discounting was the exception rather than the rule (see for example Neild, 1964; Corner and Williams, 1965). The payback method was particularly popular. However in the mid 1970s Carsberg and Hope suggested from their survey work that there had been a significant move towards DCF, although interestingly they found that where more than one method was used, some version of the payback method was the most popular (1976, pp. 43–47).

The most recent evidence on this issue comes from a survey of 150 finance directors of the largest UK companies in the late 1970s and early 1981 by Pike (1983). The results are shown in table 11.3. Over three-quarters of the companies represented used payback in 1980. Pike also showed, however, that only in 11 per cent of firms was it the *sole* criterion. The slight increase in the percentage using payback over the period 1975 to 1980 is interesting given the Confederation of British Industry's evidence to the Committee to Review the Functioning of

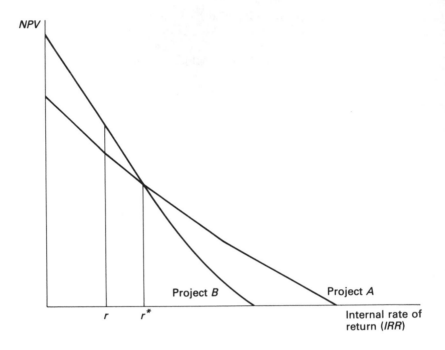

Figure 11.1   *NPV* vs *IRR*
Project *A* is preferred to project *B* on the *IRR* criterion. However at cost of
capital *r*, project *B* is preferred to project *A* on the *NPV* criterion. At any cost of
capital greater than *r**, the two methods yield the same ranking.

Financial Institutions in the middle of this period that increased
uncertainty and pressure on prices and profits had led some companies
to attach more attention to payback and less to DCF (HMSO, 1977b, p.
9). This suggests not surprisingly that the payback method has a greater
relative attractiveness where liquidity and/or uncertainty considerations
are important.

As indicated above Pike's survey was limited to large companies. At
the other end of the size distribution, the use of DCF techniques is
unusual. For example Hankinson's study (1984) of 52 small engineering

Table 11.3 Investment appraisal techniques in a sample of large UK companies (% of companies using technique)

Method	1975	1980
Payback	71	79
Accounting rate of return	51	51
NPV	42	54
IRR	32	38
Other	5	7

Source: Pike, 1983.

firms in the South of England found that only 8 per cent used DCF. Of the rest, 48 per cent used 'trial and error' or no appraisal at all.

The evidence that DCF is still not the dominant technique and is unusual among smaller businesses – Pike found that even *within* his sample, DCF is more popular among the larger businesses – may be variously interpreted. It *may* be evidence of managerial incompetence or lack of knowledge. On the other hand it may indicate that, for some reason not immediately apparent to the appraisal 'technician', businesses find other techniques more appropriate for the conditions in which they operate.

The Presence of Uncertainty

Virtually all investment decisions are made under conditions of uncertainty. Investment costs, profits and interest rates are all subject to unforeseen change. The sources of uncertainty include the general economic and business climate, demand conditions, technological developments and the reactions of rivals. A firm may attempt to cope with uncertainty in various ways. At a general level it may calculate (for the appraisal methods it is using) a *range* of possible outcomes for a given project and see how *sensitive* appraisal results are to different assumptions on the scale and pattern of revenues and costs. However, even when it has undertaken such an exercise, it still needs some rules by which it decides whether or not to go ahead with a particular project. More specifically it may short-circuit sensitivity analysis by adapting the particular appraisal method it is using. It may raise the discount rate in *NPV* calculations. Or, if it is using payback, it may shorten the period that is acceptable to it. This latter response to uncertainty seems to be particularly attractive to businesses in that it is simple and concentrates on a vital consideration in the firm's survival and success, its cash flow. However, whatever a firm does as far as formal evaluation techniques are concerned, it will almost invariably combine it with some form of qualitative assessment. It must always be remembered that increasing the sophistication of the appraisal techniques themselves cannot provide a substitute for the business judgements that underlie the estimates that are fed into the appraisals.

The presence of uncertainty may not only affect the appraisal methods used. It may also influence the nature of the investment itself. For example a firm may decide only to finance projects which allow it some flexibility of response in the future, even though the built-in flexibility raises the initial cost of investment. Again, a firm may undertake diversifying investment in order to spread its risks.

11.4 SOURCES OF FUNDS

Internal vs External Sources

A business may obtain finance for investment in a variety of ways. However, a distinction is usually made between internal and external sources of funds. The main component of internal funds are those profits which are not distributed to shareholders. Other internal sources include interest on loans and rents. External funds cover a wide variety of sources including new issues of shares, long term loans, bank lending (traditionally regarded as short term in nature, although in recent years, loan periods have become longer), trade credit and hire purchase.

Table 11.4 shows the relative importance of these sources for UK industrial and commercial companies in 1983. Clearly, internal funds were the most important sources. It should be noted that the internal funds referred to in the table exclude stock appreciation which is that part of the change in the value of stocks and work in progress which arises from increases in the prices at which these items are valued. It should also be noted that investment is only one form of expenditure from these funds. In 1983 gross investment accounted for under 50 per cent of such expenditure. Stock building, purchases of the shares of other companies and the provision of credit were the other main items for which funds were required.

The biggest single source of external funds in 1983 was from overseas. These funds arise for example through the purchases of shares for UK subsidiaries and associate companies by overseas parent companies and internal transfers within multinationals. Issues of new shares in the UK ('UK capital issues') represented less than 7 per cent of the total amount of funds.

Table 11.4   Sources of funds for UK industrial and commercial companies, 1983

	£m	%
Internal funds after deduction of stock appreciation	22,387	71.1
External funds	9,065	28.9
Receipts from government grants etc.	650	2.1
Trade credit	503	1.6
Bank borrowing	2,012	6.4
Other loans	680	2.2
UK capital issues	2,082	6.6
Overseas	3,138	10.0
Total	31,452	100.0

Source: *Financial Statistics*, 1984.

Table 11.4 relates only to one year. There is considerable variation in the relative importance of the different sources from year to year. However, it is fair to say that internal financing has nearly always provided the majority of funds (the mid–1970s was an exception). It is also the case that in obtaining external funds, companies have come to rely much more heavily in the last 20 years on shorter term borrowing (Rybczynski, 1982.)

The Costs of Different Sources

Which source of finance a business uses depends on numerous factors. First, the type of business will determine which sources of funds are in principle available. The unincorporated business cannot by definition issue shares, although it may become a company in order to do so. The private company cannot offer shares to the public. Secondly, the costs and risks of using different methods varies. (It is important in this context to realize that the use of retained profits is not 'free' since they have an alternative use.)

'Cost' should be interpreted widely. Some businesses, especially those under the control of their original owners, may rule out share issues on the grounds that the consequent 'cost' to them of losing control of their businesses is too great. New issues of ordinary or preference shares often require a heavy initial outlay on promotion, which is not required for instance for bank borrowing. On the other hand new issues do not generate an obligation to make repayment over a specified period or to pay interest charges. Sometimes interest at a fixed rate may be charged on long term loans. This can create problems for a company which borrows at times of high inflation but which repays when inflation is low.

Thirdly, the performance of the company itself will influence which sources are used. For example a very highly profitable company with a policy of maximum retention of profits is likely to obtain much of its finance internally. However, a rapid growth company even if it is highly profitable may not have sufficient funds to finance all its plans. A company with a poor record may be unable to launch a new share issue and may be forced to use other forms of finance. Fourthly, the tax structure may affect the availability of funds. For example a policy that discriminates in favour of profits that are retained by a business (as opposed to being distributed to shareholders) is likely to encourage internal financing of investment.

The Problems of Small Firms

Small firms may be at a relative disadvantage when it comes to raising external funds. Marsh (quoted in Caves, 1980, p. 315) has provided data on the cost of rights issues of different sizes. ('Rights' issues are those in which new shares are offered to existing shareholders first.) He estimated that in 1975, the cost of raising £50,000 was 13 per cent of the proceeds. For £100,000 it was 8 per cent, and for £1m, only 2.9 per cent. There is likely to be a fairly close relationship between the size of firm and size of issue.

Costs of raising loans and other forms of finance are usually relatively higher for the smaller firm for the following reasons. First, lending institutions may experience economies of scale in vetting applications for funds. The cost of vetting a £10m application is unlikely to be a thousand times more than that for a £10,000 application. Secondly, there are economies of scale in preparing applications for funds. The larger firm can often afford to employ specialist staff to deal with such applications. The manager of the small firm on the other hand may have to rely on his own non-specialist skills. Thirdly, smaller firms may present a higher risk to a potential lender. They are often less diversified and have lower reserves to see them through unexpected commercial problems. Finally, the larger firm may bring more market power to bear in dealing with financiers. The lower cost of funds that results from this power is not of course due to real economies of scale.

Much attention in recent years has been given to an examination of whether the relative disadvantage faced by small firms is simply due to the higher costs that smallness inevitably generates or whether there are biases against such firms which cannot be explained on such grounds. The Committee to Review the Functioning of Financial Institutions took the view (HMSO, 1979a, p. 39) that the banks might have been 'excessively cautious' in their assessment of the risks associated with some small firm lending. It was on the basis of this view that the Committee recommended the setting up of a loan guarantee scheme (see p. 27).

11.5 MERGERS AND ACQUISITIONS

Acquisition vs New Investment

Instead of buying new fixed assets, a firm may decide to buy all or part of an existing business. Such a strategy has the advantage that the purchasing firm is able to avoid the teething problems associated with the commissioning of new plant, and the building up of its associated labour force. It is usually a much quicker way of obtaining a given amount of capacity, and it may create fewer difficulties for the expanding firm in the market place, since existing customers, as well as capacity, are usually taken over. Thus the acquirer does not have to invade competitors' markets. On the other hand a new acquisition occurring in a single 'lump' can create absorption problems for the acquirer, especially if the acquired firm has been an unwilling victim. It may take a long period of adjustment before the two organizations are working as one.

Merger Activity in the UK

There have been several merger booms in the post-war period ('merger' here is used as a general term to include a fusion of genuine 'equals' as well as acquisition by one company of another). The last boom in terms of numbers of mergers occurred in 1972 and 1973. The number in each of these two years was around 1200 per year compared with under 500 in the 1980s. In both years expenditure on mergers exceeded net investment. Most of the mergers were of a horizontal type, although there has been an increasing trend towards conglomerate activities (HMSO, 1978b, p. 98).

The Effects of Merger

The effects of merger activity on business performance have been extensively studied in recent years (see for example Utton, 1974b, Meeks, 1977, Cowling et al., 1980). It is clear from this research that the

gains often expected from mergers – for example through the achievement of more economies of scale – have not in general materialized.
Indeed, in many cases, the evidence points to some *impairment* of cost
efficiency. These findings raise the question of why merger booms have
occurred. One plausible answer is that merger activity may in part be a
reflection of management's *own* objectives. (As chapter 7 pointed out,
these objectives may not always be consistent with profit maximization.)

Bigger size may bring higher managerial salaries, and more security in
the sense that managers may be less likely to face take-over by others. A
'quieter life' may be a further outcome of larger size, especially if
accompanied by market power. There are therefore good reasons why
bigger size is attractive to managers, even if it does not bring with it
greater efficiency. A rapid way of achieving such a status is through
merger.

Some of the public policy implications of merger activity are considered in the next chapter.

11.6 HUMAN INVESTMENT

Human investment is similar in many respects to physical investment: a
firm may finance a training programme in the expectation that the
workforce will subsequently become more efficient and thereby increase
the future flow of profits. In the case of human investment however the
firm does not own the labour on whom the expenditure is made. It
cannot ultimately stop an employee from moving to another firm, or
setting up in business on his own account. When the employee leaves he
takes the investment with him. Training is said to be specific to the firm
in which it occurs when it is of no value outside that firm. General
training on the other hand raises the efficiency of the trainee both inside
and outside the training firm. Apprenticeships are usually regarded as
primarily general in character. Most training schemes however have
both specific and general elements. The distinction between specific and
general training may have important implications for the financing of
training. In the case of specific training the firm knows that the
employee cannot use his newly acquired skills elsewhere. It may
therefore be willing to meet the training expenditure itself, provided it
can ensure that the employee will stay with the business, at least until
satisfactory returns can be obtained. It may offer various incentives - for
example, long service awards or good promotion prospects - to stop the
employee moving. The employee knows for his part that his specific
training does not give him command over higher salaries elsewhere. His
employer is thus able to obtain the return on the training investment by

paying him (after training) less than the value of his work to the business.

General training is rather different. Since this kind of training raises the efficiency of the employee not only in the business doing the training but also elsewhere, the employee's post-training wage in the training firm will have to reflect what he could obtain elsewhere given his enhanced productivity. There would thus be no scope for the training firm to obtain a return on any investment. In these circumstances a firm would be unwilling to finance general training. The *trainee*, however, *does* have an incentive to pay for his training as the latter raises his future earnings. As Becker has shown, (1975, pp. 16–37) the general trainee 'pays' by accepting, during training, a wage lower than the value of his output to the firm.

11.7 SUMMARY

Investment in fixed assets may take many different forms. One important distinction is that between gross and net investment, the difference between these two being accounted for by replacement investment. Gross investment as a percentage of Gross Domestic Product at market prices fell steadily between 1974 and 1982. During the same period the share of net investment in gross investment also fell dramatically. In 1982 net investment accounted for less than a quarter of gross investment and in some industries, notably manufacturing, it was negative.

The investment decision is often highly complex. However, a number of appraisal techniques have been developed in industry. Surprisingly perhaps, those techniques which take the timing of profits and outlays into account have not achieved overwhelming acceptance in industry; indeed their use is often unusual, particularly among small firms. This may in part be a reflection of the fact that sophisticated appraisal techniques are inappropriate or have only limited relevance for many business conditions, especially where uncertainty is widespread.

Finance for investment may be obtained in many ways. However, internal sources represent the principal source in the UK. Banks have become relatively more important in providing external finance. Most of the relative disadvantages that small firms face in raising external finance may be due to the higher costs that are involved, although there are some grounds for arguing that banks may have been too cautious in assessing the risks associated with such firms.

Merger activity may be seen as an alternative to expenditure on new assets. There have been several merger booms in the UK, the latest being in 1972/73. Studies of mergers show that in general the expected gains in efficiency have not been forthcoming. One reason for these findings may be that merger activity is meeting the non-profit maximizing objectives of managers.

Human investment activity by firms is complicated by the fact that the labour in which that investment is made is not owned by the firms. This means that a profit maximizing firm will be reluctant to incur training expenditures which raise the trainee's productivity not only in the training firm, but elsewhere. In these cases the trainee himself may pay for the training.

This and the previous five chapters have considered various aspects of competitive activity among firms. The last two chapters now focus on policy issues associated with that activity.

PART III
Industrial Policy

12

Competition Policy

This part of the book is concerned with some issues of industrial policy. This chapter focuses on those policies which affect the nature and extent of competition between UK firms. The next chapter considers policies designed to raise the international competitiveness of UK firms. The two types of policy are of course closely related: policies which affect the ways in which firms compete in the UK are also likely to influence the competitiveness of such firms in an international context. The reverse is also likely to be true.

12.1 A THEORETICAL BASIS FOR COMPETITION POLICY

Competition policy is based on the argument that allowing the market to operate without constraints may lead in some circumstances to results that are contrary to the public interest. (The 'public interest' is a term capable of a wide variety of meanings; its particular legal expression in the UK is discussed later.)

Much of the case for competition policy has focused on the supposed adverse effects of monopoly and it is these effects which are first considered. Later in the chapter, however, oligopolistic markets are briefly discussed.

Monopoly

To simplify the following analysis, a monopoly which is not threatened by either entry of other firms or government action is considered. Thus the monopolist's behaviour is unconstrained by the possibilities of external control. Although monopoly of this 'pure' kind is rarely encountered in practice, it nevertheless serves as a useful framework which may be more or less useful in the circumstances of any particular industry. It is assumed that the costs incurred by the monopolist fully reflect the costs of production to society, that market demand reflects social demand, and that only one price is charged in the market, i.e. there is no price discrimination. The case against monopoly has been argued on many grounds. Three are singled out for separate treatment here. They are that monopoly generates allocative inefficiency (see p. 11) by causing price and output distortions; that it leads to cost inefficiency (see p. 11) and that it reduces the rate of innovation.

Allocative inefficiency

(1) *The theory* In long run equilibrium, i.e. after the firm has made all desirable adjustments to its factor inputs, the profit maximizing monopolist charges a price that is higher than its long run marginal cost (LMC). In perfect competition on the other hand, price is equal to LMC in long run equilibrium. It is on the basis of this distinction that monopoly is said to be allocatively inefficient. To show why this may be so it is necessary to introduce the concept of consumers' surplus. This surplus is the difference between the total monetary value that consumers place on the consumption of a given quantity of a good or service and the amount they have to pay to purchase that quantity. The relevance of consumers' surplus for the analysis of monopoly is considered in figure 12.1, which examines the effects of the monopolization of a previously perfectly competitive industry.

The perfectly competitive industry faces the demand (AR) curve shown. The industry's long run supply curve LRS_C is drawn as a horizontal line for ease of exposition. (A horizontal industry supply curve of this kind does not, however, necessarily imply that each individual's firm LMC curve is also horizontal.)

Industry price and quantity are P_C and Q_C respectively. Now the total value consumers place on that quantity may be approximated by the area ABQ_CO, i.e. the area under the demand curve for the given quantity. The amount they have to pay to purchase Q_C is $P_C \times Q_C$, i.e. the area P_CBQ_CO. Thus consumers' surplus is the area ABP_C.

What would be the position if the perfectly competitive industry were monopolized by a (profit maximizing) firm whose LMC curve (LMC_M) was identical to LRS_C? (Such a change is of course highly artificial; but it does help to highlight some important differences between the two market situations.) Industry price would rise to P_M and output would fall to Q_M where LMC_M is equal to marginal revenue (MR). Such changes result from the divergence between the monopolist's AR and MR. This divergence is in turn a consequence of the direct influence that the monopolist exercises on price.

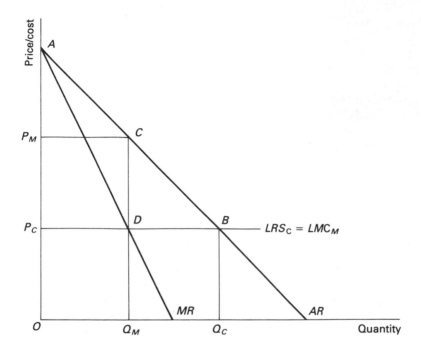

Figure 12.1   The deadweight loss: monopoly and perfect competition compared

In perfect competition, industry price and output at P_C and Q_C respectively. Consumers' surplus is area $APBc$. On monopolization, output would fall to Q_M, and price would rise to P_M. As a result, some of the consumers surplus (P_MCDP_C) would go to the monopolist. The consumer would retain ACP_M. However, there would be a deadweight loss of surplus of CDB; no one would receive this in the monopolized industry.

As a result of the switch to monopoly, some of the consumers' surplus obtained under perfect competition goes to the monopolist as profit or producer's surplus. (Under perfect competition the producer receives no surplus.) This transfer is equal to the area P_MCDP_C in figure 12.1. It may be regarded as redistribution of surplus (from consumers to the monopolist) which has no effect on the total size of the surplus and which can therefore be ignored if every £1's worth of the monopolist's surplus, or profits, is given the same weight as every £1's worth of consumers' surplus. The consumers' surplus under monopoly is reduced to area ACP_M. Total (consumers' and producers') surplus under monopoly is therefore area $ACDP_C$. This area is smaller than the total surplus (which is received only by consumers) under perfect competition. The difference is the triangle CBD. No one receives this; it is lost in the transfer from perfect competition to monopoly. It is sometimes referred to as the deadweight loss (DWL).

The crucial point to note is that if the monopolist were to increase output to Q_C, and thereby to allow price to fall to P_C, the increase in the surplus of consumers would put them in a position not only to provide full compensation to the monopolist for the loss of profits resulting from the change (P_MCDP_C), thereby ensuring that he is no worse off, but also to gain themselves. In this sense monopoly is allocatively inefficient (consumers could gain without making the monopolist worse off). No such gains could, however, be obtained under perfect competition.

Why do consumers not 'bribe' monopolists to produce the competitive level of output? The answer lies in the transactions costs that would be involved in making the necessary arrangements. Customers are typically widely dispersed and some might think that they could obtain 'a free ride' by increasing their surplus without contributing to the monopolist's compensation.

(2) *Nationalized industry pricing* It is primarily because of the allocative inefficiency that results from the price–LMC divergence under monopoly, that attempts were made in the 1960s to require nationalized industries, many of which have considerable market power, to adopt LMC pricing (HMSO, 1967). However, an investigation in the mid-1970s (NEDO, 1976) found that few of the industries had adopted this principle, in part because of the practical difficulties involved. In 1978 (HMSO, 1978a) the nationalized industries were released from the requirement to conform to a particular pricing policy. Instead, all that was required was that an industry's pricing structure should be 'sensibly related to the costs of supply and the market situation', a formula which may be interpreted in an almost infinite variety of ways.

(3) *The Measurement of the Deadweight Loss* The empirical measurement of the DWL can present formidable difficulties. However where the demand curve is linear and costs constant, as in figure 12.1, the measurement becomes more straightforward. Since the MR curve bisects the horizontal distance between the vertical axis and the demand curve (Reekie and Crook, 1982, p. 9), $P_CD = DB$. Also, $CD = P_MP_C$. Thus $CDB = \frac{1}{2} P_MCDP_C$ or half monopoly profits. The snag with this approach is that the identification of monopoly profits is not easy.

Company accounts, on which most investigators have to rely, make no distinction between monopoly profits and those profits that could be regarded as 'normal' under competitive conditions. Furthermore in reality there will always be a spectrum of cost efficiencies among companies in an industry. At any one time therefore some companies may be earning higher profits than others simply because they are more efficient. Thus estimates of DWL must be treated cautiously. These problems have not however prevented attempts at the measurement of the DWL. For example Cowling and Mueller's study (1978) based on the analysis of the top 103 firms in the UK for the period 1968–9 found that the DWL represented nearly 4 per cent of gross corporate product. (Gross corporate product is the gross value added of companies.)

(4) *The Deadweight Loss: Some Difficulties* The use of the DWL as a measure of the allocative inefficiency of monopoly has been questioned on a number of grounds. It is, for example, argued that it *under*estimates the loss from monopoly since it does not include the costs involved in gaining (and maintaining) such a position (Posner, 1975). These costs may take various forms, including those resulting from advertising, product differentiation and even lobbying government. They arise simply because the monopolist wishes to see some consumers' surplus become producer's surplus. They do not give rise to any increase in the sum of consumers' and producer's surplus.

Another line of criticism, presented for example by Littlechild (1981), is that the type of comparisons on which figure 12.1 is based is inappropriate. There are several arguments here. First, there is no guarantee that, in the switch from perfect competition to monopoly, the demand and cost curves would remain unchanged. For example, the incentive to advertise might change. As shown in chapter 9, advertising changes both demand and costs. Secondly, the analysis in figure 12.1 rules out (by assumption) the possibility of future entry. Even where a monopoly is based on a patent or on sole ownership of a factor, the profits may act as an incentive to potential entrants to 'invent round' the monopoly position. If the monopolist is unsuccessful in deterring such entry, the DWL will disappear in the long run as price and output eventually settle at their competitive level. (The analysis in figure 12.1 assumes that the DWL is permanent, i.e. is repeated period after period.) Thus, the contestability of a market (see pp. 117–8) will play an important part in determining how much allocative inefficiency exists. In a perfectly contestable market, there will be no DWL. Of course, even when entry is possible, there may still be a temporary DWL.

Thirdly, the calculation of even a temporary DWL assumes that the good or service in question would otherwise have been produced under competitive conditions. This may not be the case. A firm may identify a market gap where it thinks it can, at least for a time, make monopoly profits. It only attempts to fill that gap because of the prospect of such profits. Without the initial monopoly profits, the good would not be produced at all, or only after an interval. In this case, the total surplus from the new product (assuming that a pound of the monopolist's surplus receives the same weight as a pound of consumers' surplus and that there are no effects of the innovation on *other* products) becomes $ACDP_C$ in figure 12.1. The calculation of a DWL here is inappropriate. Indeed, if the initiative of the first firm leads to other firms coming in and the competitive output being achieved more quickly than would otherwise have been the case, then the consumers' surplus on output $Q_C - Q_M$, i.e. the deadweight loss in figure 12.1, is enjoyed *earlier*. The monopoly profits may, of course, be *more* than sufficient to attract the firm into the market gap.

How appropriate the use of the DWL concept is in any particular monopoly is clearly going to depend on numerous factors whose relative importance will differ from industry to industry. However, an examination of barriers to entry, and an appreciation of the dynamic nature of business activity are both likely to be essential ingredients in any assessment.

Cost inefficiency

In chapter 7, it was argued that managers' objectives may differ from those of shareholders and that this divergence may lead to firms not maximizing their profits. One way in which managers may achieve non-profit maximizing outcomes is by raising costs above their minimum level i.e. they may not seek to maximize cost efficiency. Managers may go for less than maximum cost efficiency either explicitly – for example by having more staff or better company cars than necessary – or implicitly, by opting for greater X inefficiency (see p. 11). Leibenstein has argued (1966) that market power tends to generate X inefficiency.

Figure 12.1 assumed maximum cost efficiency. Some effects of dropping that assumption are illustrated in figure 12.2, where LRS_C, P_C and Q_C are (again) the long run supply curve, price and output respectively of the competitive industry. LRS_C is assumed to be equal to LMC_{M1}, the long run marginal cost of a monopolist with no X inefficiency. If the industry were to be taken over by such a monopolist, price would rise to P_{M1} and output would fall to Q_{M1}. However, if as a result of monopolization, X inefficiency developed and costs rose to LMC_{M2}, price would be even higher at P_{M2}, and output even lower at Q_{M2}. If it is assumed that the monopolist's managers derive benefit from the slack equal to the increase in costs, area $Q_{M2}(LMC_2 - LMC_1)$, then the loss of surplus in this case becomes area EFB. How far this is a valid measure of the loss from a monopoly with X inefficiency depends on similar factors to those discussed in relation to the price and output

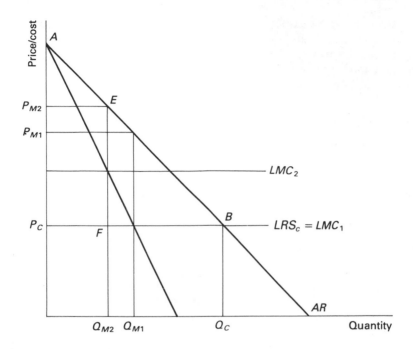

Figure 12.2 *X* inefficiency and the deadweight loss
The perfectly competitive price and output are P_C and Q_C respectively. If the
industry is monopolized, *X* inefficiency is assumed to raise the *LMC* curve from
LMC_1 to LMC_2. The monopolist maximizes profits on the new cost level by
charging P_{M2} and producing QM_2. Assuming that the managers derive benefit
from the increase in costs of QM_2 ($LMC_2 - LMC_1$), the loss in surplus that
results from the shift from perfect competition to monopoly is *EFB*.

distortions illustrated in figure 12.1. Managers may incur expenditure
which is designed solely to provide them with the market power which
enables them to raise costs. New entry may eventually destroy the
monopoly position and hence the scope for *X* inefficiency. At the same
time, the prospect of such inefficiency may itself act as an inducement to
managers to engage in innovative activity that would not otherwise
occur. Higher costs may also arise as a direct result of policy measures
designed to control reported profits.

Against the 'monopoly causes X inefficiency' argument, however, may be set the possibility that a monopoly may be able to achieve lower unit costs than several *separate* firms producing the same output, if natural monopoly conditions are present (see p. 115). The extent to which such lower costs offset the X inefficiency effect is an empirical matter.

Reduced innovation

The relationship between market structure and innovation was considered in chapter 10. It was suggested there that while some market power may encourage innovations, very high levels of concentration do not in general appear to assist the innovative process. This is not to say, however, that *some* monopolies are not highly innovative. Nevertheless they are likely to be the exception rather than the rule.

Other issues

The effects of monopoly may be expressed in ways that do not fit in easily to the above framework. For example, the monopolist's market power may enable it to adopt tactics which reduce the likelihood of competition from potential entrants. One possibility is for the monopolist to refuse to supply any firm that buys from an entrant firm. Customers of the monopolist may then be reluctant to experiment with alternative sources of supply.

Oligopoly

So far only monopoly has been considered. Many of the arguments may also be appropriate to oligopolistic markets in which firms are able to practice either implicit or explicit collusion. There may, however, sometimes be additional factors to be taken into account. For example, competitive duplication of advertising or other market expenditures may occur. This duplication may not increase market demand and the market shares of each oligopolist may remain unaffected. A substantial cut in the relevant expenditures would not, therefore, have any effect on each firm's demand, although it would release resources for other uses. At the same time, duplication is likely to raise entry barriers, since newcomers may have to match the current levels of expenditure.

12.2 THE 'NO POLICY' ALTERNATIVE

It is sometimes argued that, provided entry is not artificially restricted (for example by licensing laws or statutory monopolies), a *laissez-faire* system will automatically ensure that, in the long run at least, allocative and cost inefficiency are eliminated. Entry is seen as the mechanism by which this is achieved. This essentially is the philosophy behind the current attempts to deregulate many markets through the removal of legal restrictions on entrants. Such deregulation is not without its costs – several airlines in the US have been liquidated as a result of their over-ambitious plans to take advantage of the removal in recent years of route licensing restrictions – but such costs have to be set against the substantial gains that customers may obtain from greater competition.

Support for the view that the market mechanism will itself ensure maximum efficiency, provided entry is unrestricted, need not imply that there are no benefits to be obtained from having a competition policy, merely that its costs would outweigh any benefits. Even if it could be shown for example that there was a short run DWL in markets in which there were no artificial entry restrictions, the costs of 'policing' the market to ensure that it behaves in the public interest, may be greater than this loss. 'Costs' here include not only those of the regulatory body, but also those incurred by the offending firms in conforming to (and possibly fighting) the regulations.

Deregulation and the maintenance of 'free' markets may, of course, be regarded as a form of competition policy. However, the latter is usually restricted (as it is in this book) to the regulation of more specific aspects of market structure or behaviour. Successive post-war governments in the UK have supported a competition policy of this latter kind.

12.3 WHAT TYPE OF COMPETITION POLICY?

Two main approaches may be identified.

The Prohibition Approach

Certain types of market structure or behaviour may be declared illegal. For example in the UK, all forms of collectively enforced resale price maintainance (rpm) are outlawed. It is simply necessary for the authorities to show that such a practice is being followed for the firms concerned to be guilty of an offence. No assessment is made of the advantages and disadvantages of individual cases of collective rpm. Such a prohibition approach need not necessarily imply that all instances in which firms engage in the proscribed practice are contrary to the public interest but simply that the cost of separating out those that have beneficial (or no adverse) effects are greater than any benefits that might come from having a system of exemptions from general prohibition.

The Case by Case Approach

The second type of approach evaluates particular forms of structure and behaviour on their individual merits. Such a policy may be decribed as pragmatic. The case by case approach, which dominates UK competition policy, implies that it *is* worthwhile distinguishing between the 'good' and the 'bad' in this area. Such distinctions do of course require some criteria against evaluations are to be made. In the UK these criteria are summarized in the term 'the public interest', the nature of which is discussed in section 12.5.

The legislative framework within which the case by case approach operates may not itself be neutral in its stance on particular types of structure or behaviour. For example, as shown below, there is a strong legal presumption against agreements among firms. In respect of monopolies, however, there is no such presumption.

12.4 WHAT TYPE OF INSTITUTION?

Review of structure and behaviour may be carried out by a court, under judicial procedures, or by an administrative body. The latter can have a much greater flexibility in its approach. Administrative procedures are more attractive in cases where the 'public interest' issues are complex and where a clear presumption (either for or against) would be difficult to sustain.

12.5 UK POLICY

There are five main areas in which UK competition policy currently operates. These areas concern dominant firms (monopolists and oligopolists), mergers, agreements between firms, anti-competitive practices and the nationalized industries. Before each of these areas is dealt with below, it is important to realize that UK competition policy has developed in a piecemeal fashion. It would be a mistake to assume that the policy has been worked out and developed according to some 'master plan' (Borrie, 1982). (A brief historical review of UK competition policy is contained in Creedy et al., 1984, pp. 192–5.)

Dominant Firms

Monopolies and oligopolies are not prohibited by law. However, under the present legislation – embodied in the Fair Trading Act, 1973 – where a business or group of inter-connected businesses supply at least 25 per cent or more of a particular good or service in the UK, they can be referred for review by the Director General of Fair Trading (DGFT) to the Monopolies and Mergers Commission (MMC). The MMC is an administrative body, whose members are chosen by a government minister.

This power of review also applies to groups of businesses supplying at least 25 per cent of the market who act in such a way as 'to prevent, restrict or distort competition'. No formal agreement between such firms has to be shown. (Certain specified goods and services fall outside the scope of the Act.)

There is no legal requirement that firms coming within the scope of the legislation should notify the authorities to that effect. It should be noted that only a small percentage of cases which could be referred by the authorities to the Commission are, in fact, referred. However, even the small number of referrals may have a deterrent effect on a wider business population.

The MMC has usually to decide two things when considering a particular reference: first, whether 'a monopoly situation' as specified above actually exists; and, secondly, whether it operates or may be expected to operate against the public interest. The Fair Trading Act gives the MMC a number of broad guidelines on the nature of the public interest. These are set out in the appendix to this chapter. It is important to note that the MMC is given no guidance on what weight to attach to any individual guideline. This point is particularly important where a case under investigation satisfies one guideline but does not meet another. In these cases the MMC must provide its own weighting system. Furthermore it is worth noting that the MMC need not limit itself to these guidelines. The Act requires it to take into account 'all matters which appear in the particular circumstances to be relevant'. This fairly free approach to the definition of the public interest reflects the view that a wide range of factors needs to be taken into account in any dominant firm assessment. Such market structures are not necessarily against the public interest and each case must be treated on its merits. The approach to dominant firms is therefore on 'a case by case' basis, with no presumption either way. The wide definition of the public interest may, however, create problems. For example MMC investigations carried out at different times and in different industries need not be consistent with each other, since different public interest criteria may be applied. It should be noted that the Fair Trading Act only requires the MMC to analyse whether a dominant firm is operating or may be expected to operate *against* the public interest.

Once the MMC has reported and made its recommendations, the Secretary of State may use a wide range of powers to implement these recommendations if he so wishes. Included in these powers are the right to prohibit or modify a certain practice, or to keep it under surveillance and to order the breaking up of a business. (How effective these powers can in fact be in practice is, of course, another matter.)

The reports of the MMC show only too clearly the complexity of modern industrial competition. They also illustrate the importance of keeping a fairly open mind in reaching any assessment of a monopoly situation. The importance of such a pragmatic approach can be seen in the MMC's interpretation of profits data. In some cases, relatively high profits have not attracted unfavourable comment from the Commission, since they have arisen, in the MMC's view, from such factors as greater cost efficiency, better technical development and the risky nature of the business. For example the MMC accepted that the rate of return obtained by Rank Xerox – the virtual monopoly suppliers of indirect electrostatic reprographic equipment – in the late 1960s and early 1970s had been substantially higher than the average for manufacturing as a whole but argued that such profits would not have been made 'if the company had not been as efficient as we judge it to have been' (HMSO, 1976b, p. 103). On the other hand, in other industries, high profits have been interpreted as excessive in the context of the firm's business performances and environment. For example, the profits earned by Automotive Products on clutch mechanisms of which it was a dominant supplier, were criticized by the MMC on the grounds that they reflected the combination of the firm's monopoly position and its practice of price discrimination between customers (HMSO, 1968, p. 51). Interestingly Automotive Products' average rate of return in the period under consideration was lower than that of Rank Xerox.

While any firm assessment of the MMC's work in this area is difficult, it seems reasonably clear that it has served to reduce some of the more serious abuses arising from the possession of market power. (For a useful survey, see Pass and Sparkes, 1980.) Certainly, there have been few reports in which the behaviour of the firms concerned have been given a completely clean bill of health. Remedial action following dominant firm investigations has been initiated on a wide front and has led, *inter alia*, to reductions in price, a closer relationship between cost and price, the ending of price discrimination, wider consumer choice and the removal of practices designed to inhibit entry.

Mergers

All proposed mergers which would lead to at least 25 per cent of a market being supplied by one firm or which would involve assets taken over of £30m or more must be considered for possible referral to the MMC by the Office of Fair Trading which advises the Secretary of State on whether he should allow a merger or refer it for a public interest judgement. The MMC is required to use the same public interest guidelines in its consideration of mergers as those applicable to dominant firm investigations. In considering a merger, the MMC has to engage in some crystal ball gazing: it has to come to some judgement on how a proposed change in market structure *is likely to* affect the public interest.

After the Commission's report, the Secretary of State then has to decide whether or not to allow a merger to go through. He is not bound by the Commission's recommendations. Only a small minority – about 3 per cent (HMSO, 1978b, p. 24) – of eligible mergers have been referred to the Commission. Most of these have been found to be against the public interest. The low referral rate implies that over the period during which the merger legislation has been in force, i.e. since 1965, there has been a presumption in favour of merger activity in the initial vetting procedures. This presumption has received little support from a wide range of studies on the effects of mergers (see pp. 181–2) and there can be little doubt that many mergers which could have been referred to the MMC have gone ahead without clear gains in efficiency being obtained. Assessment of the possible effects of a merger by the firms concerned has often been superficial. Certainly, a number of firms have been unwilling to argue their case before the MMC, preferring instead to abandon their merger proposal. One possible explanation for this preference is that the case for merger was insufficiently strong or thought out. But even taking into account the deterrent effect of the legislation, it is probably fair to say that merger policy has not been especially effective in stopping increases in market power where there have been no offsetting gains in efficiency. One of the difficulties with UK merger policy has been that political considerations have sometimes played an important role in both the initial decision whether or not to refer – it should be noted that in the case of dominant firms it is the DGFT, rather than the Minister that makes a reference – and subsequent action on the MMC's report. For example, the 1976 merger between Britain's only two sugar cane producers was not referred because it was supported by the Ministry of Agriculture (*The Economist*, 5 February 1983).

Agreements Between Firms

The statutory presumption in relation to the public interest implications of dominant firms and mergers is fairly neutral. However, agreements between firms relating either to goods or services come in for much harsher treatment. The presumption (under the Restrictive Trade Practices Act, 1976) is that they are against the public interest *unless* it can be shown that they provide one or more fairly narrowly defined benefits *and* that overall, these benefits outweigh the detriments (see the appendix to this chapter). Agreements which simply exchange information are covered by the legislation as are those of an informal nature.

The presumption against agreements is reflected in the institutional arrangements made to implement the legislation. *All* agreements under which at least two or more of the parties accept certain specified restrictions, must be registered with the DGFT and the onus for registration lies with the participating firm. The public interest implications of registered agreements are considered in judicial proceedings before a Restrictive Practices Court. (Every registered agreement must be referred to the court except in certain narrowly defined circumstances.)

When the legislation on agreements was first introduced in 1956, a significant number of agreements were abandoned or modified to avoid registration (Swann et al., 1974, pp. 153–6). Furthermore, the vast majority of those agreements which were, in fact, registered, were abandoned before they could be brought to court, and only a very small minority were permitted to continue after their case had been examined. Firms may, of course, find ways of co-ordinating their activities which do not involve registrable agreements. Price leadership is one such method (see p. 111). In the last resort merger may be the answer for firms whose common interest is very strong, but who cannot satisfactorily achieve co-ordination of policies. However, there is no evidence to indicate that firms have responded in this way (O'Brien et al., 1979, pp. 140–1). If none of these options can be pursued, or is worth pursuing, firms may enter into illegal agreements. As Borrie (1982) has pointed out secret agreements in such diverse fields as telephone cables, bread and polyester resins have been uncovered in recent years. It is very unlikely that all agreements of this kind have been identified.

Despite these problems, there is a good deal of case study evidence to suggest that allocative and cost efficiencies have been increased and that the rate of technological development has improved (Swann et al., 1974, chapter 4). Interestingly, however, these developments do not appear to have had an adverse effect on the fortunes of the firms themselves. There is, for example, no evidence to suggest that firms whose agreements have been struck down by the court have experienced a decline in their profits over time as a direct result of the operation of the legislation. Furthermore, the legislation appears to have had no detectable effect on their growth or sales (O'Brien et al., 1979, chapter 8). This finding suggests that firms have been quick to adapt to the effects of the legislation.

Anti-Competitive Practices

Under the Fair Trading Act, investigation of particular aspects of a firm's behaviour though possible is rather cumbersome and time consuming. The 1980 Competition Act sought to provide a remedy for these difficulties. It defined an anti-competitive practice as one which 'restricts, distorts or prevents competition'. *Any* firm, whether or not it is a monopolist or oligopolist, may pursue an anti-competitive practice, although it is more likely to be those firms with a substantial market share who follow such practices. The procedure under the Act is a two-stage one. The DGFT first undertakes a preliminary investigation to see whether a particular course of conduct amounts to an anti-competitive practice. At this stage the DGFT makes no judgement on the public interest issues. If the DGFT identifies an anti-competitive practice, he can refer it to the MMC, or obtain an undertaking from the firms concerned.

In reporting on any reference the MMC is required first to establish whether an anti-competitive practice is, or was being, operated and, secondly, if so, whether it is against the public interest. (The guidelines on the public interest are the same as those used in dominant firms and merger investigations.) The Secretary of State can make an order prohibiting or modifying the practice after the MMC has responded. Alternatively, the DGFT may seek an undertaking from the firm concerned.

There can be little doubt that the 1980 Act has given a greater flexibility to the MMC's work. However, it is still too early to reach a firm view on what impact the legislation will have. The first signs are that the legislation will lead to the removal, or lessening, or restrictions on competition.

The MMC's recent report on Sheffield Newspapers (HMSO, 1982b) provides a useful illustration of this effect. Sheffield Newspapers Ltd (SNL), which was the dominant supplier of local and property advertising newspapers in Sheffield made it one of its conditions of supply that newsagents would not handle any free publications which SNL considered detrimental to its interests. The MMC concluded that such a restriction was against the public interest as it led to higher advertising charges (free publications would find distribution difficult); less pressure on, or incentive for, SNL to improve and maintain its standards and the variety of services it offered to advertisers and the public; and less choice of advertising media for both advertisers and public.

The Nationalized Industries

Under the Competition Act 1980 nationalized industries may be referred by the Secretary of State for investigation by the MMC. The MMC may be asked to consider any question relating to (1) the efficiency and costs of; (2) the services provided by; or (3) possible abuse of a monopoly position by a nationalized industry.

The MMC may be asked whether in respect of these matters, the industry is acting against the public interest as defined under the Fair Trading Act. The MMC is, however, excluded from considering any question relating to the appropriateness of financial obligations, or guidance on those objectives given to the industry by government. These are to be taken as given.

The MMC has already published several reports on nationalized industries, or parts of them. In some cases, it has uncovered substantial inefficiencies and shortcomings in management practices. For example, in its report on British Rail's London and South East Commuter services, the MMC made 36 recommendations covering a wide variety of topics including suggestions for improving the control of maintenance costs, the cleaning of rolling stock, information dissemination among travellers, the productivity of manpower, and investment appraisal techniques (HMSO, 1980b, pp. 176–87). In this respect the MMC has already had a useful impact and the response from the industries themselves has often been positive (Chiplin and Wright, 1982). However, the fact that the MMC is excluded from considering issues associated with financial objectives, that there is no mechanism, apart from the possibility of follow up reports, for ensuring that recommendations are taken on board; and that references can only be made by a government minister, must limit the Act's effectiveness in this sphere.

The Effects of Competition Policy: An Overview

The overall effects of the above policies are virtually impossible to evaluate in any precise way. There have clearly been benefits – for example in allocative and cost efficiency, and in the easing of entry into some industries. The costs, both direct and indirect of operating these policies have, however, received much less attention. Furthermore, it is far from clear how alternative policies would alter the ratio of benefit to cost. Given the difficulties of assessment and the fact that, rightly or wrongly, there is a system already in operation, there is a strong case for allowing it to evolve by piecemeal rather than wholesale changes.

12.6 SUMMARY

The case for a competition policy rests on the view that free markets will not always operate in the public interest. More specifically, it is argued that monopoly may generate allocative and cost inefficiencies and retard the rate of innovation. These arguments have, however, been subject to some dispute and it is sometimes argued that the market can itself provide an effective form of regulation, i.e. that there is no need for a specific competition policy. This has not been the view of successive post-war governments in the UK.

A 'case by case' approach dominates UK competition policy, and, except in the case of agreements between firms, there is no legal presumption that any particular structure or behaviour is against the public interest. The harsher treatment of agreements is reflected in the fact that they are subject to review by a court, whereas in the other main areas of competition policy review is carried out by an administrative body.

UK competition policy has developed in a piecemeal fashion. However, there can be little doubt that some improvements in cost and allocative efficiency and in technical progressiveness have resulted and that entry has been made easier. Nevertheless it is probably fair to say that merger policy has not been particularly effective. It is also still too early to assess the impact of the policy as far as anti-competitive practices and the nationalized industries are concerned. Whether, overall, the benefits of competition policy exceed the costs must remain an open issue.

12.7 APPENDIX: PUBLIC INTEREST PROVISIONS OF COMPETITION POLICY LEGISLATION

Fair Trading Act, 1973

(Applicable to all investigations by the Monopolies and Mergers Commission)

SECTION 84

(1) In determining for any purposes to which this section applies whether any particular matter operates, or may be expected to operate, against the public interest, the Commission shall take into account all matters which appear to them in the particular circumstances to be relevant and, among other things, shall have regard to the desirability–

    (a) of maintaining and promoting effective competition between persons supplying goods and services in the United Kingdom;

    (b) of promoting the interests of consumers, purchasers and other users of goods and services in the United Kingdom in respect of the prices charged for them and in respect of their quality and the variety of goods and services supplied;

    (c) of promoting, through competition, the reduction of costs and the development and use of new techniques and new products, and of facilitating the entry of new competitors into existing markets;

(d) of maintaining and promoting the balanced distribution of industry and employment in the United Kingdom; and

(e) of maintaining and promoting competitive activity in markets outside the United Kingdom on the part of producers of goods, and of suppliers of goods and services, in the United Kingdom.

Restrictive Trade Practices Act 1976

(Applicable to cases before the Restrictive Practices Court)

SECTION 10

(1) For the purposes of any proceedings before the Court under Part I of this Act, a restriction accepted or information provision made in pursuance of an agreement to which this Act applies by virtue of this Part shall be deemed to be contrary to the public interest unless the Court is satisfied of any one or more of the following circumstances–

(a) that the restriction or information provision is reasonably necessary, having regard to the character of the goods to which it applies, to protect the public against injury (whether to persons or to premises) in connection with the consumption, installation or use of those goods;

(b) that the removal of the restriction or information provision would deny to the public as purchasers, consumers or users of any goods other specific and substantial benefits or advantages enjoyed or likely to be enjoyed by them as such, whether by virtue of the restriction or information provision itself or of any arrangements or operations resulting therefrom;

(c) that the restriction or information provision is reasonably necessary to counteract measures taken by any one person not party to the agreement with a view to preventing or restricting competition in or in relation to the trade or business in which the persons party thereto are engaged;

(d) that the restriction or information provision is reasonably necessary to enable the persons party to the agreement to negotiate fair terms for the supply of goods to, or the acquisition of goods from, any one person not party thereto who controls a preponderant part of the trade or business of acquiring or supplying such goods, or for the supply of goods to any person not party to the agreement and not carrying on such a trade or business who, either alone or in combination with any other such person, controls a preponderant part of the market for such goods;

(e) that, having regard to the conditions actually obtaining or reasonably foreseen at the time of the application, the removal of the restriction or information provision would be likely to have a serious and persistent adverse effect on the general level of unemployment in an area, or in areas taken together, in which a substantial proportion of the trade or industry to which the agreement relates is situated;

(f) that, having regard to the conditions actually obtaining or reasonably foreseen at the time of the application, the removal of the restriction or information provision would be likely to cause a reduction in the volume or earnings of the export business which is substantial either in relation to the whole export business of the United Kingdom or in relation to the whole business (including export business) of the said trade or industry;

(g) that the restriction or information provision is reasonably required for purposes connected with the maintenance of any other restriction accepted or information provision made by the parties, whether under the same agreement or under any other agreement between them, being a restriction or information provision which is found by the Court not to be contrary to the public interest upon grounds other than those specified in this paragraph, or has been so found in previous proceedings before the Court; or

(h) that the restriction or information provision does not directly or indirectly restrict or discourage competition to any material degree in any relevant trade or industry and is not likely to do so;

and is further satisfied (in any such case) that the restriction or information provision is not unreasonable having regard to the balance between those circumstances and any detriment to the public or to persons not parties to the agreement (being purchasers, consumers or users of goods produced or sold by such parties, or persons engaged or seeking to become engaged in the trade or business of selling such goods or of producing or selling similar goods) resulting or likely to result from the operation of the restriction or the information provision.

13

Improving International Competitiveness

13.1 RELATIVE DECLINE: A COMMON POST-WAR THEME

Chapter 6 presented evidence to show that there has been a fairly long term decline in the UK's share in world exports and a rise in import penetration. It also showed that output, output per head and labour productivity had all grown more slowly than in competing countries. Successive post-war governments (of both parties) have seen the reversal of this downward trend in the UK's international position as a major objective of their economic policies. For example, the Labour government's ill-fated *National Plan* launched in 1965 (see p. 28) stated in its Introduction: 'we must pay our way in an increasingly competitive world in which we have for too long been losing ground steadily to other industrial countries' (HMSO, 1965, p. 1). A range of interventionist policies followed.

The Conservative government came to power in 1970 committed to a policy of disengagement from industry. However, within two years it had given itself very wide powers to provide assistance to industry under the 1972 Industry Act. (The relevant powers are now contained in the Industrial Development Act, 1982; the principal provisions under which aid may be given to industry are identical to those contained in the 1972 Act.)

One of the major reasons for the Industry Act 1972 was, according to the government, that 'the economic performance of the UK has been falling behind that of other major industrialized countries for a long time. Our rate of growth has been comparatively low. Modernisation has lagged. Productivity has been slow to rise' (HMSO, 1972a, p. 1).

When a Labour government was re-elected in 1974 it soon embarked on a plan for an 'industrial strategy' (see section 13.3). Its reasons for having a strategy had a familiar ring: 'the performance of British industry has been steadily deteriorating ... in comparison with its competitors' (HMSO, 1975a, p. 1). The aim of the government was 'nothing less than to reverse the relative decline of British industry which has been continuous for many years' (ibid).

In 1979, the Chancellor of the Exchequer in the new Conservative government emphasized a similar theme in his first budget speech:

> Only a quarter of a century ago ... the United Kingdom enjoyed higher living standards than the citizens of any of the larger countries in Europe. Britain was then second only to the United States in economic strength. It is not so today ... in the last few years, the hard facts of our relative decline have become increasingly plain and the threat of absolute decline has gradually become very real. That is not a prospect I am prepared to accept. (*Hansard*, 12 June 1979, vol. 968, col. 237).

The above quotations show only too clearly that a halting of the UK's relative decline has long been a major objective of UK governments. A wide variety of policies and institutions have however been tried and some of these are outlined in more detail below. However, any success they may have had so far has been insufficient to lead to the abandonment of this objective on the grounds that it is no longer appropriate.

13.2 THE IMPORTANCE OF A CORRECT DIAGNOSIS

The introduction of policies designed to raise the UK's competitiveness does of course require some diagnosis, which may only be implicit, of *why* the UK has the record it has. Faulty diagnoses can lead to misconceived policies. For example suppose that, relative to the position in other countries, investment in a UK industry is low, and that this is due to management's low demand for funds because it is unable – perhaps as a result of its own incompetence – to identify profitable opportunities. Now if the low investment is *incorrectly* diagnosed as resulting from the unwillingness of financial institutions to provide funds, and governments take action on this basis – for example by setting up new, state backed institutions – the underlying problem will not be solved.

As chapter 6 points out, a number of (related) explanations have been put forward to explain the UK's post-war experience. This fact of itself should make governments wary of accepting 'single cause' analyses. In practice undisputed diagnoses of the UK's economic performance are simply not possible. It is important therefore for governments to monitor the effects of their policies (see section 13.6).

13.3 GOVERNMENT POLICIES AND INTERNATIONAL COMPETITIVENESS

Some Preliminary Issues

Many of the policy measures that have been introduced to raise the international competitiveness of UK industry have involved intervention in specific firms or industries in such areas as innovation, investment, industrial restructuring (usually involving the merging of firms), planning advice and training. Some examples are given later in this section.

This chapter largely concentrates on such 'interventionist' measures, and pays particular attention to those of a financial nature. However, it is important to note the following points. First, some Conservative governments have taken the view (not always put into practice) that the best way to improve international competitiveness is through the establishment of a favourable economic environment for industrial activity and through general economic measures, rather than through detailed government involvement in the decisions of firms. General economic measures work through such instruments as the money supply, interest rates, taxation and government expenditure. Investment incentives – loans, grants or tax relief – that are available to *all* firms may be classified in this way.

Secondly, interventionist measures in the UK have usually been motivated by a large number of interrelated considerations. The raising of international performance has sometimes only featured indirectly and sometimes not at all. The government rescue of Rolls Royce in 1971, after that company had overstretched itself with its development of the new RB211 engine for the (then) new generation of wide bodied aircraft, provides a good illustration of some of the wider issues at stake in the government decision:

> The failure of the old Rolls-Royce company had confronted the Government with a situation of immense gravity, affecting not only our own armed forces and national airlines, but many overseas governments and airlines as well. Our reputation as a trading nation and as leaders in technology would have been damaged if the Government had not stepped in quickly and effectively to preserve the physical resources of the company and to provide finance and leadership for continuing on a new basis. Something of the order of 100,000 jobs would have been at stake at Rolls-Royce and their suppliers, of which around a quarter was attributable to the RB211 project, with contingent risks in respect of economic and social costs; if uncertainty had been prolonged,

the solvency of many major firms would have been at risk and business confidence would have been gravely impaired throughout the country. (HMSO, 1972b, p. 20)

Some of the factors mentioned in this quotation also played a part in the rescue of other companies, notably British Leyland in 1974. Clearly, these rescues had important implications for international competitiveness – for example, Rolls Royce was able to launch a new engine – but there were other considerations to be taken into account.

Other motivations for state intervention have included the elimination of abuses of market power (see chapter 12); the extension of industrial democracy and public ownership; and the reduction of unemployment in regions where it is particularly high. This last objective has been a particularly important one for government intervention. Section 7 of the Industry Act 1972 (now Section 7 of the Industrial Development Act 1982) gave wide powers to government to provide selective assistance to firms in the affected areas where it could be shown that the assistance would cause employment to be maintained or increased. (These powers were in addition to the general non-selective regional development grants given to *all* firms in premises on which 'qualifying activities' were carried on in the depressed regions.) Again, such measures may have some implications for international competitiveness, but these implications are usually indirect.

In this chapter consideration is restricted to those measures where improved competitiveness has been an important and explicit aim, even though it may not have been the only aim. Attention is also restricted to government involvement with the private sector of the economy. Nationalized industries are not considered. However, it should be noted that public ownership either directly by the state, or by a state owned agency, has sometimes been used as a tool for intervention. For example when the government set up the Industrial Reorganisation Corporation (IRC) in 1966 to promote 'industrial efficiency and profitability' and to assist 'the economy of the United Kingdom', it was given very wide powers including share ownership in private businesses, to enable it to achieve its objectives by promoting or assisting 'the reorganisation or development of any industry'. (These quotations come from the Industrial Reorganisation Corporation Act 1966.)

The IRC's power to purchase shares to achieve what it saw as the desired industrial restructuring were sometimes used (see Young, 1974, pp. 74–5). The National Enterprise Board (NEB) set up by the Labour government in 1975 (see p. 211) also had similar powers. Indeed the promotion of public ownership was explicitly stated as a function of the Board. For the purposes of this chapter, however, the exercise of such powers is regarded as being part of the government's involvement in the private sector of the economy.

Government Policies Since 1974

In the last decade or so governments have adopted a wide variety of approaches and measures to increase international competitiveness. It may therefore be helpful to review the way in which policies have developed and changed over these years.

The Labour government (1974–9)

In 1975, the Labour government published a White Paper which contained its analysis of the decline in the UK's international position and its proposals for reversing this decline (HMSO, 1975a). The White Paper acknowledged a wide range of reasons for the relatively poor performance; most of the possible causes outlined in chapter 6 (such as insufficiently skilled labour, inadequate investment, pre-emption of resources by the public sector, and frequent changes in government policy) were included in its analysis.

On the basis of this White Paper the government proposed to develop 'an agreed national strategy for industry on a long term basis' (HMSO, 1975a, p. 6). Three elements in this strategy are particularly worth noting. First, it was intended to identify key industrial sectors, i.e. those most important for achieving 'our economic objectives both for the Government's purposes and for those of private industry'. These key sectors would be used as a focus for selective financial assistance and other aid. Such a strategy has often been referred to as one of 'picking winners'. It is not at all clear from the White Paper, however, precisely what criteria were to be used to identify key sectors or why government involvement would be necessary. This lack of clarity was most apparent in the proposed grouping of the sectors. They were to be put into the following three categories (HMSO, 1975a, p. 8).

– Industries which, judging by past performance and current prospects, are intrinsically likely to be successful.
– Industries which, though they fall short of the first category, have the potential for success if appropriate action is taken.
– Industries whose performance (as in the case of component suppliers) is most important to the rest of industry.

'Success' and 'appropriate action' were not explicitly defined. It was not made clear whether government involvement was necessary in 'intrinsically' successful industries, and if it was, in what form. Nor was it indicated why industries in the second category did not take appropriate action *themselves*. Industries in the third category were classified in terms of their position in the economy, a criterion rather different from the first two. (Presumably a component supplier could also be 'intrinsically ... successful'.)

The main agencies to be used in the development of plans and policies for the key sectors were to be Sector Working Parties, bodies made up of representatives of management, trade unions and government. These Working Parties were to operate under the aegis of the National Economic Development Council (see p. 29).

Secondly, the government intended to provide a wide range of selective finance. Under the Industry Act 1975 it established the National Enterprise Board, one of whose statutory purposes was 'the promotion of industrial efficiency and international competitiveness'. The activities of the NEB were to be the focus of extensive public ownership in industry. The Board was given very wide powers including those to acquire shares and to make loans and guarantees. Many government shareholdings were transferred to the NEB. The government also used the provisions of Section 8 of the 1972 Industry Act to develop schemes of selective financial assistance to encourage modernization and rationalization. (The 1975 Industry Act gave the government powers to ask the NEB to act as its agent for Section 8 assistance.)

The purposes for which assistance might be given under Section 8 were so wide that the government decided to publish more specific guidance under its *Criteria of Assistance to Industry* in 1976 (reprinted in HMSO, 1976a, pp. 35–40). Under these criteria, all decisions were to have regard to the objective of enabling British industry to compete more successfully. Profitability and return on capital were to be used as the prime test of the efficient use of resources and the amount of financial assistance needed to bring an enterprise to profitability were to be measured against the social and other benefits that might arise. Prospects for commercial viability (after selective assistance on a once-for-all basis had been given) were always to be part of any assessment. These guidelines were very similar to those originally laid down by the previous Conservative government in 1972 (see HMSO, 1975b, p. 17).

Between 1975 and 1979, 16 selective assistance schemes were developed. They included schemes in the clothing, paper and board, electronic components and footwear industries. In 1976 the government also launched the Selective Investment Scheme designed to assist commercially viable projects in manufacturing that would not have gone ahead with the same timing, nature or scale. Projects were to be examined against the aims of the Industrial Strategy and had to result in a 'significant improvement' in performance. (This scheme closed in 1979.)

To give itself greater freedom in providing finance under Section 8, the government (in 1975) repealed the general requirement laid down in the 1972 Act that assistance should only be forthcoming where the Secretary of State was satisfied that it could not be obtained in any other way.

Thirdly, the government wanted to see planning agreements between itself and major firms. The idea behind such agreements was that this would enable a two-way flow of information between firms and government. It was intended that these agreements should cover such topics as company strategy and investment plans, sales and exports prospects, and likely technological developments. The 1975 Industry Act gave Ministers power to require companies to disclose information on their activities.

It is clear from the above discussion that the Labour government's approach to the restoration of the UK's international position rested on the view that governments have a vitally important role to play in selective intervention in the affairs of industry. Industry's own decision makers could not be relied on to achieve that restoration by themselves.

The Conservative government (1979–)

The incoming Conservative government of 1979 explicitly rejected the idea that government intervention in such areas as investment and planning could improve the UK's international performance. Indeed in its view many of the *failures* in industry could be attributed to government action in that the latter could stifle enterprise and initiative. Instead it saw its main task as one of strengthening incentives and reducing reliance on the state. This was to be accompanied by moves towards greater privatization (see pp. 82–3) and less regulation in industry. Two early moves towards the latter were the abolition of the Price Commission in 1980 and the Industrial Development Certificate in 1982. (These certificates had been used as a means of controlling the location of industry.)

The previous government's attempts to develop an industrial strategy were abandoned. The Industry Act 1980 substantially reduced the role of the NEB. It was now charged with promoting the *private* ownership of interests in industrial undertakings by the *disposal* of its securities and other properties; its powers to acquire shares were substantially reduced; it could no longer act as the government's agent under Section 8 of the Industry Act 1972; and its powers to 'reorganize' industry were repealed. Many of its shareholdings were transferred to the government. In 1981 the role of the NEB was further reduced when it was merged with the National Research Development Corporation – a body (set up in 1949) to provide state support for invention and innovation – to form the British Technology Group.

The particular selective investment schemes of the previous government were allowed to run their course but were not renewed. However, the Conservative government has since introduced a number of new schemes under Section 8 of the Industrial Development Act 1982. Most of the new schemes, such as the Small Engineering Firms Investment

Scheme and the Loan Guarantee Scheme for small firms (see p. 27) are, however, targetted more closely than their predecessors.

The Conservative government also tightened the criteria under which Section 8 aid could be given. Assistance was only to be given to commercially viable projects where there was a genuine choice of international location; or which would lead to very substantial improvements in performance, usually productivity; or which would lead to the introduction of new products. The first criterion is outside the scope of this chapter. The other criteria are clearly closely related to the objective of achieving greater international competitiveness. In addition to meeting one of these criteria, assisted projects were expected to make a substantial net contribution to output which might take the form of exports or import substitution, or of meeting new or increased demands, or introduce a significant degree of innovation to the UK. The government also reinstated the condition that assistance could only be provided if it was not obtainable from elsewhere.

Planning agreements were dropped and the provisions of the Industry Act 1975 which gave the Minister power to obtain information from companies were repealed.

In parallel with this attempt at disengagement, and the general tightening up of conditions under which government financial assistance could be provided, a range of advisory and information services, mainly in the small firms and innovations fields has been developed. Many of these services, however, have their genesis in the activities of earlier governments. For example, the Small Firms Centres (see p. 27) which the present government has developed were started by the Labour government in 1976.

1974–85: An overview

It may at first sight appear that the Labour and Conservative governments have pursued radically different policies to improve the UK's international performance. In some respects this is true, particularly as far as the role of public ownership is concerned.

There have also been important changes in the institutional framework. For example, the setting up of the NEB by Labour and the subsequent dismantling of most of its powers by the Conservatives represented major discontinuities in that framework. (The establishment of the NEB would have represented an even more radical innovation if the Labour Party's plans in opposition had not been diluted when they came to power.) However, as Cairncross, Henderson and Silberston (1982) have pointed out, the policies of successive governments have also shown some continuity. The Sector Working Parties set up in the mid-1970s really represented an extension of the existing Economic Development Committees set up in the early days of

what was a Conservative creation: the National Economic Development
Council. (The Working Parties have now been converted back into
Economic Development Committees.)

Again, it must be remembered that the selective financial assistance
schemes of the Labour administration were produced under the provisions of Section 8 of the Conservatives' 1972 Industry Act. Indeed the
Conservative government was the first to set up such a scheme (for
Wool Textiles) in 1973, and as shown above it has developed further
schemes since coming to power in 1979. In the small firms field, the
Conservative government has become *more* involved than its predeces-
sor. It is worth noting too that administrative discretion continues to
play an important part in the provision of assistance. For example, the
terms under which Section 8 assistance is now given still leave considerable scope for discretion. (For example, what does 'commercially
viable' actually mean? How is a judgement to be made on such viability
as far as projects *yet to be undertaken* are concerned?)

In any assessment of government involvement in the industrial field
since 1974 it is important to keep the size of the expenditure involved in
its right perspective. Table 13.1 shows that over this period the

Table 13.1   Percentage of government expenditure going to industry,
energy, trade and employment, 1973/4–1982/3

Year	%	Year	%
1973/4	8	1978/9	5
1974/5	7	1979/80	4
1975/6	6	1980/81	4
1976/7	6	1981/2	5
1977/8	4	1982/3	5

Source: *Economic Trends,* November 1983, p. 147.

percentage of government expenditure going to industry, energy, trade
and employment – the smallest category for which a time series of any
length is available but one which covers a field far wider than the subject
of this chapter – has never been higher than 8 per cent. Furthermore this
percentage *halved* between 1973/4 and 1977/8. Probably less than a
quarter of the percentage in 1982/3 could be attributed to the kinds of
intervention discussed in this chapter.

13.4 THE CASE FOR INTERVENTION

In essence, government intervention in industry is designed to encourage firms and industries to do what they would not otherwise do. Existing market forces are seen as 'failing' to bring about the required result. The possibility of market failure may be argued on a number of grounds. Some of these arguments are examined below. In considering them, however, the following points should be remembered. First, the arguments listed below are primarily economic in character. Governments may, however, introduce policies for political reasons, for example to attract (or keep) votes. Secondly, only those reasons which may be relevant for government intervention designed to raise international competitiveness are considered here. Thirdly, it should not be assumed that simply because a government intervenes it has clear reasons for doing so. A wide variety of influences are likely to be at work and the government may not be operating according to any coherent strategy.

Market Failure: Some Key Arguments

Private firms are less well informed than governments

According to this argument firms lack knowledge which would improve their competitiveness. This knowledge (which governments are assumed to have) may concern areas such as domestic and export market opportunities, available technologies, the efficiency gains that would be obtained from industrial restructuring, scope for invention and innovation and the value of industrial training and outside advice. Lack of knowledge may characterize firms producing not only goods, but also services. For example, financial institutions may not be aware of profitable opportunities. This argument does of course raise the question of why private firms do not have such information in the first place and why governments are necessarily better informed.

Externalities exist

Even if they are as fully informed as governments, private decision takers may not take into account all the social costs and benefits that flow from their decisions. For example, firms may not have to bear the costs that arise from the considerable social disruption caused by too rapid shedding of labour and/or the closing down of plants. Furthermore, the substantial costs to the individuals who lose their jobs will not be reflected in accounts of firms. In these circumstances, governments may attempt to slow down the pace of adjustment. By so doing, they may actually *enhance* the possibility for increased competitiveness in the long run, as their actions may be regarded as indicating willingness to alleviate some of the costs of change. On the other hand, social costs considerations may lead a government to intervene to speed up change. For example individual decision makers may be reluctant to permit industrial restructuring for instance because of the personal cost to them. However, such restructuring might bring benefits which may then outweigh these costs.

Markets do not provide optimal quantities of output with 'public good' characteristics

Public good characteristics were described on pp. 5–6. The possibility of 'free riding' means that market demand is unlikely to reflect social demand. This argument is particularly important in the justification of government support of R & D, particularly at the basic research end (see p. 156). Such support may have important implications for international competitiveness.

Private firms have shorter time horizons than governments

Private firms may be unable to look as far ahead as governments. Thus a firm which is commercially viable in the longer term may be allowed to fail in a market system. This is essentially the argument which lies behind the protection of 'infant industries'. Young industries are seen as needing a period of protection from foreign trade to give them time to find their feet. (In recent years the discussion in the UK has been more in terms of protection for '*geriatric* industries'; the argument here is that industries suffering from chronic problems need a period of protection to 'rejuvenate' themselves.)

The idea that governments have longer time horizons than private firms does of course ignore political considerations. Five years however is the maximum life of a Parliament; some might argue that this effectively imposes *shorter* horizons on government action.

Private firms are less well placed than governments to take risks

Governments may be in a better position to spread their risks than private firms. This proposition lies behind the provision of launching aid (see below), given to assist firms (most notably in the aircraft industry) to develop a new product or process.

The market does not generate optimum co-ordination of business plans

No firm operates in isolation from others. If each firm is to plan its operations efficiently it needs to come to some view of the plans of other firms. Without co-ordination between firms (it is argued) each individual firm is making decisions in unnecessary ignorance. Such isolation can lead to a waste of resources. Yet private firms may find it difficult to set up a mechanism for the co-ordination of plans. It is essentially this argument that has formed the basis of various attempts at planning in the post-war period (see p. 28).

Government co-ordination may also be important in another area: the setting of standards. No one firm can unilaterally impose standards on other firms, yet the existence of such standards may play a role in (for example) ensuring compatibility between manufacturers' products. Such compatibility may be an important element in some international sales.

Assessing the Case for Intervention

It would probably not be difficult to find *some* economic argument which justified virtually any form of intervention. Rarely, if at all, is it possible to test conclusively whether in any particular situation some or all of the above arguments are valid. However, even if they were, it may nevertheless be the case that the cost of implementing an interventionist policy may outweigh any benefits. Such costs include the costs of administration. Implementation may also generate other unintended costs some of which are considered in the next section. Thus in some circumstances it may be less costly not to implement a policy, and to live with the deficiencies it would be designed to solve. (For the application of the same argument in relation to competition policy, see p. 195.)

13.5 SOME PROBLEMS OF POLICY IMPLEMENTATION

'Government Failure'

Government failure is a general term which may be applied to unanticipated side effects of a policy which raise the costs of its implementation. It may arise for a number of reasons. First, it must be remembered that the officials involved in the implementation of policy may have their *own* objectives which may mean that the stated aim of the policy may not be achieved. Niskanen (1968) for example has suggested that maximization of a departmental or agency budget may be sought because it is through such maximization that officials also maximize their own prestige and income. Officials may also become so committed to a policy, especially if they have had a hand in its formulation, that they may be reluctant to see it dropped even if it has served its purpose (or proved to be a failure).

Secondly, the quality and quantity of information available to government officials may be insufficient for them to implement a policy measure satisfactorily. A firm making applications for funds may be able to restrict or distort the flow of information. This puts officials in a disadvantaged position even though they may not know it. Outside advice may be sought (for example from management consultants) but even then the applicant for funds is often in a stronger position. A particular difficulty over information arises in any assessment in which it has to be demonstrated *before* any funds are forthcoming that the project would not otherwise go ahead either at all or in the form proposed. (In official jargon 'additionality' has to be demonstrated). There is no cast-iron way of knowing *in advance* what would happen if public funds were not provided: heavy reliance has to be placed on the undertakings of the applicant. This difficulty has been acknowledged by the Industrial Development Advisory Board which advises the Minister on Section 8 assistance (HMSO, 1983a, p. 14).

Differences between the information possessed by an applicant firm and that available to the government officials responsible for vetting applications may be at their greatest where advanced technological developments are involved.

Thirdly, the government and its advisers may have to make assessments under considerable pressure of time because of political and other considerations. This in turn may lead to bad decisions. One illustration of this pressure is given by the timetable for the assessment of an application for public funds to finance the building of a luxury sports car by the De Lorean company in Northern Ireland. McKinsey and Co, the firm of management consultants retained by the Northern Ireland Department of Commerce in 1978 to identify the risks associated with the project were given only six days to complete their job. In the private sector a proper investigation (according to McKinsey) would have taken some four to six man months (HMSO, 1983b, p. 18). The crash of the company in 1982 cost the Exchequer over £76m.

Fourthly, officials may not have the necessary skills or experience required to make good commercial judgements. Running an administrative operation may not be the most appropriate background for the assessment of business proposals. The limitations of officials in this respect is brought out clearly in the De Lorean affair. They have recently been criticized for accepting a very tight timetable for the assessment of the project; deciding to go ahead without adequately investigating Mr De Lorean's background and finances or the viability and merits of the sports car; for being outmanoeuvred in the agreement that set up the project; and for not paying enough attention to the reports of outside consultants (HMSO, 1984, pp. xxx–xxxi).

Other Problems

Other difficulties over policy implementation may arise in areas not entirely within the government machine. For example, Young has pointed out (1974, p. 34) that in the mid-1960s, despite the numerous policy initiatives that had been launched, few seemed to be affecting activities at the firm level because trade associations, and other 'filtering' agencies were being used to promote policy. It was partly for this reason that the Labour government formed the IRC in 1966 to deal *directly* with firms.

Another problem may arise when industrialists from established firms or trade unionists play a key role in the formation of government policies for their industries. Inevitably perhaps, they will tend to view proposals from the viewpoint of their own firms or unions and they may therefore impede the development of policies which are likely to impose costs on them, and to promote those which yield benefits to them. In this context, it is worth noting that it is not necessarily 'insiders' who are best placed to see market opportunities; there is a good deal of evidence to show that 'outsiders' have played an important role in industrial innovation (Johnson, 1975, p. 65.)

Some Adverse Effects of Intervention

The most obvious adverse effect of intervention is unintended Exchequer losses. Attention has already been drawn to the losses incurred in the involvement in De Lorean. (These losses were, however, small compared with those associated with Concorde, Rolls Royce, or British Leyland, for instance.)

One area where unintended losses have been analysed is in the provision of launching aid. Gardner (1976) has examined such aid for airframes and aero engine development. He found that government revenue for post-1945 projects from which no further return was expected and which were designed to provide a commercial return to the government, was only 60 per cent of the total government outlay. (Resources and outlay were both measured in 1974 terms.)

Gardner argued that one of the reasons for this low recovery was the particular formula used for estimating how much should be paid back to government. This formula based the share of the proceeds that government was to receive on the *money* value of the original assistance, without making any allowance for inflation or for interest on any outstanding debt.

Another unintended effect may occur under measures in which public money is only intended to provide funds *in addition* to those from private sources. As indicated earlier it is very difficult to ensure that this

condition is adhered to. In consequence firms may succeed in using
public funds as a substitute for their own.

In a broader sense, detailed government intervention may have some
adverse effect on enterprise. If firms become too heavily dependent on
public funds, the skills necessary for seeking out new market opportunities on their own may become eroded.

13.6 THE EVALUATION OF POLICY

Given the complex nature of the causes of the UK's relative economic
decline, and the possibility that policy initiatives may generate the kind
of unintended effects outlined in the previous section, it is important to
evaluate the effect of such initiatives. (In some cases the evaluation
exercise itself may outweigh any benefits that come from it, but this
possibility is ignored here.)

Evaluation may be attempted in many different ways. At the most
basic level, an assessment may be restricted to analysing the extent to
which the specified objectives of the policy have been met. These
objectives may sometimes be of a quantitative kind. For example,
governments may wish to see x new businesses formed over some time
period, or productivity growth increased by y per cent per annum.
Similarly evaluation of an *institution* may be conducted in terms of the
objectives set for that institution. A publicly owned financial institution
for instance may be evaluated in relation to a set target on the
disbursement of funds to industry or on the public ownership of shares.
It is clear however that while such evaluation exercises may provide a
useful starting point for assessment they nevertheless have severe
limitations. They avoid any analysis of the objectives or targets themselves. Furthermore, they do not identify a policy effect. Such an effect
requires an assessment of what would have happened in the absence of
policy. It is not usually easy to establish this 'without policy' position.
For example, assume that a firm receives a grant towards an investment.
What investment would it have made without that grant? Asking the
firm may not be particularly helpful especially if the investigators are
providing the grant! It may be possible to look at the firm's investment
levels *before* the grant was given but to use this as the 'without policy'
reference level involves the assumption that this level would also have
prevailed at the time the grant was made.

The measurement of the difference a policy measure makes is further
complicated by the fact that the policy may not only change the
behaviour of the immediate beneficiary of the policy. Other firms may
also be affected. For example a firm that undertakes an investment as a
result of a grant may increase the demand for the goods and services of
other firms. It may also lead to competitors *not* in receipt of a grant

reducing their investment. The importance for evaluation purposes of estimating the difference a policy measure makes has not always been appreciated. For example, in a statement on a training programme designed for people intending to set up in business, a government minister pointed out that well over 1,600 jobs had been created by the 350 trainees who had been on the course (*Employment Gazette*, December 1981, p. 502). Such figures give no indication of the *net* effect on jobs, i.e. after deducting what would have happened to jobs in the absence of the training.

Even when the difference a policy makes is accurately identified, this represents only a first stage in the overall evaluation process. Some assessment must also be made of the costs of the policy, and comparisons made *across* policies. The latter almost inevitably involves placing a monetary valuation on the costs and benefits.

The Overall Effects of Policy on UK Competitiveness

It is not possible to say how much *less* competitive the UK would now be in world markets if successive governments had not introduced policies designed to raise competitiveness. However, it remains true that the UK's relative position has continued to decline and that neither Labour nor Conservative governments have succeeded in their stated objectives of reversing this decline.

13.7 SUMMARY

Successive governments have endeavoured to halt the decline in the UK's international competitiveness. Labour and Conservative governments have adopted very different viewpoints in the role that should be played by government and publicly owned institutions in industrial policies, although there has also been some continuity in many of the measures that have been adopted.

The economic case for intervention may be made on a number of market failure grounds. However, it is rarely possible to assess at all accurately how valid these arguments are in any particular instance. And even if they are valid, the costs of intervention may sometimes exceed the gains. A number of unintended costs may arise as a result of government failure or other reasons.

Any evaluation of a particular policy measure requires, as a first step, an estimate of its net effects not only on the immediate beneficiary but also on those firms indirectly affected by the measure. Evaluation of the *overall* effect of policy is not possible because it is not known what the 'without policy' position would be. However, it can be said that successive governments have not yet achieved their stated aim of reversing the decline in the UK's relative international position.

References

Albu, A. (1980) 'British Attitudes to Engineering Education: A Historical Perspective', in Pavitt, K. (ed.) (1980) 67–87.

Baumol, W.J. (1967) *Business Behaviour, Value and Growth* (rev. edn), Harcourt, Brace and World, New York.

Baumol, W.J. (1982) 'Contestable Markets: An Uprising in the Theory of Industry Structure', *American Economic Review*, 72(1), 1–15.

Becker, G. (1975) *Human Capital: A Theoretical and Empirical Analysis With Special Reference to Education* (2nd edn), National Bureau of Economic Research, New York.

Beesley, M. and Littlechild, S.C. (1983) 'Privatization: Principles, Problems and Priorities', *Lloyds Bank Review*, 149, 1–20.

Benham, L. (1972) 'The Effects of Advertising on the Price of Eyeglasses', *Journal of Law and Economics*, 15(2), 337–52.

Blackaby, F. (ed.) (1979) *De-Industrialisation*, Heinemann, London.

Bloch, H. (1974) 'Advertising and Profitability': A Reappraisal', *Journal of Political Economy*, 82(2), 267–86.

Borrie, G. (1982) 'Competition Policy in Britain: Retrospect and Prospect', *International Review of Law and Economics*, 2(2), 139–49.

Bright, A.A. and Maclaurin, W.R. (1943) 'Economic Factors Influencing the Development and Introduction of the Fluorescent Lamp', *Journal of Political Economy*, 51, 429–50.

Brown, C.J.F. and Sheriff, T.D. (1979) 'De-industrialisation: A Background Paper', in Blackaby, F. (ed.) (1979) 233–62.

Buck, T. (1982) *Comparative Industrial Systems*, Macmillan, London.

Cairncross, A. (1979) 'What is De-industrialisation?', in Blackaby, F. (ed.) (1979) 5–17.

Cairncross, A., Henderson, P.D. and Silberston, Z.A. (1982) 'Problems of Industrial Recovery', *Midland Bank Review* (Spring) rep. in Matthews, R.C.O. and Sargent, J.R. (eds.) (1983) *Contemporary Problems of Economic Policy*, Heinemann, London, 88–95.

Carsberg, B. and Hope, A. (1976) *Business Investment Decisions under Inflation*, Institute of Chartered Accountants in England and Wales, London.

Caves, R.E. (1980) 'Productivity Differences Among Industries', in Caves, R.E. and Krause, L.B. (eds) (1980) *Britain's Economic Performance*, Brookings Institution, Washington, 135–92.

Chiplin, B. and Wright, M. (1982) 'Competition Policy and State Enterprises in the UK', *Anti Trust Bulletin*, 27(4), 921–56.

Clark, J.M. (1926) *The Social Control of Business*, University of Chicago Press, Chicago.

Clarke, R. (1984) 'Profit Margins and Market Concentration in UK Manufacturing Industry: 1970–6', *Applied Economics* 16(1), 57–71.

Clarke, R. and Davies, S.W. (1983) 'Aggregate Concentration, Market Concentration and Diversification', *Economic Journal*, 93(369), 182–92.

Comanor, W.S. and Wilson, T.A. (1979) 'The Effect of Advertising on Competition: A Survey', *Journal of Economic Literature*, 17(2), 453–76.

Corner, D.C. and Williams, A. (1965) 'The Sensitivity of Business to Initial and Investment Allowances', *Economica*, 32(1), 32–47.

Cosh, A. (1975) 'The Remuneration of Chief Executives in the United Kingdom', *Economic Journal*, 85(337), 75–94.

Cowling, K. and Mueller, D.C. (1978) 'The Social Costs of Monopoly Power', *Economic Journal* 88(352), 727–48.

Cowling, K., Cable, J., Kelly, M. and McGuinness, T. (1975) *Advertising and Economic Behaviour*, Macmillan, London.

Cowling, K., Stoneman, P., Cubbin, J., Cable, J., Hall, G., Domberger, S. and Dutton, P. (1980) *Mergers and Economic Performance*, Cambridge University Press, Cambridge.

Creedy, J., Evans, L., Thomas, B., Johnson, P. and Wilson, R. (1984) *Economics: An Integrated Approach*, Prentice Hall, London.

Curry, B. and George, K.D. (1982) 'Industrial Concentration: A Survey', *Journal of Industrial Economics*, 31(3), 203–47.

Dalton, J.W. and Penn, D.W. (1976) 'The Concentration–Profitability Relationship: Is there a Critical Concentration Ratio?', *Journal of Industrial Economics*, 15(2), 133–41.

Davies, S. (1979) *The Diffusion of Process Innovations*, Cambridge University Press, Cambridge.

Denison, E.F. (1967) *Why Growth Rates Differ*, The Brookings Institution, Washington.

Dilnot, A. and Morris, C.N. (1981) 'What do we know about the Black Economy?', *Fiscal Studies*, 2(11), 58–73.

Doyle, P. (1968) 'Economic Aspects of Advertising: A Survey', *Economic Journal*, 78(311), 571–602.

Enos, J.L. (1962) 'Invention and Innovation in the Petroleum Refining Industry', in National Bureau of Economic Research (1962) *The Rate and Direction of Inventive Activity*, Princeton University Press, Princeton, 299–322.

Fleming, M. (1980) 'Construction', in Johnson, P.S. (ed.) (1980) 254–79.

Fothergill, S. and Gudgin, G. (1979) *The Job Generation Process in Britain*, Research Series 32, Centre for Environmental Studies, London.

Freeman, C. (1979) 'Technical Innovation and Trade Performance', in Blackaby, F. (ed.) (1979).

Freeman, C. (1982) *The Economics of Industrial Innovation* (2nd edn), Frances Pinter, London.

Galbraith, J.K. (1958) *The Affluent Society* (Penguin edn, 1962), Harmondsworth.

Gardner, N.K. (1976) 'Economics of Launching Aid', in Whiting, A. (ed.) (1976) *The Economics of Industrial Subsidies*, HMSO, London, 141–55.

Gentry, S. and Rodger, L. (1978) *How British Industry Promotes*, Industrial Market Research Ltd, London.

George, K.D. (1974) *Big Business, Competition and the State*, Inaugural Lecture, University College, Cardiff (13 November).

Hall, R.L. and Hitch, C.J. (1939) 'Price Theory and Business Behaviour', *Oxford Economic Papers*, 2, 12–45.

Hankinson, A. (1984) 'Small Firms Investment: A Search for Motivations', *International Small Business Journal*, 2(2), 11–24.

Hart, P.E. and Clarke, R. (1980) *Concentration in British Industry 1935–1975*, Cambridge University Press, Cambridge.

Heald, D. (1984) 'Privatisation: Analysing its Appeals and Limitations', *Fiscal Studies*, 5(1), 36–46.

HMSO (1965) *The National Plan* (CMND 2764) HMSO, London.

HMSO (1966) *Household Detergents* Monopolies Commission (HC 105: 1966/67) HMSO, London.

HMSO (1967) *Nationalised Industries: A Review of Economic and Financial Objectives* (CMND 3437) HMSO, London.

HMSO (1968) *Clutch Mechanisms for Road Vehicles*, Monopolies Commission (HC 32: 1968/69) HMSO, London.

HMSO (1971) *Small Firms*, A Report of the Committee of Inquiry on Small Firms (CMND 4811) HMSO, London.

HMSO (1972a) *Industrial and Regional Development* (CMND 4942) HMSO, London.

HMSO (1972b) *Rolls Royce Ltd and the RB211 Aero Engine* (CMND 4860) HMSO, London.

HMSO (1973a) *Chlordiazepoxide and Diazepam*, Monopolies Commission (HC 197: 1972/73) HMSO, London.

HMSO (1973b) *Development and Production of the Concorde Aircraft*, Public Accounts Committee Sixth and Seventh Reports (HC 335 and 353: 1972/73) HMSO, London.

HMSO (1973c) *Parallel Pricing*, Monopolies Commission (CMND 5330) HMSO, London.

HMSO (1975a) *An Approach to Industrial Strategy* (CMND 6315) HMSO, London.

HMSO (1975b) *Annual Report: Industry Act 1972* (HC 620: 1974/75) HMSO, London.

HMSO (1975c) *The Future of the British Car Industry*, Central Policy Review Staff, HMSO, London.

HMSO (1976a) *Annual Report: Industry Act 1972* (HC 619: 1975/6) HMSO, London.

HMSO (1976b) *Indirect Electrostatic Reprographic Equipment*, Monopolies and Mergers Commission (HC 47: 1976/77) HMSO, London.

HMSO (1977a) *Cat and Dog Foods*, Monopolies and Mergers Commission (HC 447: 1976/77) HMSO, London.

HMSO (1977b) *Evidence on the Financing of Industry and Trade* (vol. 2), Committee to Review the Functioning of Financial Institutions, HMSO, London.

HMSO (1978a) *The Nationalised Industries* (CMND 7131) HMSO, London.

HMSO (1978b) *A Review of Monopolies and Mergers Policy* (CMND 7198) HMSO, London.

HMSO (1979a) *The Financing of Small Firms*, Interim Report of the Committee to Review the Functioning of Financial Institutions (CMND 7503) HMSO, London.

HMSO (1979b) *Petrol*, Monopolies and Mergers Commission (CMND 7333) HMSO, London.

HMSO (1980a) *Appendices* to the Report of the Committee to Review the Functioning of Financial Institutions (CMND 7937) HMSO, London.

HMSO (1980b) *British Railways Board: London and South East Commuter Services*, Monopolies and Mergers Commission (CMND 8046) HMSO, London.

HMSO (1980c) *Domestic Gas Appliances*, Monopolies and Mergers Commission (HC 703: 1979/80) HMSO, London.

HMSO (1980d) *Engineering: Our Future*, Report of a Committee under the Chairmanship of Sir M. Finniston (CMND 7794) HMSO, London.

HMSO (1980e) *The Inner London Letter Post* (HC 515: 1979/80) HMSO, London.

HMSO (1981) *Ready Mixed Concrete*, Monopolies and Mergers Commission (CMND 8554) HMSO, London.

HMSO (1982a) *Annual Report: Industry Act, 1972* (HC 503: 1981/82) HMSO, London.

HMSO (1982b) *Sheffield Newspapers Ltd*, Monopolies and Mergers Commission (CMND 8664) HMSO, London.

HMSO (1983a) *Annual Report: Industrial Development Act* (HC 72:1983/84) HMSO, London.

HMSO (1983b) *Financial Assistance to De Lorean Motor Cars Ltd, Minutes of Evidence*, Public Accounts Committee (HC 127–iv: 1983/84) HMSO, London.

HMSO (1984) *Financial Assistance to De Lorean Motor Cars Ltd Vol. 1: Report together with the Proceedings of the Committee and Minutes of Evidence*, Committee of Public Accounts (HC 127–I: 1983/84) HMSO, London.

Hewer, A. (1980) 'Manufacturing Industries in the Seventies: An Assessment of Import Penetration and Export Performance', *Economic Trends*, 320, 97–109.

Hood, N. and Young, S. (1979) *The Economics of Multinational Enterprise*, Longman, London.

Jewkes, J., Sawers, D. and Stillerman, R. (1969) *The Sources of Invention* (2nd edn), Macmillan, London.

Johnson, P.S. (1975) *The Economics of Invention and Innovation*, Martin Robertson, London.

Johnson, P.S. (ed) (1980) *The Structure of British Industry*, Granada, St Albans.

Johnson, P.S. and Apps, R. (1979) 'Interlocking Directorates among the UK's Largest Companies', *Anti-Trust Bulletin*, 24(2), 357–69.

Kirzner, I. (1973) *Competition and Entrepreneurship*, University of Chicago Press, Chicago.

Knight, F. (1921) *Risk Uncertainty and Profit*, Houghton Mifflin, Boston.

Koutsoyiannis, A. (1982) *Non-Price Decisions*, Macmillan, London.

Kravis, I.B. and Lipsey, R.E. (1971) *Price Competitiveness in World Trade*, National Bureau of Economic Research, New York.

Layton, C. (1972) *Ten Innovations*, George Allen and Unwin, London.

Leibenstein, H. (1966) 'Allocative Efficiency vs. "X Efficiency", *American Economic Review*, 56(3), 392–415.

Littlechild, S.C. (1981) 'Misleading Calculations of the Costs of Monopoly Power', *Economic Journal*, 91(362), 348–63.

Livesey, F. (1980) 'Retailing', in Johnson, P.S. (ed.) (1980) 280–303.

Maddison, A. (1980) 'Phases of Capitalist Development', in Matthews, R.C.O. (ed.) (1980) *Economic Growth and Resources Vol. 2: Trends and Factors*, Proceedings of the Fifth World Congress of the International Economic Association, Macmillan, London, 3–33.

Mann, H.M., Henning, J.A. and Meehan, J.N. (1967) 'Advertising and Concentration: An Empirical Investigation', *Journal of Industrial Economics*, 16(1), 34–45.

Matthews, R.C.O. (1982) *Slower Growth in the Western World*, Heinemann, London.

Matthews, R.C.O., Feinstein, C.H. and Odling-Smee, J.C. (1982) *British Economic Growth, 1856–1973*, Oxford University Press, Oxford.

Maunder, P. (1980) 'Food Manufacturing', in Johnson, P.S. (ed.) (1980) 80–105.

Meeks, G. (1977) *Disappointing Marriage: A Study of the Gains from Merger*, Cambridge University Press, Cambridge.

Meeks, G. and Whittington, G. (1975) 'Director's Pay, Growth and Profitability', *Journal of Industrial Economics*, 24(1), 1–14.

Morgan, A.D. (1982) 'Productivity in the 1960s and 1970s', in Matthews, R.C.O. (ed.) (1982) 17–28.

Mueller, A. (1977) 'Industrial Efficiency and UK Government Policy', in Bowe, C. (ed.) *Industrial Efficiency and the Role of Government*, HMSO, London, 259–74.

Mueller, W.F. (1962) 'The Origins of the Basic Inventions Underlying Du Pont's Major Product and Process Innovations, 1920 to 1950', in National Bureau of Economic Research (1962) *The Rate and Direction of Inventive Activity*, Princeton University Press, Princeton, 323–46.

Mueller, W.F. (1982) 'Conglomerates: A Non-industry', in Adams, W. (ed.) (1982) *The Structure of American Industry* (6th edn), Macmillan, New York, 427–74.

NEDO (1976) *A Study of UK Nationalised Industries*, NEDO, London.

NEDO (1977) *International Price Competitiveness, Non Price Factors and Export Performance*, NEDO, London.

NEDO (1980) *British Industrial Performance*, NEDO, London.

NEDO (1984) *Trade Patterns and Industrial Change*, NEDO, London.

Neild, R.R. (1964) 'Replacement Policy', *Economic Review*, (30), 30–43.

Nevins, J.A. (1976) *Ford: The Times, the Man, the Company* vol. 1 (reprint edn), Arno Press, New York.

Niskanen, W.A. (1968) 'The Peculiar Economics of Bureaucracy', *American Economic Review* (Papers and Proceedings), 68(2), 293–305.

Nove, A. (1977) *The Soviet Economic System*, George Allen and Unwin, London.

O'Brien, D.P., Howe, W.S. and Wright, D.M. (1979) *Competition Policy, Profitability and Growth*, Macmillan, London.

Pass, C.L. and Sparkes, J.R. (1980) 'Dominant Firms and the Public

Interest: A Survey of the Reports of the British Monopolies and Mergers Commission', *Anti Trust Bulletin*, 25(2), 437–84.

Pavitt, K. (ed.) (1980) *Technical Innovation and British Economic Performance*, Macmillan, London.

Phelps-Brown, H. (1977) 'What is the British Predicament?', *Three Banks Review*, 116, 3–29.

Phlips, L. (1983) *The Economics of Price Discrimination*, Cambridge University Press, Cambridge.

Pike, R.H. (1983) 'A Review of Recent Trends in Capital Budgeting Processes', *Accounting and Business Research*, 13(51), 201–8.

Posner, R.A. (1975) 'The Social Costs of Monopoly and Regulation', *Journal of Political Economy*, 83(4), 807–27.

Prais, S.J. (1981a) *The Evolution of Giant Firms in Britain* (with a new preface), Cambridge University Press, Cambridge.

Prais, S.J. (1981b) *Productivity and Industrial Structure*, Cambridge University Press, Cambridge.

Pratten, C.F. (1971) *Economies of Scale in Manufacturing Industry*, Cambridge University Press, Cambridge.

Pratten, C.F. (1976) *Labour Productivity Differentials within International Companies*, Cambridge University Press, Cambridge.

Pryke, R. (1981) *The Nationalised Industries*, Martin Robertson, Oxford.

Pryke, R. (1982) 'The Comparative Performance of Public and Private Enterprise', *Fiscal Studies*, 3(2), 68–71.

Ray, G.R. (1969) 'The Diffusion of New Technology', *National Institute Economic Review*, (48), 40–83.

Reekie, W.D. (1975) 'Advertising and Market Structure: Another Approach', *Economic Journal*, 85(337), 156–64.

Reekie, W.D. (1980) 'Pharmaceuticals', in Johnson, P.S. (ed.) (1980) 106–30.

Reekie, W.D. and Crook, J.N. (1982) *Managerial Economics* (2nd edn), Philip Allan, Oxford.

Rees, G. (1969) *St Michael. A History of Marks and Spencer*, Weidenfeld and Nicolson, London.

Rees, R.D. (1975) 'Advertising Concentration and Competition: A Comment and Further Results', *Economic Journal*, 85(337), 165–72.

Robinson, C. and Rowland, C. (1980) 'North Sea Oil and Gas', in Johnson, P.S. (ed.) (1980) 28–56.

Rybczynski, T.M. (1982) 'Structural Changes in the Financing of British Industry and their Implications', *National Westminster Quarterly Review*, (May) 25–36.

Sargent, J.R. (1979) 'UK Performance in Services', in Blackaby, F. (ed.) (1979) 102–16.

Sawyer, M.C. (1981) *The Economics of Industries and Firms*, Croom Helm, London.

Scherer, F.M. (1980) *Industrial Market Structure and Economic Performance* (2nd edn), Rand McNally, Chicago.

Schumpeter, J. (1939) *Business Cycles* (vol. 1), McGraw Hill, New York.

Schumpeter, J.A. (1954) *Capitalism Socialism and Democracy* (4th edn), George Allen and Unwin, London.

Senker, P. (1980) 'Forklift Trucks', in Pavitt, K. (ed.) (1980) 159–67.

Silberston, Z.A. (1970) 'Price Behaviour of Firms', *Economic Journal*, 80 (319), 511–82.

Silberston, Z.A. (1972) 'Economies of Scale in Theory and Practice', *Economic Journal*, 82(325s), 369–91.

Singh, A. (1975) 'Take-overs, "Natural Selection" and the Theory of the Firm', *Economic Journal*, 85(339), 497–515.

Smith, A.D., Hitchens, D.M.W. and Davies, S.W. (1982) *International Industrial Productivity*, Cambridge University Press, Cambridge.

Smyth, R.L. (1967) 'A Price–Minus Theory of Cost', *Scottish Journal of Political Economy*, 14(2), 110–17.

Steel, D.R. (1984) 'Government and the New Hybrids: A Trail of Unanswered Questions', University of Exeter, mimeo.

Steiner, P.O. (1966) 'Economics of Broadcasting and Advertising: Discussion', *American Economic Review (Papers and Proceedings)*, 66(2), 472–75.

Stoneman, P. (1980) 'Computers', in P.S. Johnson (ed.) (1980) 154–78.

Sutton, C.J. (1974) 'Advertising, Concentration and Competition', *Economic Journal*, 84(333), 56–69.

Swann, D., O'Brien, D.P., Maunder, W.P.J. and Howe, W.S. (1974) *Competition in British Industry*, George Allen and Unwin, London.

Swords-Isherwood, N. (1980) 'British Management Compared', in Pavitt, K. (ed.) (1980) 88–99.

Taylor, C. and Silberston, Z.A. (1973) *The Economic Impact of the Patent System*, Cambridge University Press, Cambridge.

Telser, L.G. (1964) 'Advertising and Competition', *Journal of Political Economy*, 72(6), 537–62.

Townsend, J., Henwood, J., Thomas, G., Pavitt, K. and Wyatt, S. (1982) *Innovations in Britain since 1945*, Science Policy Research Unit, Sussex University Occasional Paper No. 16.

Utton, M.A. (1974a) 'Aggregate versus Market Concentration', *Economic Journal*, 84(333), 150–5.

Utton, M.A. (1974b) 'On Measuring the Effects of Industrial Mergers', *Scottish Journal of Political Economy*, 21(1), 13–28.

Utton, M.A. (1979) *Diversification and Competition*, Cambridge University Press, Cambridge.

Utton, M.A. (1982a) 'Domestic Concentration and International Trade', *Oxford Economic Papers*, 34 (3) 479–497.

Utton, M.A. (1982b) *The Political Economy of Big Business*, Martin Robertson, Oxford.

Waterson, M.J. (1982) 'Advertising/Sales Ratios in the UK, 1969–80', *Journal of Advertising*, (1), 53–5.

Waterson, M.J. (1983) 'Advertising Expenditures in the UK: 1982 Survey', *International Journal of Advertising*, (2), 159–68.

Wildsmith, J.R. (1973) *Managerial Theories of the Firm*, Martin Robertson, London.

Wilson, C. (1954) *The History of Unilever* (vol. 1), Cassell, London.

Wragg, R. and Robertson, R. (1978) *Post War Trends in Employment, Productivity Output, Labour Costs and Prices by Industry in the UK*, Department of Employment, London.

Young, S. (1974) *Intervention in the Mixed Economy* (with A.V. Lowe), Croom Helm, London.

Author Index

231

Subject Index